THE ESSENTIAL
WORLDWIDE LAWS OF LIFE

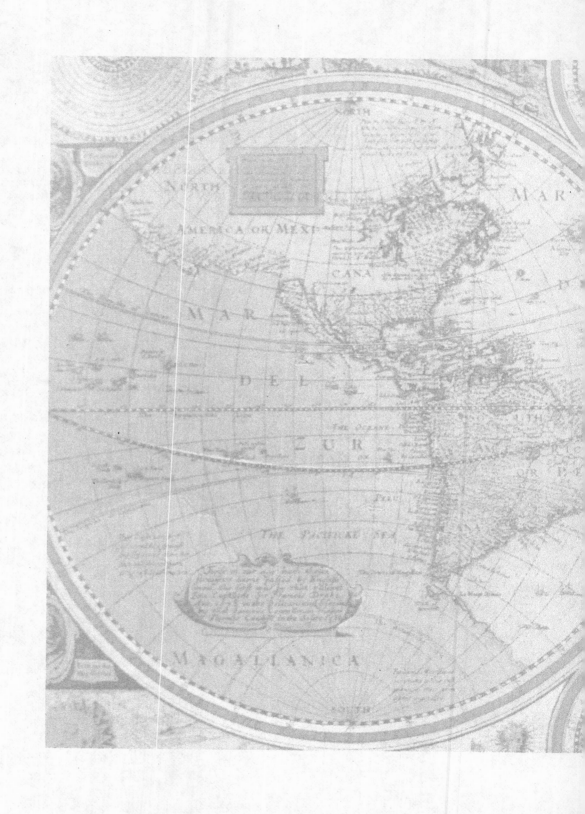

The Essential
Worldwide Laws of Life

Sir John Templeton

With a Foreword by Stephen G. Post

TEMPLETON PRESS

Templeton Press
300 Conshohocken State Road, Suite 550
West Conshohocken, PA 19428
www.templetonpress.org

Designed and typeset by Gopa & Ted2, Inc.

Library of Congress
Cataloging-in-Publication Data

Templeton, John, 1912-2008.
  The essential worldwide laws of life / Sir John
Templeton ; with a foreword by Stephen G.
Post.
    p. cm.
  Includes bibliographical references.
  ISBN 978-1-59947-382-6 (hbk. : alk. paper)
  1. Conduct of life. 2. Conduct of life—Quota-
tions, maxims, etc. 3. Spiritual life—Quotations,
maxims, etc. I. Title.
  BJ1581.2.T4263 2012
  170'.44—dc23

                                    2011036871

Printed in the United States of America
12 13 14 15 16 17   10 9 8 7 6 5 4 3 2 1

Contents

Contents

vi

Foreword

N DECEMBER 1962, the message on the Templeton family Christmas card was as follows: "On the 1962nd birthday of Christ, we invite you, our friends, to ponder with us this little question: Are you in control of your mind?" While a tad unusual for a Christmas card greeting, the question is filled with wisdom. Sir John Templeton meant a control from within, a free self-focusing of mind and emotion, in contrast to anything imposed from outside. In *The Essential Worldwide Laws of Life,* Sir John applies this same wisdom in a practical, user-friendly book that teaches us how we can live better if we take a bit of time each day to concentrate on time-honored principles of human flourishing. The key ingredients underlying *The Essential Worldwide Laws of Life* are these three: (1) our thoughts are carried forward into manifestation in our daily living; (2) the thoughts that will be most helpful to us are ones that focus on the future in clear terms, and on helping, as well as on humility, forgiveness, gratitude, joy, perseverance, and other key virtues; and (3) we are each ultimately responsible as free individuals for what we allow into our minds and, hence, for creating our lives.

Sir John Templeton was a global investor who understood that the very best investment we make is in our minds, which we can determine to cultivate with thoughts that enable us to prosper and grow, no matter what obstacles and challenges we confront. Sir John worked just as hard at idea picking as he did at stock picking. He wanted ideas that had proven themselves by providing high dividends to those who might be fortunate enough to own them as long-term investments of the soul. He selected a set of principles or "laws of life" that he felt were truly valuable assets, like blue-chip dividend-paying stocks that expand in value regardless of the peaks and valleys of the markets. Sir John was not interested in short-term investments in fashionable ideas that do not stand the test of time. He investigated these ideas or "laws of life" scientifically; he analyzed them philosophically and theologically; he sought out expert advisors from every corner of the globe; he reflected on them at the level of everyday experience; and he took each of them into his own soul. Sir John was an investment genius who cared deeply for every client and was also a great healer who understood that the right thoughts, properly prescribed and modeled especially early in life, could replace spiritual poverty, misery, and bitterness with abundance, joy, and resilience. He knew that the best investment any of us ever make is in a mind full of the thoughts that build up our lives and the lives of others rather than tear them down. He understood that there can be no lasting freedom without responsibility and that, ultimately, each of us can enhance our futures though the astonishing influence of our thoughts.

Sir John Templeton wanted to encourage ideas that heal our lives. *The Essential Worldwide Laws of Life* is Sir John's healing prescription for humanity. Its inspiring contents can change lives and cultures for the better and prevent the behaviors that contribute to illness, disease, and violence. Sir John read the newspapers, and he was painfully aware of how the messages in contemporary culture are destructive and self-destructive. He placed his hope in the perennial laws of life that shaped him from youth and that can do the same for the many young people today who are in desperate need of a positive philosophy for practical living.

To reach youth, Sir John put tireless energy and substantial resources into the Laws of Life Essay Competition, focusing on students in grade schools, junior highs, and high schools across the United States.

In 1987, he founded the first contest in Franklin County, Tennessee, to encourage young people to write about the laws of life and how they have influenced their lives. In twenty-five years, the contest has reached millions of youth and, today, organizations such as Junior Achievement China, Learning for Life, and Georgia Rotary Districts Character Education Program operate large-scale Laws of Life contests.

Why did these laws of life mean so much to Sir John? As a Tennessee teenager during the 1920s, Sir John discovered a truth that arches across the ages in a trajectory from the philosophers of antiquity such as the Roman Marcus Aurelius, who wrote "Your life becomes what you think," to more recent spiritual leaders such as Charles Fillmore, who said, "Thoughts held in mind produce after their kind." Indeed, these are both passages that Sir John cites in *The Essential Worldwide Laws of Life*. Could anyone seriously doubt that our thoughts have immense implications for how we focus our energies and creativity in every domain of life?

Sir John, a mainstream Presbyterian all of his life and for many years a board member of Princeton Theological Seminary, did not need to quote anything more than this beloved passage: "As he thinketh in his heart, so is he" (Prov. 23:7). He saw value in many methods of focusing the mind on the laws of life, including the rituals, prayers, meditations, music, art, verse, or forms of worship that he collected from around the world in an impressive edited book, *Worldwide Worship: Prayers, Songs, and Poetry* (2000). Indeed, world religions at their best are designed to "prime" our minds and hearts for good living. Of course, he knew that religions can sometimes bring out the worst as well as the best in people. He wanted to see the best.

With its many branches and leading lights, Sir John's laws of life fit loosely within the Americanist pragmatic philosophical genre known as "New Thought," and within what is termed "cognitive priming" by contemporary psychology. This emphasis on the power of brief affirmations cultivated through daily meditation entered Sir John's young life through a small booklet that arrived monthly addressed to his beloved mother. *The Daily Word*, published by the Unity School of Christianity, has been inspiring people across the world since its first publication in July 1924. This handy little booklet includes an inspiring affirmation for each calendar day, followed by a paragraph of contemplative reflection and a passage from Scripture. Even a few minutes at the beginning of each day for such a spiritual exercise can set the tone of our interactions and attitudes, "priming" our responses to interactions and events, and focusing our energies on the things that matter most.

Unity was founded by Charles and Myrtle Fillmore in Kansas City, Missouri, in 1903, although the informal beginnings of Unity go back to the 1880s when the couple, struggling with economic and health challenges, found solutions in spiritual currents of the time, such as the writings of Emmanuel Swedenborg and Ralph Waldo Emerson as well as in Theosophy, Hinduism, and Quakerism. Fillmore believed that spiritually progressive individuals should welcome relationships with people of all religious persuasions, and that they should accompany creeds with simple "spiritual principles." He recognized a phrase found in the Hindu Upanishads, a sacred text: "What you think you become." If we think good, we become good; if we think bad, we become bad. Thought has always been held to be creative, and may even be as real as matter—a point suggested these days by quantum physics. But such speculation aside, mastery of one's thoughts is mastery of one's soul and fate. It is by practicing concentration (*Dharana* in the Sanskrit) that we achieve control over our thoughts and a deeper unity with them. This unity enables us to unleash more energy in actualizing our vision for a meaningful and generous life.

The interface of the laws of life and science fascinated Sir John. The influential national and international research initiatives that Sir John initiated through his eponymous philanthropic foundation on love, forgiveness, gratitude, joy, self-control, character, hope, humility, purpose, and prayer are all well identified in the laws of life. He often sought out premier scientists who might be able to make "spiritual progress" by learning more about one of these laws, which he sometimes described as the "invisible realities" that are so influential in each of our lives. One can connect Sir John's fascination with the benefits of bringing science to spiritual principles and laws of life to Unity. As one of Sir John's close associates, Unity minister Glenn R. Mosley, notes in his book *New Thought, Ancient Wisdom*, "Fillmore believed that an *appropriate* understanding of and belief in Scripture did not preclude embracing scientific research" (p. 30). Indeed, in 1933 Fillmore gave a major address at the World Fellowship of Faiths entitled "Unity of Religion and Science," in which he asserted that as science progresses, we must refine our beliefs accordingly. Sir John's diligent, deeply loyal, kind, and tireless son Dr. John M. Templeton Jr. continues this astonishing legacy of spiritual progress through scientific discovery as president of the John Templeton Foundation today.

Sir John freely pursued his dreams for improving the world. He knew that many philanthropists did marvelous work in contributing to needy organizations that tend to the weak, infirm, and vulnerable. He too was generous in helping others. But his bright and creative vision was to help all people, without exception, by slowly bringing the world to greater knowledge and practice of the laws of life. Sir John knew that with these principles of living planted in each of our minds and practiced in our daily lives, we could flourish at every level—interpersonally, emotionally, physically, economically, and spiritually. He felt that engaging the laws of life is crucial to human well-being and progress, and that their expansion into lives and culture is absolutely imperative for the future of civilization.

Were any objective observer to review the portfolio of research the John Templeton Foundation has funded in its twenty-five year history, it would be clear that most of the major initiatives are extensions of *The Essential Worldwide Laws of Life*. These laws constitute the backbone of Sir John's life work, and he clearly saw fit to investigate them with diligence. He was always seeking to strengthen our understanding of these laws as human assets in living well. They are the essence of "progress in religion," or "spiritual progress," and of the "invisible realities" that shape our actions. These are our human strengths, but they are laid out in the context of a spirituality that relates them not just to living better, but being closer to God.

The overarching principle of *The Essential Worldwide Laws of Life* is that our minds and thoughts are tremendously powerful in shaping the reality around us. This principle and spiritual discipline made its way from New Thought into Protestant Christianity through Norman Vincent Peale, whom Sir John knew personally for many years. It made its way into the business world through the writings of Napoleon Hill. It resonates with the mainstream "rational emotive therapy" movement of Albert Ellis. Sir John especially invited youth into this way of life. Indeed, in 1997 he handed me an autographed copy of *Worldwide Laws of Life* to give as a present to my then fourteen-year-old daughter Emma.

Sir John—and New Thought generally—have always stressed the centrality of agape love. A contemporary example of this core aspect of New Thought can be found in Dr. Michael Beckwith's Agape International Spiritual Center in Culver City, California, and throughout other entities loosely associated with Unity. This emphasis on agape love is not only central in Fillmore's work, but also in another New Thought pioneer, James Allen, who understood agape love as the chief source of happiness. Allen, in his 1903 classic *As a Man Thinketh*, articulated a line of thinking central to Sir John as follows: "The heart that has reached utter self-forgetfulness in its love for others has not only become possessed of the highest happiness but has entered immortality, for it has realized the Divine" (p. 122). Allen continues, "Lose yourself in the welfare of others; forget yourself in all that you do; this is the secret of abounding happiness" (p. 125).

The Essential Worldwide Laws of Life is all Sir John, but is now organized thematically into chapters and reduced a bit in length by the elimination of nonessential embellishments here and there. Now the words of his classic work flow more easily and jump right off the page to touch mind and heart with sage wisdom. *The Essential Worldwide Laws of Life* is an abridgement of Sir John's *Worldwide Laws of Life: 200 Eternal Spiritual Principles* (Templeton Press, 1997). Though Sir John passed away in 2008, he was always looking for ways to present his laws of life more effectively, and I feel certain that he would have been ecstatic with this essential edition. Sir John knew that life can be hard and circumstances difficult, but he recognized that we each have gifts and noble purposes that can move us forward, and that we can persevere and flourish best when we can use our minds effectively.

Stephen G. Post

Introduction

**W**HAT IS TO BECOME OF ME? What does the future hold? How can I set out on my own into a world that seems filled with conflict and strife? How do I cope with day-to-day pressures? How do I find peace in the midst of turmoil? What will allow me to be in the world, but not of the world? How can my life be useful and happy?

These are questions asked by many people today. Fortunately, there are positive responses and definite guidance that can enrich the life of every individual who sincerely seeks to learn. To be a happy and useful person, it is important to understand and practice the laws of life. These laws are simply the "set of rules" by which we should live. They come from a vast array of sources—the major sacred scriptures of the world; various schools of philosophical thought, both ancient and modern; storytellers, such as Aesop; scientists, such as Isaac Newton; and from various artists and historians—to name a few. There seem to be literally hundreds of such laws, and most families and religions seek to teach the laws they were taught. Some laws are so clear that most people can agree they are true. For example, honesty and truthfulness rank high as values in cultures and societies around the world.

Our stay on this small planet called Earth is a brief one, and we have an excellent opportunity to leave the world a better place than we found it through our choice of how we live our lives. One way to accomplish lasting improvement is to master the laws of life. The poet Henry Wadsworth Longfellow wrote:

> Lives of great men all remind us
> We can make our lives sublime,
> And, departing, leave behind us
> Footprints on the sands of time.

The truth of this statement can be demonstrated if we look to the lives of the famous as well as those of the unsung heroes of the past and present. Here we find many models for useful, happy living. And, when we examine their words and deeds, we often discover the principles that inspired and sustained their benefits to present and future generations.

The world operates on spiritual principles just as it operates on the laws of physics and gravity. It is up to us to learn what these principles are and then choose to live by them. You might ask, "What is spiritual law?" We may answer that it is an invisible law and, being of spirit, is not dictated by the laws of our physical world. Spiritual law isn't shaped by current opinion or whim. It is not determined by people. Spiritual laws are impartial because they apply equally to everyone throughout our world. They work without prejudice or bias at all times and in all places. These laws are self-enforcing and are not dependent on human authority or commandments.

Followers of the ancient Chinese sage Lao Tzu understood spiritual law as the Tao. The simplest interpretation of Tao, or spiritual law, is "This is how things work." One way to comprehend this law is to realize the relationship between the mind and its thoughts, feelings, and ideas and the physical activities that give those thoughts, feelings, and ideas expression. There is a relationship between the invisible thoughts and feelings of our minds and the visible actions we take as a result of them.

The Essential Worldwide Laws of Life is aimed at assisting people of all ages to learn more about the universal truths of life that transcend modern times or particular cultures in the hope that it may help people in all parts of the world to make their lives not only happier but more useful. The laws of life that were chosen for this book are important and possible to apply in one's life. Each quotation that serves as the title of an essay points to a particular law that holds true for most people under most circumstances. The material is designed to inspire as well as encourage you, to help you consider more deeply the laws you personally live by, and to reap the rewards of their practical application.

The laws described herein may be used as effective, practical, and workable tools. When you apply them consistently, you can draw forth the power to transform your life into a more deeply useful and joyful experience. Even if your life is already working well, it's possible that it can work even better as you incorporate more of the wisdom contained in these pages. If I had found a book of the basic laws of life during my college years, I could have been far more productive then and in the years that have followed. Possibly one of the laws in this book may encourage you to try something that, until now, you may have only dreamed of attempting!

In my youth, I was inspired by the courage and vision of Rudyard Kipling's poem "If." This poem taught me to dream but also to be master of my dreams. I learned from the great English poet that the earth belongs to us all and that, with courage and enthusiasm, progress is likely to follow. The final stanza of "If" still rings in my ears:

> If you can fill the unforgiving minute
> With sixty seconds' worth of distance run,
> Yours is the Earth and everything that's in it,
> And—which is more—you'll be a Man, my son!

Behind this book is my belief that the basic principles for leading "a sublime life," to paraphrase Longfellow, can be examined and tested just as science examines and tests natural laws of the universe. By learning the laws of life and applying them to everyday situations, more and more people may find themselves leading joyful and useful lives. It has been well said that "life is a tough school because the exams come first and the learning afterwards." This book is a sincere attempt to provide some opportunities for learning before the exams arrive!

Acknowledgments

Without the help of many individuals who shared their ideas and wisdom with me, this book would not have been possible. Over the years I have employed most of these people for their help in providing ideas, writings, explanations, examples, and editing for this collection of laws. Some of these contributors were ministers and laypeople associated with religious groups; others were private individuals who share a similar hopeful outlook on life and a fundamental belief in the principle that "life works better when you play by the rules."

THE ESSENTIAL
WORLDWIDE LAWS OF LIFE

CHAPTER I

Controlling Your Mind

When you rule your mind, you rule your world
—BILL PROVOST

REAT TEACHERS through the ages have described the importance of our minds and of mastering our thoughts. Buddha said, "The mind is everything; what you think, you become." Philosopher and psychologist William James wrote, "The greatest discovery of my generation is that a human being can alter his life by altering his attitudes of mind."

If you desire to understand the reason behind the statement "When you rule your mind, you rule your world," take a look at what some religious teachers and spiritual philosophers call Infinite Mind and the Law of Mind Action. Some say there is only one Mind, sometimes called Spirit, or God Mind. This Mind is the life, intelligence, power, and creativity that suffuses the entire universe. Yet they say the Law of Mind action holds that we are individual and yet remain a part of the whole.

We have free will. Here is the starting point of our actions, our spoken words, our thoughts, even our feelings. That makes a great deal of difference in what we think about God, our self, our family, our neighbors, our acquaintances, our work associates—everything. As English essayist Joseph Addison said, "One of the most difficult things for a powerful mind is to be its own master!"

A positive attitude toward life can be difficult for some people to adopt, for it may seem unrealistic. These skeptics may find it hard to believe that positive thinkers can accomplish almost anything they set their minds to. But, with a positive attitude, your chance for success in any situation is greater if you look for workable solutions rather than allowing negative thinking to limit your decision making. Zig Ziglar, a sales motivation expert, says, "Your business is never really good or bad out there. It's either good or bad right between your two ears!" He describes the most essential component of successful selling as the ability to understand and meet the other person's needs, saying, "You can get everything in life you want if you will just help enough people get what they want." The ability to listen to others and appropriately interpret their needs depends to a great extent on a receptive mental attitude. Ralph Waldo Emerson, the nineteenth-century essayist, emphasized the importance of the spiritual perspective in our life as well as the power of the mind.

Mary Kay Ash, founder of Mary Kay Cosmetics, was one of the most remarkable success stories of our time. Since 1963, her company grew from a modest storefront in Dallas to an international, billion-dollar operation with a sales force numbering in the millions. Her approach to management was based on meeting the needs of others. With well-grounded Christian values undergirding her business philosophy, she asked everyone in her organization to focus on meeting the needs of others as their top priority.

Selfishness overlooks a key principle of success—helping others. Successful people meet the needs of others because it makes them feel good about themselves. Then, by subordinating any selfish motives to the greater motive of being of service, they successfully navigate their way through life. As with successful men and women throughout the world, our success is proportionate to the number of people we have helped to grow and prosper.

Our thoughts are, most assuredly, things. They are conceived in the mind and travel through time and space like ripples in a pond, affecting all they touch. Thoughts are the building blocks of our experience. The world we see is the one we have created with our thoughts, for "Mind is the builder."

Your life becomes what you think
—MARCUS AURELIUS

Thought—the act or process of thinking—is one of the greatest powers we possess, and, like most powers, it can be used for good or evil, as we choose. Many people have never been taught how to use thought, to master the power of the mind. It is just as essential to know how to think correctly as it is to know how to speak or act correctly.

The mind, which is invisible, directs the thinking process. It tells the brain how to sort experience and fact, and how to give shape and form to new ideas. The indirect action of thought is easy to understand, for people must think before they can do anything. Thought is the motivating power behind an action, just as electricity is the motivating power behind lighting our home. Thought also has a direct effect on matter. Regardless of whether or not we translate our thought into action, the thought itself has already produced some kind of effect.

Have you ever had an original idea and wondered where it came from? It's as if your mind planted a seed of the idea in the brain. Your brain recalled your experience and knowledge and developed the idea in a way that could finally be expressed by you coherently and persuasively. You probably honed the idea as you tested it under various conditions.

In the same way, the mind tells the brain what to think about. It's tempting to believe that we have no control over what comes into our heads but, in reality, we do. If a thought comes to you that is not in your best interest, you can, with practice, begin thinking something else, so that the undesirable thought will simply go away.

Sound difficult? Try the following experiment. If someone says to you, "Don't think about bananas!" you immediately conjure up a mental image of a banana. To tell yourself to stop thinking about something doesn't do a great deal of good then, does it? The undesirable thought must be replaced by a desirable thought. If you don't want to think about bananas, try thinking about Valentine hearts. Once these two words are planted in your mind, you can picture the Valentine heart, in all its beauty, and the bananas are gone.

This is called the *crowding-out technique*. If you fill your mind to capacity with thoughts that are good and productive, you won't have room for the bad ones. The thoughts you can "crowd out" are those of envy, hatred, covetousness, self-centeredness, damaging criticism, revenge, and any time-wasting thoughts that are counterproductive to your ultimate goals in life. Another method for crowding out negative thoughts is to quietly release them. You might affirm, "I lovingly release you to the vast nothingness from whence you came." Then let them go.

Be kind to yourself in this process. If you've worked at changing your thoughts and the negative ones seem to keep roosting in your mind, laugh at yourself. Accept that you're doing your best, and return to thinking your replacement thought. As you become more adept at controlling your thoughts, your positive, good thoughts will change your life for the better.

What we focus on expands
—ARNOLD PATENT

When we focus on a particular thought, our mind often immediately responds by calling up similar thoughts. Positive and loving thoughts and feelings spark a whole range of thoughts and feelings that can lift our spirits. If, on the other hand, we concentrate on negative thoughts and fearful emotions, we may conjure up an ever-greater negativity.

Whatever we choose to focus on, our mind automatically expands that image for us.

Given this truth, wouldn't you rather focus on positive images than on negative ones? In a short scenario, suppose you are faced with a complicated task, and your mind focuses on the word *failure*. Suddenly, an image might be evoked in which you fail at your task. This image could expand to the point where you may fail at other tasks and, possibly, to the point where people may ridicule you for your failure. Now, clear your mind, and visualize that you are faced with the same task, and decide to focus on the word *success*. Let positive images of accomplishing the task fill your mind. You see images of others appreciating your success, shaking your hand, smiling with admiration. This success image snowballs, and you can see yourself succeeding at other, more difficult, tasks.

But can these thoughts affect your actual performance? Absolutely. When you focus on a particular image, you tend to talk about what's on your mind. Thus, if your mental focus is on positive images, you're more likely to mention these ideas and images in communication with others. A good listener, who focuses on what is being said, can absorb your positive words and actions, and many constructive images or ideas might come to him. Like the spark that ignites the flame, he may share these good ideas with others, and they, in turn, may share them with still others. Thoughts expand not only within our own minds but expand through others as well.

Many spiritual teachers know that the human mind is molded from an omnipresent element that takes form, shape, and intelligence, and becomes a part of our thought world. The knowledge and awareness that compose your world often come from what you have held in mind as your inner ideal. Be confident about your mental focus. Are you really alive, alert, awake, and enthusiastic about life? If so, the harvest of abundant living can fill your world with gladness.

As you think, so you are

—CHARLES FILLMORE

The condition of your health, your finances, your relationships, your livelihood—all of these reflect the fruit of certain attitudes. If you don't like the fruit you're harvesting—for example, poor health, financial struggle, difficulty in maintaining meaningful relationships, unhappiness with your work—it's essential that you harvest from another tree.

The writer of Proverbs said, "As [a man] thinketh in his heart, so is he" (Prov. 23:7, KJV). He understood that it's what we think in our heart that expresses itself in our lives. What you believe about yourself, what you believe about life, can work itself into and through everything you do. Successful living begins by believing yourself worthy of success.

A young woman named Marianne believed she was inferior and her life bore the fruit of that belief. She had grown up on the so-called wrong side of the tracks. Throughout her young life, well-meaning friends warned her not to expect too much because life was hard and it was unfair. For years her life bore the fruit of that belief. She became a prostitute and a drug addict. She was in and out of jail regularly. One day, while walking through a shopping mall, Marianne stole a wallet from another woman's purse. The wallet contained a few dollars, some credit cards, and, among other things, a small pamphlet. Intending to take only what was of immediate value and get rid of the rest, a sentence from the pamphlet caught her attention, "As a child of God, you are worthy of the best life has to offer."

In the moments that followed, something strange began to happen to Marianne. Her cold, bitter attitude toward life and people began to thaw. Somehow those words struck a chord that had long been lost but not quite forgotten. She was further surprised when she found herself desperately feeling the need to return the wallet to the woman. Getting the phone number from a blank check in the wallet, Marianne phoned the woman that day. She explained what she had done and said that she wanted to bring the wallet over to her home immediately.

To Marianne's surprise, there was no bitterness in the woman's attitude. Instead, there was compassion and understanding. Marianne told the woman about her hard life, and the woman listened to her with tender sympathy. The woman offered Marianne a job in one of the many dress shops she owned in the city. She went out of her way to help Marianne shed the harsh feelings from her past and begin to believe in herself. In time, the young woman's life began to bear a whole different kind of fruit. She gradually gained confidence in herself and was able to begin to trust others and see the good in them.

Another person's faith in us can strengthen our faith in ourselves. The mother of a fifteen-year-old named Doug became increasingly worried when her son's temperature kept rising until it reached 105 degrees. Doug was taken to the hospital, where blood tests revealed leukemia. The doctors were frank, telling Doug that for the next three years he would have to undergo chemotherapy. He might go bald and gain weight. Learning this, Doug became discouraged; although he was told that there was a good chance of remission, he was smart enough to know that leukemia can be fatal.

On the day Doug was admitted—his first time in a hospital—he had opened his eyes, looked around the room, and said to his mother, "I thought you got flowers when you are in the hospital." Hearing this, an aunt called to order an arrangement. The voice of the sales clerk was high-pitched, and she sounded young. The aunt imagined an inexperienced person who may be unaware of the arrangement's significance. So she said, "I want the planter especially attractive. It's for my teenage nephew who has leukemia."

"Oh," said the sales clerk, "Let's add some fresh-cut flowers to brighten it up."

When the arrangement arrived at the hospital, Doug was feeling strong enough to sit up. He opened the envelope and read the card from his aunt. Then he saw another card. His mother said it must have been meant for another flower arrangement, but Doug removed it, opened it, and began to read. The card said, "Doug—I took your order. I work at Brix Florist. I had leukemia when I was seven years old. I'm twenty-two years old now. Good luck. My heart goes out to you. Sincerely, Laura Bradley." Doug's face lit up. For the first time since he entered the hospital, he felt inspired. He had spoken with many doctors and nurses, but this one card was the thing that made him believe he might beat the disease.

This story was reported in the *Chicago Tribune* newspaper by Bob Greene:

> It's funny; [Doug] was in a hospital filled with millions of dollars of the most sophisticated medical equipment. He was being treated by expert doctors and nurses with medical training totaling hundreds of years. But it was a sales clerk in a flower shop . . . who—by taking the time to care, and by being willing to go with what her heart told her to do—gave Doug hope and the will to carry on. The human spirit can be an amazing thing, and sometimes you encounter it at its very best when you aren't even looking!

Pay close attention to what your heart tells you. If you are working toward prosperity and harmony in life, be certain you truly believe you are worthy of having them. This inner conviction, coupled with action, may produce the fruit in life you so deeply desire. Remember, as you think, so you are!

Your thoughts are like boomerangs
—EILEEN CADDY

The continent of Australia has given us many unusual things. Cut off from the rest of the world by vast ocean waters for millions of years, even animal life there has developed into strange forms—for example, the kangaroo and the platypus, the goose-billed, fur-bearing animal that lays eggs and feeds on earthworms.

Australia's indigenous people have their own unique customs and inventions. Of the latter, the boomerang is the most famous. It is a "stick that comes back." When thrown by a skilled handler, a boomerang, which comes in a variety of different shapes, may sail far away and still return to the thrower's hands. Some Australian natives are so skilled in its use that they can kill birds and other game for food with the boomerang.

Our conduct, the way we act, may be similar to the boomerang—especially acts of loving-kindness. For kindness has a way of returning to those who express it to others. You may have heard of the old fable of the lion and the mouse. One day a hungry lion caught a tiny mouse who pleaded for its life, saying, "I am such a tiny mouthful for you, O great lion. Besides, if you release me, some day I may be able to do you a return favor." The lion laughed at the mouse and let it go.

Sometime later, the lion was caught in a rope net trap which had been set by hunters. And who do you think gnawed the ropes apart and saved the lion? The tiny mouse, of course.

It is the truly brave, the truly great, the truly unafraid who often exhibit the greatest kindness in their activities. Many are rewarded with kindness from others and with positive things that happen to them. When a job opening, or an opportunity for advancement becomes available, or a chance to accompany a friend on a trip or to a special event, the friend who has acted kindly toward others generally receives the special invitation first.

That which returns to us may often be decreed by what we send out. The Good Samaritan in the Bible narrative could have walked by the injured man lying beside the road and sincerely prayed that the man would somehow be helped. Instead, he did the practical thing by stopping to assist a fellow traveler and proved to be a noble instrument of God, binding the man's wounds and helping him to shelter.

God has given his children so many blessings. We may draw forth from the reservoir of spirit as much as we choose to receive and use. When we begin to realize and appreciate spiritually the wonders of God's creation, we become like an explorer who visits a new country filled with abundant, amazing, and beautiful opportunities. As we abide in this consciousness of love and kindness, we begin to pass along to others our love and our blessings in many ways. This energy may then return to us, like a boomerang. It might take years to return, and the blessings may come from a different direction, but the law of life of giving and receiving can do its precious work in our lives.

Thoughts held in mind produce after their kind
—CHARLES FILLMORE

Many ago comedian Flip Wilson made famous the phrase "What you see is what you get." While this is a common belief, it would perhaps be more accurate to say, "What you think is what you get!"

Thoughts, like seeds, sprout and blossom according to their variety, and the thoughts you cultivate create your experiences of life. Just as a seed planted in fertile soil produces healthy fruit, your mind may be lightened or darkened depending on the type of thoughts planted in it. If apple seeds are planted and nurtured, you can harvest delicious, juicy apples. If you plant and nurture thistle seeds, you get prickly thistles. This analogy also holds true for the mind. Positive thoughts can produce positive results, whereas negative thoughts can lead to negative results. Understanding this cause-and-effect relationship can help you "think into being" the kind of life you wish to have.

Each of us is born with the freedom to choose the thoughts we want to direct our lives. We can choose the path we desire to pursue; we may choose the pace at which we wish to travel, and also what we wish to carry along the way. Have you ever realized that you have the ability to precondition your mind to success? When you precondition your mind, you invest in the process of transforming your life. This is a basic principle of positive thinking. You can forecast whether you find future success or failure by your present type of thinking. How? Because what you consistently think is likely to happen, tends to happen. Let's take a further step and define the meaning of success. In its deepest sense, success means to live graciously, humbly, orderly, lovingly, and compassionately as a person and to use fully your talents to help others, not merely to achieve things.

Napoleon Hill, the best-selling American author of *Think and Grow Rich*, was born and raised in a one-room log cabin in the mountains of southwest Virginia. Young Hill's home was so isolated that he was twelve years old before he saw his first railroad train. Adding to his impoverishment was the loss of his mother when he was only ten.

Dr. Hill, in his later years, remembered the day, a year after his mother's death, when his father brought home a new wife. "My father introduced her to the relatives. When my turn came, I was standing in the corner with my arms folded and a scowl on my face. I was all set to show her how tough I could be.

"Father walked up to me and said, 'Martha, here is your son, Napoleon, the meanest boy in Wise County. I won't be surprised if he starts throwing rocks at you by tomorrow morning.'" All the relatives roared with laughter.

"My stepmother walked up to me," Hill recalled, "put her hand under my chin, and lifted my head upward so she could look squarely into my sullen face. 'You are wrong about this boy,' she said. 'He is not the meanest boy in Wise County. He is a smart boy, who has not yet learned how to make the best use of his wisdom.'"

With his stepmother's encouragement, Napoleon Hill traded his rifle for a typewriter. She taught him to type, to do research, and to express his ideas in writing. When he said, "There is but one thing over which man has complete control. That is his own mental attitude," it was his own experience speaking. For when Napoleon Hill replaced the belief that he was mean with the seed-thought that he was wise and could do great things, he became the successful person he was meant to be. He went on to advise kings and presidents and to inspire millions through the power of the written word.

As you read this book, reflect on what your thoughts have created over a period of time. Defeatist thoughts, angry thoughts, dishonest thoughts, self-centered thoughts, and failure thoughts are destructive. Loving thoughts, honest thoughts, service thoughts, and success thoughts are creative.

Just as fruit generated from the best kind of seed is the most delicious and pleasing, so, too, the life most worth living is cultivated from the best and most loving thoughts. Before you can utilize the positive power of your thoughts, it is necessary to become aware of your current pattern of thinking. You may not have a stepmother who was as helpful as Napoleon Hill's in pointing out negative thought patterns. Nevertheless, in quiet times on your own, observe your habits of thought, and begin to weed out those that do not suit your higher purposes.

You can train your mind to nurture positive, loving, and unselfish thought patterns and, through them, develop a deeper, richer personality that may be the fulfillment and fruition of your greatest creative potential.

Whether you think you can or not, you are right
—HENRY FORD

Would it surprise you to learn that everything in your life right now may be pretty much the way you made it? Have you thought recently that from hundreds of options, you choose your responses to whatever situations present themselves? Would you agree that you have exercised the capacity to choose what you have received? If so, doesn't it stand to reason that if you made the choice in the first place, you can change your mind and change a situation?

What a powerful notion! Whatever happens to you, you can say, "I am the master of my life." In order to meet life joyously and successfully, we need to cultivate a positive attitude toward life. This can give us a feeling of being in tune with our good and can help bring that good into being. After all, our attitude in life plays a big part in bringing us joy in living.

If we allow negative or restrictive thoughts to live in our minds, our self-made limitations can sometimes cause us to forget that we can fly with the freedom of thought. Our invisible mental prisons remind us from time to time, "You can't do that. It isn't practical. You're not smart enough. It will cost too much. People will laugh at you. You're too young. You're too old. Your health won't allow it. Your parents won't allow it. It will take too long. You don't have the education."

It sometimes seems true that many people have become accustomed to searching out, examining, and even magnifying signs of trouble in their lives and in their world. It can be easy to see unpleasantness around us if this is where we choose to place our focus. Anne Frank, who underwent great hardship during World War II, wrote in her diary that in spite of all she had been through, she still believed in the basic goodness of people. This is the kind of optimism that we can live with and that can help us to live. The world we live in has been in existence for a long time. There may be some facets of it that we cannot change, and, of course, they may have an effect upon us. Yet each of us creates an important part of the world in which we live—our own inner world.

Are we willing to consider that we just might attract to ourselves whatever our minds are focused on? That if we think we can do something, we can; and if we think we cannot do something, often we can't?

Life is not all chance; life is mostly choice. We can be the "builders of our lives," with the freedom to choose our thoughts and thereby establish our habits and our attitudes. These attitudes then can determine the direction and quality of our lives. We are thinking and feeling beings. Through the power of our minds, we become more able to experience and accomplish that on which we place our attention. There may be few subjects that we know and understand less about than the formative power of the mind. Whether we think we can or not, we are right!

Change your mind to change your life
—SIR JOHN TEMPLETON

What does your mind have to do with your life? Everything! To illustrate: if you believe you're unworthy of love and happiness, you may attract to yourself situations that disappoint, frustrate, and hurt. Conversely, healthy self-esteem can build positive results. The mind is considered to be the starting point of every act and thought and feeling.

Thinking is a creative force that is constantly at work in humanity and in creation. That magnetic atmosphere of thought travels with you and is a part of you. To cultivate a positive attitude toward life, it is important to put your faith in strong and positive ideas, rather than allowing circumstances and conditions to rule and create unhappy and resistant attitudes toward things that happen.

It's important to move from negative to positive thinking if a person wants the quality of her life to improve. You can think in a new way and begin finding the good that exists in you and in others by making a decision to change. You only need to be willing to try. Your mind can be powerfully creative. It is capable of continually higher levels of thinking. Exercise your mental muscles! You are the one who controls the attitudes your mind will hold, express, and project. You have the freedom and authority to create the best life and attitude you can possibly envision.

In the book *Macro-Mind Power*, author Rebecca Clark emphasizes:

> Begin now to school your impulses and feelings into desired areas. Your dreams and ideals are the parents of your impulses and feelings. What you think concerning people, places, situations, and things can take shape in

your life. Refuse to entertain a thought about someone else which you would not have objectified in yourself. You are the assemblage of your thoughts!

If you desire to change your life to a more positive living experience, examine your thinking processes. Change your mind, and you can find life's unlimited good in every situation, awaiting your recognition and acceptance.

You create your own reality
—JANE ROBERTS

Do you believe that "reality" may be something outside yourself? We often hear people refer to the "real world out there." To be sure, there can be a world beyond our own personal reality—an outer world that may have an appearance and distinction of its own. However, another world, an inner one, may be much more real. This is the place where your beliefs, thoughts, and feelings reside. Your happiness, peace of mind, and enjoyment of work, friends, and loved ones often depends more on this inner world than on the outer one.

Two people could have similar *external* circumstances and have very different internal experiences. Suppose, for example, two men were given the task of speaking before a large audience. Mr. Smith may enjoy speaking in public, and the experience can be a most pleasant one for him. Mr. Jones, on the other hand, may be extremely fearful of public speaking and find the experience a harrowing test of willpower. Both men share a similar reality, but their internal realities may be far removed from each other.

An unhappy person may see things that tend to justify his unhappiness. The pessimist may see discouraging signs wherever he looks. The positive person usually seeks to find the good in a situation. And the honest person can find the truth in the situation at hand and create his own reality.

We have far more control over our inner world than our outer world. Not to say that changing our inner world is necessarily easy. We may have developed thinking and feeling patterns or belief systems that are deeply ingrained. Change may not always be easy, but it can be accomplished. Examining our beliefs and attitudes and observing our thoughts and feelings can be a useful place to begin. Change often starts to happen when we recognize false beliefs and make an effort to bring them in line with reality; when we recognize negative thoughts and choose not to listen to them; and when we recognize negative feelings and choose to give them no power over us. We have the power to create our own reality by choosing thoughts and beliefs that are positive and true. So, in truth, we do create our own reality, our inner reality, the only reality in which we truly live.

The mind can make a heaven into a hell, or a hell into a heaven
—JOHN MILTON

An article in *Sunshine* magazine mentioned the way most people talk. It said that they use *D*'s instead of *P*'s. The string of *D*'s that people vocalized every day included debt, doubt, disease, disaster, discouragement, depression, decay, deception, danger, defeat, difficulty, discord, deception, disappointment, distrust, disagreement, dread, dejection, destitution, and desolation!

The article then went on to say we would be much better off talking about the *P*'s: peace, prosperity, plenty, power, pluck, persistence, purpose, promotion, possession, proficiency, progress, perseverance, prayer, and possibilities.

Which of the two types—those who use the *D*'s or those who use the *P*'s—do you think lives in a more heavenly state of consciousness?

Living on the "right" side of life, or the "heavenly" side, can bring sparkle and beauty to the many facets of our individuality and the way our lives unfolds. Maybe you know someone who lives in a "heavenly" state of consciousness, and things seem to work out well for him. He enjoys splendid health. The affairs of his life seem to be happy and harmonious, and the much-desired "good things of life" have a habit of coming his way.

However, there seem to be other people who somehow manage to get on the "wrong side of life," regardless of their desire for things to be otherwise. They experience times when nothing seems to work out in their favor. The harder they try, the further away they seem to be from good health, happiness, success, or whatever good they may be seeking. What makes the difference between these two seemingly opposite ways of life?

The truth is that our attitude of mind can actually help the good things of life either to gravitate toward us or move away from us. Our mind and our thinking processes can make a heaven into a hell, or a hell into a heaven. How, then, can we cultivate and develop the right attitude of mind?

The first step is to pause right where we are, stop the chattering noise of our thoughts, and allow our thinking to adjust.

A second step is to reaffirm your faith, lift your consciousness—and your thoughts—to a higher level of expression. Suppose you are experiencing some difficulty. Daily living may seem to be hard going at the moment, and you may feel uncertain about what you need to do next. Instead of beginning to panic and put pressure on yourself, pause for a moment and affirm, "Spirit goes before me, guiding and directing my efforts and my direction." Lifting your thoughts to a higher level can renew and restore the peace and serenity of your awareness—and your life!

One further step is often necessary: this is to go forward with confidence and courage, trusting the inner guidance that you receive and knowing that the way may indeed be made clear.

Beautiful thoughts build a beautiful soul
—SIR JOHN TEMPLETON

A person may be born in poverty, but by mastering and controlling his destiny through his thoughts, feelings, actions, and choices, he can rise above his limitations, and make the transition to a more spiritually evolved soul. Isn't this potential worth the effort to properly use the tremendous gift and power of your mind?

There are certain good ideas, or laws of life, that we need to learn, practice, and cooperate with to lead a happy and successful life. Seeing the good in everyone and everything is one such idea. Recognizing and appreciating the beauty that is all around us is another. These ideas, when believed in, begin to work a kind of magical transformation in our lives. For example, if we look at ourselves and find that we could be more loving individuals, we may entertain in our minds the idea of love. We may give our minds and hearts to this idea. We may let it have its way with us as if it were some kind of living entity.

It is a law of life that whatever we give our attention to, and believe in, tends to become our experience. The law of good ideas instructs us to begin to practice the art of giving our attention and belief to such good ideas. As we practice abiding by the ideas of abundance, wisdom, strength, love, faith, imagination, life, and health, we begin to see positive and distinct changes for the better transforming our lives.

Thoughts are things
—CHARLES FILLMORE

Thoughts are things. Thoughts create things. Thoughts shape things. Thoughts are real. The invisible process going on inside our heads that we call thinking produces objects as real as the ground we walk on or the food we eat. Consider for a moment your thoughts as a flowing mountain stream. The life-giving stream begins high in the mountain, flows down to the valley below, and then empties out into the fields and orchards of your life. You want to keep that stream as pure and fresh as when it emerged from its source. You wouldn't dream of pouring polluting chemicals or refuse into that lovely stream because you know you would reap the results in terms of an unhealthy and scanty harvest in your fields and orchards.

Your personal world depends on your stream of thought for its prosperity, health, beauty, harmony, and well-being in the same way that a farmer's field depends on fresh water to produce its maximum yield. We can look around our planet and see problems caused by pollution. Consider what might be happening in our minds and bodies as a result of the polluted thoughts and feelings that we allow to reside in our minds! *Pollution* may sound like a negative word, so perhaps we could think in terms of mental ecology. *Webster's Dictionary* defines the word *ecology* as "a branch of science concerned with the interrelationship of organisms and their environments." Mental ecology, then, means the branch of study that deals with the relationship between human thoughts and their environment. The Bible hints at the importance of mental ecology when it states the relationship between human thoughts and their environment in this manner: "As [a man] thinketh in his heart, so is he" (Prov. 23:7, KJV). And a proverb from the Buddhist Tripitaka reminds us, "All that we are is the result of what we have thought: It is founded on our thoughts and is made up of our thoughts."

Mental pollution refers to negative thoughts, feelings, and attitudes. Emotional responses of anger, hate, envy, jealousy, guilt, fear, resentment, and recrimination are pollutants that disrupt the mental and spiritual ecology of our mind. And the eventual suffering these pollutants cause mirrors the problems brought on by unabated pollution of the atmosphere, land, and waters of our earth.

Let's consider thoughts now from a different perspective. Thoughts can shape things. Almost everything that we use and come in contact with each day was originally a thought. For example, the car we drive, its motor, tires, wheel, and mechanical parts came into being as thoughts in someone's mind. The material things we take for granted in life and that make living easier or more pleasant—pencils, ballpoint pens, chewing gum, magazines, textbooks, candy, ice cream, cell phones, television, radios and DVD players, computers, houses and apartment buildings, schools, churches, and so much more—started as thoughts, as ideas.

Because thoughts are invisible, we may not be aware of their tangible existence. Also, the material manifestations of thoughts may come hours, days, months, or even years after their inception as ideas. It would be a mistake to underestimate the power of the mind. Our thoughts mold the kind of people we become and are as important as our behavior. In fact, our thoughts are a form of behavior. If we think negative thoughts, we can become negative, reactive, and uncreative. But if we think positive thoughts and seek to see the good in every situation, our attitude and response to life reflect a sunny and pleasant disposition.

Learn to discipline and direct your thinking. Focus on thoughts and actions that build up rather than tear down. Think of St. Paul's words to the Philippians (4:8): "Finally, brethren, whatever is true, whatever is honorable, whatever is just, whatever is pure, whatever is lovely, whatever is gracious, if there is any excellence, if there is anything worthy of praise, think about these things."

CHAPTER 2

Building Character

The measure of a man's real character is what he would do if he would never be found out
—THOMAS MACAULAY

 F THE MEASURE of a person's real character is determined by what he would do if he weren't found out, the only person capable of judging his actions is the person himself and God. If he can look at himself in the mirror each day and know he is living as honestly as he can, that honest and positive assurance will be reflected in his eyes. Our conscience can often be our friend and our guide. It nudges us when we contemplate doing something wrong. It warns us of the danger that could be done to us or to others if we stray from our true path. It is important to listen to that inner voice. The person who learns or chooses to ignore his conscience often forsakes his best friend and lifetime guide.

We've been building our character since we were children, and part of the building process can be learning to listen to our conscience and following its guidance. We know there may be times when we can do something wrong and not be found out. We also know that if we get away with doing something wrong, *we* will know what we did, and we have to live with ourselves twenty-four hours a day. Every time we put a chink in our character, we become diminished, and our pride and self-esteem suffer.

Our real character can be measured by us. If we do a self-inventory and find we may be lacking in desired personal attributes, we can make the conscious choice to grow in areas of integrity, honesty, humility, sincerity, or other positive traits we desire. We can determine to live honestly with ourselves and others. We can determine to be as honest in secret as we are when others are present. We can determine that our character will be of value to *us*.

You alone live with your motives and secret actions, and only you can set the standard of your personal integrity. Eventually, the temptation to abandon your high standards will arise. It may be prompted by unexpected circumstances, a friend, a coworker, a mate, or even an employer. It may come unexpectedly, and it may even seem like the logical thing to do. Certainly it may appear to be the easiest answer to a complicated situation. At such times you would do well to ask yourself if you will be able to look back later, satisfied that you did your best. Will you be able to review your conduct and feel successful deep within? Perhaps no one may ever find out how you performed—whether you cut corners or, instead, went the "extra mile" to do the appropriate thing. But *you* know. Will you be inwardly proud of your performance or have the gnawing feeling that you could have been more honest?

Each person is here for a purpose. Each of us has a place to fulfill and a job to do that can improve the world just because we are living. Can you feel this inner longing? The accomplishment doesn't have to be a big, spectacular job, but it can be important for you to feel that you are doing something to make the world a little better than it was before. Listen carefully to the inner promptings of conscience.

Never do anything that you'll have to punish yourself for
—ANONYMOUS

Have you ever noticed that when you cheat, or lie, or don't support a friend, and then realize what you've done, an inner alarm goes off? It's a kind of moral wake-up call! What if your friends found out what you'd done? If the person you respected most in the world discovered you had let him down?

Hiding a cruel, selfish, uncaring, or unloving act deep down inside doesn't make it go away. Often it festers, and you begin to feel guilty and full of shame. Even if no one knows but you, those bad feelings come back to haunt you whenever you think about them.

Unfortunately, these bad feelings about ourselves rarely go away without some kind of self-examination. And it's by experiencing the emotions and accepting the ramifications of what you've done that you can begin to accept and change yourself. There are several ways you can come to terms with yourself. First, you can admit the truth, even if it's only to yourself and one other person, perhaps a counselor or a minister. Talking about a painful situation with someone you trust can pull the situation out into the open and remove a weight from your mind and heart. You're being honest and have a chance to forgive yourself.

Second, if it's something that can be corrected by telling the truth, then do so. The truth in any situation can clear the air. Speaking the truth is an affirmation of light and can release the emotions of shame and guilt. It takes a lot of courage to be honest, and many friendships have grown deeper because of honesty between the people involved in a situation.

Lastly, you can choose to make a contract with yourself to only do things you can be proud of in the future. This contract is a commitment to live with integrity, regardless of whether or not others around you choose to live that way. Remember that, ultimately, you are the one who benefits by living with honor and integrity. It is a powerful key to good health, good relationships, and self-esteem.

The truth will make you free
—JOHN 8:32

Like a person in a hypnotic state, everyone may be suggestible to a certain extent, which is why advertising is so effective, and why it is important to examine your beliefs from time to time to see where they originate. How much of what you believe is the result of what others told you? How much of what you believe about yourself comes from what others believe about you?

What is a great truth that can make you free? Possibly this. No matter what your condition, your environment, or your situation may be; no matter how unhappy or miserable you might think you are; no matter what you may be facing in the way of problems; the answer and the remedy are right within yourself. Those who have chosen to believe this truth and practice the principles underlying it can become people of peace and joy and happiness and abundant living. They know that within them is an unconquerable spirit. They have been touched by its power, and they have felt its presence. They live by this truth constantly.

The Indian spiritual and political leader Mohandas K. Gandhi said this about truth: "In the dictionary of the seeker of truth there is no such thing as being 'not successful.' He is or should be an irrepressible optimist because of his immovable faith in the ultimate victory of Truth, which is God."

It is important to bring our thoughts, feelings, words, and actions into alignment with our understanding of God's will. Through these applications we may invite the presence of Spirit and victorious living into our lives. The truth really can make us free once we realize that much of what we believe, especially about ourselves, is not necessarily the truth but is instead a "hypnotic suggestion" we have accepted from others.

Seek to become aware of what you believe about yourself, about others, and regarding the world around you. Ask yourself, "Is this really true or is it an illusion?" If your beliefs seem to be limiting your options in life by keeping you in bondage, they probably do not represent the truth. When you know the truth about who you really are, you are indeed free!

Honesty is the best policy
—MIGUEL DE CERVANTES

In African legend, an old chief needed to test the wisdom of the young man he had chosen to be his successor as head of the tribe. He asked the young man to prepare two meals for him. The first meal was to contain the very best ingredients life had to offer; the second meal would contain the worst.

On the appointed day, the chief sat down to his first meal and was served a delicious plate of sliced cow tongue with vegetables. The chief was delighted with the food, and upon finishing, asked the young man why he had chosen tongue.

"The tongue is one of the finest parts of our being," the young man replied. "It can speak wonderful words of truth that can help our people grow and prosper. The right words can give our people courage and bolster their integrity. Tongues can speak of love and harmony and hold our village together."

The chief was quite impressed and waited for his second meal with eager anticipation. On the appointed day, the chief sat down to eat his second meal and found it to be identical to the first. When he finished the meal, he asked the young man why he had prepared the same food twice.

The young man answered:

> The tongue can be the best part of us, but it can also be the worst. The tongue can speak words of anger and discouragement that can tear people down and rob them of hope. It can weave deceit; it can speak untruths that may cause disharmony. The tongue, more than any other weapon, could destroy our village life.

The old chief listened closely and slowly nodded his head. He knew he had chosen the next leader wisely.

There may be times when it seems that one little lie—what is called a "little white lie"—might make life easier. "After all, who would know?" is a rationalization we may use when considering taking the easy way. But deceptions can become linked to further, and more damaging, deceptions, which may cause our thoughts and actions to become confused and impure. Deceit often takes a terrible toll on our sense of integrity and self-worth.

Even if our lies are only "little white lies," the tangled web of dishonesty can choke the joy and spontaneity from our lives. We may try to convince ourselves they weren't really lies at all, but at some level of awareness, truth whispers to us that the path of honesty can be a peaceful policy.

Jordan's late King Hussein, during a conference of Arab chiefs of state, commented, "We should face reality and our past mistakes in an honest adult way. Boasting of glory does not make glory, and singing in the dark does not dispel fear." And Fanny Brice, American comedian and singer, promoted honesty by saying, "Let the world know you as you are, not as you think you should be, because sooner or later, if you are posing, you will forget the pose, and then where are you?"

The ability to choose lies or truth can, indeed, be a powerful weapon, as the old African chief understood well in naming his successor. The young man did not sugarcoat the truth. He refused to make a white lie out of it. What we may not realize is that by choosing deceit, we often end up hurting ourselves. There may be times when we might be tempted to believe that a lie could protect us. But the best protection—that which can assure us of a happy and successful life—is the knowledge that, in every circumstance, honesty is the best choice.

Honesty is the first chapter in the book of wisdom
—THOMAS JEFFERSON

Great philosophers and sages begin with one truth—be honest and "all things will be added unto you." They understood that people share the same basic drives: a need for love, for freedom and respect, and the desire to feel as if their lives have meaning. By looking within, the keys to understanding human behavior can be revealed if you are courageous enough to search your innermost heart.

But how many of us know where that heart is? How many of us have fallen out of touch with what we intuitively know? Often this seems to be most true when we apply it to knowing our own feelings. The noisy hustle and bustle of the outer world can distract us so much that we have a hard time listening to that still, small voice that knows the truth of any situation.

Thomas Jefferson wrote as follows in a letter to one of his contemporaries:

> He who permits himself to tell a lie once, finds it much easier to do it a second and third time, til at length it becomes habitual. He tells lies without attending to it, and truths without the world's believing him. This falsehood of the tongue leads to that of the heart, and in time depraves all its good dispositions.

Jefferson tried to be as farsighted as possible so that a nation of honest men and women would endure. "Sometimes it is said," he wrote, "that a man cannot be trusted with the government of himself. Can he, then, be trusted with the government of others?" A compelling thought when we extend it beyond our small personal world. But what is any nation made up of, except the entwining of many people's small worlds? How often have we read in the newspapers of injustices in our own cities and towns, and shrugged? What can we do? How can we make a difference? Truth isn't our jurisdiction. Or is it?

One important thing we can do is make it a habit to be honest with ourselves and others at all times. When we disconnect from our feelings to avoid a scene or to appear "cool," we often silence the voice within. We may silence truth. After a while we may no longer hear its voice. This may be one reason why psychologists and psychiatrists seem to be so busy in today's world. We may be paying to learn how to reconnect to our own inner promptings.

Begin today. The following exercise can offer meaningful insights into yourself. Take a sheet of paper and divide it into two columns. On one side write down the things you *like* about human nature—the things you *honor*. You may write down qualities like tenderness, strength, humor, diplomacy, love, or hard work—whatever comes to mind. Then, in the other column, write down those qualities that you may find *offensive*—the ones that may "push your buttons." In this column you may write down anger, laziness, deception, cowardice, brutality, or jealousy.

Then take a look at both columns. In total truth, claim them both. Name the aspects of honorable character as you see them in yourself. Find where they may resonate with you. And recognize which, if any, need to be strengthened and worked on. Take the undesirable column and address these items. Recognize that you have smidgeons of these characteristics, even if they may be hidden from the sight of most people. Acknowledge them for the times when they arise. Do not deny them utterly, or they could creep up on you as the disowned enemy in yourself—sometimes coming only in the guise of the people that you draw to you, because they are denied within.

Be honest. Be true. Love all parts of yourself. You are human, and, like the rest of us, the godhood within you—the goodness within you—is in a state of coming to magnificent expression. With honesty and free will, you can claim those aspects of yourself that you choose to express in your world.

There is a part of you that can be larger than any littleness, stronger than any weakness, wiser than you may think, and more brave than any fear. There is a part of you that is of the earth—earthy—as there is also a part of you that is of the Spirit—spiritual. This is the important part of you. Be honest with yourself and others. Learn to know your real self.

A good reputation is more valuable than money
—PUBLILIUS SYRUS

Your reputation is mostly the result of how others see you. A good reputation is slowly built on a firm foundation of humility, integrity, love, and charity. Building a good reputation can be similar to building a house. You begin with a basic firm foundation and build from that point. The finished house is a product of the choices you made during the construction—from plan to completion. If your house is carelessly constructed of thin walls, then the slightest wind may destroy it. If you have chosen your building materials with attention to strength, quality, and durability, your house can withstand the strong winds that may blow.

Let's consider an example. By the time he was eighteen, John was saddled with a very poor reputation. He often lied. He would make promises to his friends and fail to keep them, no matter how important those promises were to the other person. He had even been arrested for shoplifting. Because John's father was very well off financially, John thought he had everything. He lived in a fine house, wore the latest fashions, had his own car, and had plenty of spending money.

But John did not have everything. Far from it! He did not have a good reputation. One summer, between his high school graduation and the start of college in September, John applied for a summer job in the field of his planned future career. But he didn't get the job. His poor reputation cost him the position. Then, for the first time, he fell in love. But because of his well-known reputation, the girl refused to date him.

Fortunately, John came to realize that money is not so important in life if it's accompanied by a poor reputation. Your reputation, not your money, is the most valuable currency of all. John began to make changes in his life, but many years passed before people completely accepted the "new" John.

Again, what you do in everyday life affects your reputation. It is up to you, and you alone, to make appropriate decisions. Friends, parents, coworkers, clergy, and teachers can help you, advise you, and stand by you, but they cannot act for you. If you take the time to think about what effects any action can have on your life and make your decisions based on that awareness, you can earn a good reputation. It doesn't matter if you're rich or poor, a good reputation increases your chances of leading a life rich in meaning and happiness. This doesn't mean you won't make mistakes. Everyone makes mistakes. It is important, however, to admit your mistakes when you make them and take whatever steps you can to correct them. This can keep your reputation intact.

When you have a good reputation, you exude integrity, and you like and respect who you are. Work to build that good reputation. Money cannot buy it, but hard work can earn it.

What would you like to be able to say about yourself and to have others say about you? Create a fantasy in your mind and imagine exactly how you would most like to be. Would you like to feel from within yourself that what you say is honest and true? Would you like for your friends and associates to know the integrity of your intentions? What level of confidence would you like to project as you relate with people in your everyday world? Would you like to be more loving and gentle? Create in your mind a living picture of the kind of personality and attributes that would serve you best. For a moment, know that those inner imaginings can be translated into physical behavior. That is precisely what you have been doing all along, ever since you showed up in your present physical body. Your vision of the way you wish to be and what you wish to express in your life may require giving up old habits and ways of doing things, if those ways did not reflect the image of yourself you desire. Write down the attributes of a good reputation—as you desire it. Then, look at ways you can begin living that way.

The way to mend the bad world is to create the right world
—RALPH WALDO EMERSON

Gautama Buddha, whose original name was Prince Siddhartha, grappled with the problems of human existence. Though his words had not been written down, his disciples memorized many of his teachings and passed them on to succeeding generations by word of mouth. In the principal teachings of the Buddha, called the Four Noble Truths, it is stated first that human life is intrinsically unhappy; second, that the cause of this unhappiness is human selfishness and desire; third, that individual selfishness and desire can be brought to an end; and fourth, that the method of escape from selfishness involves what is called the "Eightfold Path": right views, right thought, right speech, right action, right livelihood, right effort, right mindfulness, and right meditation. Certainly, this awareness of "rightness" and the letting go of personal negativities can go far toward creating a loving, caring, and more beautiful world.

A good way to create a better world is for each of us to be better individuals. There are certain laws of life that, when followed, can make life sweeter, more harmonious, prosperous, healthy, and free. When we choose to abide by these laws, we reap the benefits of living in harmony with the universe. When we don't, we risk experiencing sickness, war, economic insecurity, and unemployment. The problems that create turmoil, pain, misery, and suffering in our world can change when each person makes a *conscious* decision to act and think for the good of all. Personal motive is always a good guide. Ask yourself, "Why am I doing the things I do?" and allow the inherent wisdom of spirit to provide the true answer. If your motives are pure, then good should come of them. The positive ideas we believe in today can constantly expand and grow in our consciousness. This could be termed being "on beam" with life. Pilots often fly using a radio beam as a guide. As long as they remain "on beam," they are safe. If they get off the beam, they're in danger.

Each human being, too, has an inborn "beam"—a conscience. While we are in tune with the way things were designed to be, we are "safe." When we are out of tune, we may show it in the form of greed, fear, sickness, addiction, and jealousy. Some people experience a lifetime of having the flu each winter, allergies in the fall, headaches, indigestion, and all the so-called minor ailments that we accept as a part of life. Sometimes it isn't necessary for this to be so. Each of us has the inner power to cultivate health, happiness, and serenity. We are capable of reeducating our bodies and our thinking.

By always thinking and acting with good in our hearts and by becoming responsible for ourselves, we can begin to change our wrong world into a right world. It's time to stop saying that "they" need to change things around here. When we start saying, "I need to give life a helping hand," we then begin to benefit life. It has been said that "a journey of a thousand miles begins with the first step." Let each one of us take that step and make it count!

You are sought after if you reflect love, joy, peace, patience, kindness, goodness, faithfulness, gentleness, and self-control
—SIR JOHN TEMPLETON

Living is a process of learning and growing in wisdom from the lessons we learn. One of my favorite quotations from Henry Wadsworth Longfellow states:

Life is real! Life is earnest!
And the grave is not its goal;
"Dust thou art, to dust returneth"
Was not spoken of the soul!

One lesson worth learning early is that life reflects back to us what we give to it. Among the greatest gifts we may offer to our world are love, joy, peace, patience, kindness, goodness, faithfulness, gentleness, and self-control. These are the gifts of a humble and sincere individual and come directly from the heart.

Others may realize that we are trustworthy. When we deal with people honestly, and with kindness, faithfulness, and gentleness, we send the message that we care. In return, we are treated the same way, because what we give to others often comes back to us. The man who moves in accord with his inner self moves in accord with a force that no outside power in the world can alter, and he moves joyously. An internal discipline can set each individual "house" in order, allowing the self to be mastered and ruled by a power greater than the individual ego. This self-discipline breeds the stuff of which heroes are made. Tenacity and determination are results of an ingrown faith and confidence in the great and good ends of life and the worthiness of human destiny.

When we develop self-control, we gain a balance in our lives that enables us to live the other qualities more fully and completely. Without self-control we lack the ability to be patient with ourselves and with others and the ability to love unconditionally. Self-control gives us the ability to put the ego in the correct perspective so that we bring no harm to ourselves or others. When we are able to do this, we realize the true value of the ego as the vehicle for our expression and not as a tyrant that has to have its way. The ego that insists on having its own way is a destructive ego and can lead to destructive habits. Learning self-control is a key to gaining mastery over our lives.

You are only as good as your word
—SIR JOHN TEMPLETON

Much has been written about the power of the spoken word. In the Holy Bible, we are informed that the creative power of speech had its derivation in the creative power of sound. In the book of Genesis, God literally "speaks" the universe into existence. "Let there be light. Let there be a firmament" (1:3, 6). Each verse of the entire first chapter of Genesis begins with the notable acclamation, "Let there be. . . ." and with the same potency begins the Gospel of John—the most mystical of the four Gospels: "In the beginning was the Word." What is the significance of such translations? And what impact can they have on our lives today? Simply that the "Word" was not necessarily something that God "said" or "did" a long time ago; rather, the WORD of God's creative power may be ensouling, permeating, informing, and conveying God to and through all living things here and now.

When it comes to keeping your word, there is no such thing as a "small" situation. Promising you will call someone and then neglecting to do so may seem small to you, but it can loom large in the mind of the person to whom you made the promise. That person may have needed someone to talk with at the moment. Perhaps she may not be very active socially, and a telephone call could mean a great deal to her. She could simply like you as a friend and look forward to the promised chat. By failing to make that call, not only are you risking making someone unhappy, but you may also be hurting yourself. Things might go badly for you in the near future, and you may need friends more than ever. But if you were not good at keeping your word, they may have decided to give up on you. This is the negative view of "being as good as your word."

There is also a strong positive side, as Jim's case shows. Every time Jim made a promise, no matter how small or seemingly insignificant, he kept his word. If he made plans with someone and then was offered the opportunity to do something more exciting or interesting, he never hesitated. He would say, "Thank you. I would love to do it, but I already have a commitment."

Jim's behavior invariably brought two reactions—both positive.

The first friend would be pleased because he and Jim stuck to their plan, and the second friend would be impressed. While sorry that Jim couldn't join him, he appreciated that Jim could be counted on. Jim was not only well liked during his school years, but he was respected and successful as an adult. His word was his bond, and both friends and business associates liked and trusted him. "Jim's as good as his word," a professional friend said of him. Not only were his words pleasant to hear, but they carried the conviction of his integrity.

Use wisely your power of choice
—OG MANDINO

Of all the powers that you possess as a human being, the greatest power is the power to choose. What you are right now is the sum total of the choices you have made in your life.

Every choice that you make forms a building block of your life. Every act, every word, every decision becomes a part of you. The way that you see and respond to the world in which you live results from the choices you have made. So, in a sense, not only do your choices make you who you are, they make your world the way it is because the world you "see" is the world in which you live. We are given the opportunity to shape and mold our world through the use of our consciousness. We have the power of free will to determine what we want in life, and we have the authority to call forth our good through the powers of decree, imagination, enthusiasm, joy, and faith.

Pause for a moment and look at your life. Are you experiencing any kind of lack or limitation? Are you happy with your diet? Are you suffering from any type of physical ailment? Do you find your work boring or unfulfilling? Do you like your friends? Whether your answer to these questions is "yes" or "no" isn't the point. The point to consider is that you are experiencing results from that which you have already chosen! You cannot experience anything in life—positive or negative—unless you *accept* it as such. You cannot accept anything unless you make up your mind to do so. And when you make up your mind about anything, that is the action of choosing!

If it seems necessary to do something you don't like, ask yourself: is there another way to accomplish this task that might work better for me? What is the time frame? What alternatives do I have now or in the future? When you become conscious of your power of choice, you may be amazed at the variety of choices available. You have much more power over your life than you may realize. You have the power to change your life and indeed even to change who you are through your power of choice. Use it wisely!

Since you are constantly making choices every moment of every day, isn't it time to start choosing wisely? You can make a decision right now to do what you want to do, to be who you want to be, and to do what you have to do. As a friend has so aptly put it, "We are the master of our own destiny only in the measure of our ability to choose wisely and constructively."

The borrower is servant to the lender
—PROVERBS 22:7 (KJV)

The person who borrows money often finds himself nervous or uneasy in the presence of the lender. There is a comfort and confidence in managing your finances so well that you are free to choose how you spend your money. How can you enjoy spending the money when it really belongs to someone else? In their book *Owe No Man,* Ann Ree Colton and Jonathan Murro write of scriptural principles of good stewardship and divine providence, "Travel light: 'owe no man' (Rom. 13:8); hasten to leave your offering, your spiritual promises on the altar; go forth and work diligently to pay off the debt carelessly made in time of blind motive." And the words of William Shakespeare invite us to "neither a borrower nor a lender be."

Consider the situation of a person who has fallen behind on her loan payments. It has become easy to obtain credit cards, but this convenient access to money can also become a burden. If the card-holder loses her job or faces a real emergency, such as an accident or unexpected medical expenses, she may suddenly find herself unable to repay her creditors.

Phone calls may start coming from the bank with greater frequency. Often these calls assume a condescending tone that can cause the debtor to feel sorry she ever accepted the loan. Gone may be the friendly tone that was contained in the letters inviting her to "buy now and pay later." After a few months of being behind in her payments, the attitude can become "pay now or face dire consequences."

Many people have arrived at a step even farther down the ladder. When they don't want, or can't get, another loan, and they see no clear avenue to repay their creditors, bankruptcy may seem to be the only solution left. For most people, it is embarrassing to admit that they have difficulty handling their finances. And the stigma of bad credit may take much time and effort to overcome.

Abraham Lincoln stated, "You cannot keep out of trouble by spending more than you earn. You cannot establish security on bor-rowed money." A debt can be like quicksand, pulling us downward into feelings of fear, insecurity, and indignity. An increasing number of small debts can act like patches of quicksand that demand more of our time and thought. Large debts can gradually draw you emo-tionally downward until you are in over your head. When this occurs, you may find it difficult to think about important issues of daily living other than the demands of the indebtedness.

People don't like to be servants, but it's easy to forget that that is what you become when you cast your lot with such modern conve-niences as credit cards, home equity loans, revolving charge accounts, and time payments. No matter what they may be called, loans can make the person receiving them feel subservient to the person giving them.

While it may be a fact of life that for many people certain bills may seem necessary—for example, utility bills, mortgage payment, medical bills, or unexpected necessities that may arise—we can agree with R. Buckminster Fuller, "I consider it essential to pay all my bills in the swiftest manner possible."

Crime doesn't pay
—ANONYMOUS

What can you do if you recognize a possible weak area in your character that might lead you to a life of crime? For instance, fear, anger, hurt feelings, a sense of inferiority, alcohol or drug problems, or codependency. How could you turn a weak point into a strong point? Many service and support organizations are available to help. And there are some things you can personally do to turn your life around.

Dr. Norman Vincent Peale presented the following six-point formula (which was developed by H. C. Mattern) in his book *The Amazing Results of Positive Thinking*.

1. Isolate your weakness; then study and know it thoroughly. Plan a real campaign against it.
2. Precisely specify the strength results you wish to attain.
3. Picture or visualize yourself as becoming strongest at your weakest point.
4. Immediately start *becoming* the strong person you wish to be.
5. Act as though you are strongest where you have been weakest.
6. Ask God to help you and believe that He does.

H. C. Mattern was described as a thoroughly negative person, so much so that on a balmy night he walked into a lonely meadow on Long Island, New York, and tried to commit suicide. He felt that life was worthless and he was overcome by hopelessness. He lifted a vial of poison to his lips, drank it, and slumped to the ground. The next thing he knew, he was staring in astonishment into a moonlit sky. At first, he wondered if he was dead. When he realized he was still alive, Mattern suddenly wanted very much to live. He thanked God for sparing his life and dedicated himself to a life of helping other people.

Never be afraid to acknowledge your deepest feelings. It is by looking deeply and honestly into oneself and recognizing what possibilities lie within that we can make the choices that direct us on the path of self-improvement.

The dark of night is not the end of the world
—ANONYMOUS

Many of us have times when there seems to be no solid support on which we can walk, stand, or even rest. Our world may seem to be crumbling under our feet, and we might wish we were anywhere but our present place. The situation may be one where we are certain our family doesn't understand how we feel. It may be difficult to convince those close to us of the seriousness of our thoughts and feelings. And there may seem to be no outside avenue of assistance in making major decisions. We may feel completely alone in the midst of a difficult situation.

The mystic St. John of the Cross called this type of crisis "the dark night of the soul." And *dark night* is a pretty descriptive analogy. If you have been wakeful during the predawn hours while the world is still sleeping, you may know how lonely it can feel. There is no one to talk to, and the feeling can be almost as if you are the only person alive in the world. The night may seem endless, and, in those moments, you might believe that morning will never come.

Some of the crises that come into our lives may seem to be endless and without hope of a positive outcome. At such times, we might be tempted to believe that life is not worth living. Perhaps we think the world (including our family, school, job, and relationships) would be better off without us. However, this is not true! You have a reason for living. Each person in the world has a reason for living. You have a part to play in this life, as does every other person in the universe. You *do* matter.

What we often see as "no reason for living" may actually be a situation in which we may have an opportunity to learn a valuable lesson for becoming a whole person. The most stressful event can be a gift in the form of a powerful learning experience that can help us to grow in wisdom and understanding of life's true and deeper meaning.

When involved in a situation that feels like the end of the world, picture yourself standing at the beginning of a stairway. If there is no light, you do not know there are steps that can support your weight. If you ask for light, you can be shown that there is indeed a stair, with each step leading you from the problem to the solution. Empty your mind of unhealthy thoughts, and replace them with wholesome, creative concepts. Take charge of your thoughts, instead of allowing them to control you. Refrain from making emotional judgments. Pause and think objectively and dispassionately. Be aware that nothing can replace gloom as completely as the practice of caring and goodwill. Theodore Roethke had an understanding of the possible benefits of these dark times when he said, "In a dark time, the eye begins to see." As we move into the new dawn after one of these "dark nights of the soul," we may often have a clearer perspective of the situation and a greater awareness of the blessing it has brought. One man meets these challenging experiences with the following statement: "This comes to bless me!" And he looks for—and finds—the blessing!

There is a part of you that knows the right action for any problem that might arise. Remember, even if you have tried various things that haven't worked, there may still be many different ways to forge a solution. There are few insoluble problems, only those we haven't yet learned how to solve. Not knowing how to solve a problem doesn't make you a worthless person. You are simply being given an opportunity for growth.

After the darkest night, the sun always rises. What you are experiencing may be only a cloud hiding the face of the sun. Let the power and warmth of the sun within you burn away the cloud that may attempt to dim your inner light. Let the sun of belief in life energize you as you climb to the pinnacle of overcoming.

CHAPTER 3

Forging Attitudes and Beliefs

Man is what he believes
—ANTON CHEKHOV

 HERE IS A STORY about a woman who dreamed she was being chased by a large, ugly, and terrifying monster. Everywhere the lady ran, the monster would always be right behind her, drooling, making ghastly noises, and breathing down her neck. In an attempt to get away, the woman ran into a canyon that proved to be a cul-de-sac. She was trapped. With her back against the tall, mountainous wall, she watched as the monster came closer and closer. When he was within inches of her, she cried out, "What horrible thing are you going to do to me?"

The monster looked at her and said, "That's up to you. It's your dream!"

At that point she could decide to be devoured by the monster, have the monster turn into a handsome prince, or even choose to have the monster disappear. It was her dream, and she had the power to determine how it would play out.

To a certain extent, many of us create monsters out of our self-image. We come to view as wrong those aspects of ourselves that are different and unique and spend most of our lives trying to hide those "bad" qualities from the world around us. We try to run away from who we are because we feel there's something about our natural selves that isn't right.

Our lives are very much like our dreams. We have control over our thoughts and can view our lives any way we choose. If our thoughts have created a monster out of a certain aspect of ourselves, then our thoughts can take control of the monster and turn it into something that can create a positive self-image.

Whatever our inner self wants we can have in our outer world if we are willing to believe in ourselves, believe in life, and follow through with action. It isn't enough merely to wish that people love us; it is up to us to be kind, helpful, and thoughtful to others. We must do more than long to be successful; it is important to develop the skills, the interest, and the perseverance that goes into achieving success.

Make the most of yourself by fanning small sparks of possibility into flames of achievement. Do you dare to be different? Are you willing to set your own pattern? Remember the words of Shakespeare, who was divinely inspired to write:

> To thine own self be true,
> And it must follow, as the night the day,
> Thou canst not then be false to any man.

Each of us tends to become what we think we are, and if we present to the world a person whom we honestly believe is okay, the world will respond to us positively and with acceptance.

A happy person is not a person in a certain set of circumstances, but rather a person with a certain set of attitudes
—ANONYMOUS

Two young women work in the same office and receive the same salary. Anne often complains that she is underpaid. She feels she is asked to handle too many things for someone on her salary level.

She arrives, dreading the day ahead, and leaves tired and discouraged. Mary, on the other hand, is happy to have a secure job and enough money to pay her bills, with some left over for extras and savings. She looks at each task as a challenge and does her best to accomplish whatever is required of her. She arrives, looking forward to the day, and leaves, happy to be heading home to her family, feeling good about what she has accomplished. Not surprisingly, after an employee review, positive Mary received both a promotion and a salary increase. Negative Anne was let go.

Part of the makeup of our personality has to do with the things we reinforce mentally and emotionally. If we have anxiety, we may reinforce that anxiety and get caught in a circle of negativism. Habitual negative thoughts or feelings may begin to affect, and even seem to control, our life if we continually reinforce them. The same can be true from the positive perspective.

A man once stopped in the train aisle before two fellow passengers who were playing chess. One of the contestants, a teenager, was about to concede defeat when the man in the aisle remarked that there was one more move. The youth invited the man to take his place at the chessboard. Taking over, the man made one deft move that changed the entire complexion of the game. Soon he won the game, although minutes before the youth would have given up. The man remarked that, in chess, there may not always be one more move, but in life, when our best efforts have seemed to fail to bring the happiness we desire, there is always one more move. This is the move where we turn to God for inspiration, the indwelling presence to whom all things may be made possible.

Several years later the young chess player was an infantryman, cut off from his company and alone in a foxhole. Enemy patrols were closing in on him, and all seemed lost. Suddenly, he recalled the chess game and the remark about "one more move." He prayed, affirming the presence and activity of God, and consciously let go in faith. Then, he felt a surprising inspiration to call to his adversaries and demand that they surrender and save themselves. He did so, with an authority of voice that even surprised himself. Every one of them laid down their arms and became his prisoner. His one more move, letting God take over, saved several lives. His set of circumstances may not have been happy ones, but his set of attitudes saved the day!

I shall allow no man to belittle my soul by making me hate him
—BOOKER T. WASHINGTON

Each of us is responsible for controlling our outlook on life as well as our attitudes. Hate, as an emotion, can be the alternate of a most powerful kind of feeling. When we seek to understand some of the natural human attitudes, we find that the most strenuous hatreds are usually based on either a fundamental fear or a strong personal desire. Isn't it true that sometimes we may feel resentful of someone whose actions seem to deprive us of something we want? The American writer James Baldwin said, "I imagine one of the reasons people cling to their hates so stubbornly is because they sense, once hate is gone, they will be forced to deal with their pain."

African-American educator Booker T. Washington, an emancipated slave, lived in poverty so severe that he went to work at the age of nine. He could easily have blamed his situation on circumstances and used these as an excuse for hatred. Instead of permitting this emotion to fester within his soul, he harnessed his energies and channeled them into improving his own condition and that of others.

Washington worked as a janitor to obtain an education—the method that he believed would lead to self-improvement and eventual improvement of conditions for humankind. He took command of his life rather than viewing himself as a victim of his circumstances. After graduation and some teaching experience, he was eventually asked to head a new school for blacks in Tuskegee, Alabama. He accepted the position.

The challenges of little money, no equipment, and having only two converted buildings did not make the new administrator envy wealthy schools or hate those who were more fortunate. Instead, Washington began working toward his goal. During his administration, Tuskegee Institute grew to have nearly two hundred faculty members and one hundred well-equipped buildings.

While Washington's emphasis on education drew criticism from members of the black community who believed that political activism was the path to genuine progress, Washington calmly followed the direction he believed to be true. Rather than seeing the differences as an excuse to hate and fight, the educational leader continued his positive work on the academic front.

As the writer of the *Dhammapada* stated: "Hatred does not cease by hatred; hatred ceases only by love. This is the eternal law." Love knows by its own fires of devotion how to make calamities serve a useful purpose. Obstacles can often lead to success. Great moments ultimately can come out of dark periods.

Optimism has its roots in the abiding goodness
—ANONYMOUS

The intent of the optimist is to discover the good. When confronted by difficulty, the healthy optimist doesn't pretend there is no confusion, fear, or pain. She is honest about her feelings and still believes in a good outcome, even if she doesn't yet see how it may manifest itself.

Father Tom Walsh, a psychotherapist, has taught a popular course called "Humor, Hilarity, Healing, and Happy Hypothalmia" at the Franciscan Renewal Center and at various churches in Phoenix, Arizona. Walsh, who has counseled many depressed people, observes, "You cannot be depressed, or anxious, or angry when you're laughing. It can't be done."

Ralph Waldo Emerson writes fervently and eloquently about optimism, and he did so in the years following the ill health and deaths of his first wife, two brothers, and his adored six-year-old son. Such tragedies could cause some people to become bitter and cynical. But though he experienced deep grief, Emerson's love of life's goodness would not allow any warping of that high belief.

You, too, can carry what Emerson called that "infallible trust and . . . the vision to see that the best is the true. In that attitude, one may dismiss all uncertainties and fears, and trust that time will reveal the answers to any private puzzlement."

Love thy neighbor as thyself
—MATTHEW 19:19 (KJV)

The belief that you are less worthy, less attractive, less intelligent, or less good than another in any way sets you apart from those who would love you and would accept your love in return. Feelings of inadequacy, shame, and self-pity can consume your energies in an emotional tornado that destroys all your relationships. The devastation that often occurs as you live out your self-doubts only reinforces the beliefs that you hold in a vicious cycle, or a self-fulfilling prophecy. It's a law of life that says, "What you send forth, you get back." Some people grow up believing so many limitations about themselves that, after a while, their lives actually begin to manifest those limitations.

If you believe you must always be the way you have always been, you are arguing against growth. If you are convinced that your family is responsible for the kind of person you are today, you are trapped in that cycle. Although you can't eliminate the negative influences that were a part of your childhood, you can decide whether or not you will allow them to hold sway over your life today.

The human mind often breaks reality down into simple forms— black or white, good or bad, me or you. This either/or way of thinking may confuse some into believing that it's not possible to treat another with care, while at the same time giving care to ourselves. Cultural traditions that value love and thoughtfulness to other people may convince people that it is selfish to be considerate of their own feelings and needs. In truth, to love others you need to love yourself as well.

Maintaining a healthy sense of self-respect is different from being narcissistic. Narcissus, the figure in Greek mythology who spent his days pining after his own reflection in a pool, neglected everyone else in his life because he was so preoccupied with himself. He was like those who spend hours trying to get their hair perfect or their makeup flawless so that others will think of them as beautiful. The underlying assumption is that you're not good enough as you are, that you must alter and improve yourself in order to be acceptable in another's eyes.

True self-esteem belongs to each of us who looks in the mirror, not to criticize or admire, but to see past physical appearance into the essential child of God reflected there. Accept the person you are, risk sharing yourself with others, and then watch how you grow.

You find what you look for: good or evil, problems or solutions
—SIR JOHN TEMPLETON

If the outlook of a situation isn't bright, we may have been looking *out* too much, focusing too much on external appearances. The solution lies in looking within, not out; in looking up, not down; in looking for the good, not the so-called evil. In looking up, we direct our vision away from the limited beliefs of the world. We no longer see ourselves or our circumstances according to the limited viewpoint of the world.

Ask any professional athlete what attitude allows one person to win and another to lose; what separates those who try and fail from those who try and succeed. The answer? Belief. Belief is the vision of what can be accomplished. Belief is the athlete's own internal vision of himself as a winner. Belief is part of our personal perspective. As Ken Keyes writes in *Handbook to Higher Consciousness*: "A loving person lives in a loving world. A hostile person lives in a hostile world."

Accentuate the positive; eliminate the negative
—JOHNNY MERCER

When something seems to be going awry in our lives, it becomes tempting to believe that everything in our life is wrong. Unfortunately, this attitude can make us act in ways that seem to draw more negative influences to us, and we may overlook the positive aspects in our lives.

There will be times when you'll want to cry, "It's not fair!" But feeling sorry for yourself doesn't solve the problem. Better to think, "This is how it is. Now, what can I do about the situation?" Remember, anger is an emotion, and emotions seldom successfully solve problems. Instead, they may be more likely to create new ones.

As you practice thinking in positive ways, you will find that your life becomes smoother and exhibits less tension and anger. You can begin to manage your feelings, instead of allowing outer circumstances to guide your mood. You can begin at any time to shift your thinking and react positively, while still releasing negative thoughts.

Pleasant, more productive days can result from such positive thinking. Because your subconscious mind is the reservoir for your memories, you can call to mind past events and recall what your responses were at that time. When a similar thing happens today, your mind sends a remembered message, which could be a message of anger, resentment, or frustration. You have the ability to give your mind new messages as you choose to react emotionally or to address the situation with poised and balanced thinking.

CHAPTER 4

Helping Others

Enthusiasm is contagious
—SIR JOHN TEMPLETON

SMALL CHURCH in a low-income area of Brooklyn asked a businessman if the neighborhood children could play in a vacant lot he owned until another use was made for the property. The man agreed to allow the space to be used as a playground on two conditions. First, the church had to pay for insurance. Second, the church had to take responsibility for cleaning up the lot. The congregation of the church agreed to cover the insurance payments, and the entire membership decided to clean the lot on a given Saturday.

A few of the families were slightly late in arriving, and among the late arrivals was a couple with a disabled ten-year-old daughter. As the family made its way to the lot, many of the volunteers wondered why the couple had brought the girl. What could she possibly accomplish? After all, she could hardly walk!

But the young girl plunged into the project with gusto. Propping herself up by leaning on her crutches and leaving her hands free, with a huge smile and a happy expression, she held the plastic bag open while her father and mother filled it with trash. The family laughed and talked about the many sports and activities they visualized taking place on the lot. Their enthusiasm became contagious. A little disabled girl had inspired the other volunteers with her attitude. Yet a few found themselves wondering why the girl was so excited. It seemed to them unlikely that the child would be able to use the playground herself. How could she? When asked how she planned to participate when the playground opened, the little girl was totally enthusiastic. "I'll keep score and be a referee and stuff like that." She grinned.

The individual who takes up any activity as a positive adventure can inspire the same attitude in others. The worker who looks for ways to enjoy his work, to be enthusiastic about it, sets the stage for others to follow his example. Always remember that what a person does, for good or ill, can be contagious. A smile is contagious, but so is a frown. Although no one can be sunny all the time, if we take up our tasks with enthusiasm, it is likely those around us will catch our spirit. Incidentally, the derivation of the word *enthusiasm* is "filled with spirit." Enthusiasm really is contagious!

Help yourself by helping others
—SIR JOHN TEMPLETON

Select with care the area of your livelihood and make certain you love what you do. When you love your work and hold the attitude that what you do may be done on behalf of others, your life and your work can take on special meaning and deep significance. As one who gives joyously and thankfully, as one who is ever ready to assist another, you may be much more likely to be successful than the person who works simply to earn a living.

The more you work and plant, the more you can harvest. The more good you can do, the more success you can achieve. Lou Rawls, the actor and singer, talked about loving his work. He said:

> Singing has been my life, and I love to sing. Sure, I get paid
> for singing, and I wouldn't put that down. But when I put
> all that is in me into a song, and those who listen let me

know we're together, that's really living. I would suggest to anyone that if you don't love what you're doing, find something you love to do and do it—especially if it makes you feel that you and other people are together. That's been my life, and I thank God for it.

Service to others is a creative process that releases energy that can manifest itself in many ways and bring deeper meaning into your life. When we love deeply enough, coupled with the desire to be helpful to those around us and to our world, we often find fulfillment and true closeness with others that can satisfy our desire to reach the hearts of them. On the other hand, when we do not love enough to enter into this wholesome, freeing union with others, we may try to solve our basic problem of separation by seeking power over others. We may tend to live by comparison, by being overly competitive, or by feeling better or more important than others. And these attitudes do not move us toward our goals of unity, love, and helpfulness.

In Acts 3:6, the apostle Peter is speaking to a man who cannot walk. He said, "I have no silver and gold, but I give you what I have. . . ." Reflection on these words can teach us to be sensitive to the needs of the people around us. May we desire to give what is ours to give, trusting that whatever we give can be a real blessing.

I can give of my time.

I can give my love, support, and understanding.

I can give of patience and compassion.

I can share the gift of joy and laughter.

I can offer encouragement and companionship.

Most importantly, I can give my prayers and see the Spirit of God supplying the needed comfort—uplifting, upholding, and sustaining.

We can give our assistance cheerfully, abundantly, and from a heart overflowing with God's love.

God is responsible for the inborn talents you possess. From there on, the responsibility is yours. It is up to you to develop them as far and as deeply as they may go. People who use their talents completely—most of all to help and love others less fortunate—will be rewarded and find success.

Expect the best and your positive outlook
opens the door to opportunity
—SIR JOHN TEMPLETON

It is a fact of nature that winter storms can be dangerous. With freezing temperatures, snow, sleet, and wind, icy conditions on the roads pose a threat to even the most experienced driver. Sometimes car batteries freeze up, and it's hard to get the car started, or snow has fallen that must be plowed away before cars can pass. Schools are often closed to keep the students at home and safe from the hazardous roads. Yet those same conditions that close the schools may offer most children delight at the prospect of an unexpected holiday in the middle of the week! Fun-loving people can find myriad ways to play in the fluffy white stuff whether they sled, slide, or ski; roll it into balls for throwing or into boulders for building. To the expectant student, who has followed the weather reports more faithfully than a meteorologist, a snowy day is no problem. An optimistic expectation converts the problem into an opportunity for enjoyment.

Sometimes, however, a problem may cause difficulty. For example, solving a challenging engineering problem on a multimillion-dollar building project is certainly more stressful than balancing your checkbook. There may be deadlines to meet, and you may feel pressure to perform well because your job, your future well-being, and the safety of many people depend on you. These stresses can make a problem seem like something larger than life and something you aren't sure you wish to tackle. You may question your ability to meet the challenge set before you. Doubt, uncertainty, and a sense of inadequacy can make a simple problem snowball into something more complex than it is. When an avalanche of negative emotions threatens, it becomes difficult to experience a ski slope as fun to traverse! A molehill may look like an entire mountain and an obstacle rather than a challenge to your ability and skill. Because anxiety may occupy a large part of your thinking processes in tense situations, solutions might seem elusive, and your performance may falter.

Helen Keller may have had many problems, but she never allowed negative emotions to plunge her into a pit of self-pity. Imagine the optimistic expectation and hope she must have expressed to break out of a dark and silent prison to become self-expressive. With her teacher, Annie Mansfield Sullivan, Helen lectured all over the United States, answering questions from the audience that were communicated to her by Miss Sullivan. A stock question was, "Do you close your eyes when you go to sleep?" Helen Keller's stock response was, "I never stayed awake to see." She kept a high, hopeful inner eye on a light that guided her to overcome severe physical handicaps to build a life more creative than many people with full sight and hearing experience.

Look for the best in every situation, and you have the opportunity to turn any problem into a manifestation of greater good. Give thanks for the Spirit, which is working *for* you by working *through* you.

Little things mean a lot
—EDITH LINDERMAN

One morning during rush hour in a large metropolitan area, a large moving van became stuck in an underpass. The driver's estimate of the height of the opening was off by a few inches, and the truck could go neither forward nor backward. Within minutes the police arrived on the scene, and a large crowd of spectators gathered. Engineers were called to advise on the best way to free the truck. In the midst of all the noise and excitement, a small boy made his way to the truck driver.

"I can tell you how to get out, mister," he said.

"Okay! Okay! So everybody's an expert around here!" growled the driver impatiently.

"Just let some air out of the tires," said the boy.

Only minutes later, that became the conclusion arrived at by the engineers. Those few inches made a difference and the truck moved smoothly through the underpass. The solution to the problem was such a little thing—so simple that it had been overlooked.

Sometimes the solution to a problem can be one small thing. One small candle lit in the darkness can make a difference. Take friendship, for example. It's natural to want to be liked, to be popular with our friends and coworkers. But often some little thing may hold us back. We may feel stuck in present circumstances and find it difficult to move forward to make friends. Perhaps if we made one small change in some aspect of ourselves, we might become more interesting and more pleasant, and forming friendships might be easier.

Maybe we appear conceited to others, and too full of ourselves. Certainly a "nose-in-the-air" attitude can get in the way of making friends. Most people do not enjoy spending time with an "I-I-I" sort of person. Learn to drop the egotistic "I" from your vocabulary, and you may find it easier to move through the underpass to friendship.

Could it be that we have some habits that turn friends off, possibly a tendency to be overly critical of others, making catty remarks behind their backs, or saying things in front of others that may be embarrassing?

Could it be that we lack a genuine interest in others? Do we honestly like to see our friends win honors and recognitions? Are we wholeheartedly happy when good fortune comes their way? Do we let our friends know that we're sincerely interested in them and happy for them?

We need to look honestly within ourselves and conduct a personal self-examination to see if some quality might be holding us back and keeping us from making the friendships we desire. To have a friend, it is often necessary to be willing to *be* a friend. So let's take a moment to look at ourselves in the mirror and do whatever may be necessary to become the friend we want to be. Enjoying the blessings of life could depend on "just one little thing."

An old stonemason was laying a rock wall, which, because it looked natural, was a thing of great beauty. The owner of the estate, while walking in his fields, noticed that the stonemason took as much care in placing the small stones as he did in placing the larger ones. So the estate owner walked over to the worker and said, "My friend, wouldn't the wall go up much faster if you used more of the larger stones?"

"Aye, most certainly, sir," the old man replied. "But you see, I'm building for lasting beauty and strength, not for speed."

He thought for a moment and added: "Sir, these stones are like men. Many small ones are needed to support the fewer big ones and hold them in place. If you leave out the small stones, the big ones will have no support, and they will fall!"

So it often seems to be with life. It may be that the cohesion of many small and beautiful thoughts and feelings, built one upon the other, can create the ordered and well-balanced life.

You're either part of the problem, or part of the solution
—ELDRIDGE CLEAVER

It has been said that there are two kinds of people in the world: those who see a problem, define and describe the problem, complain about the problem, and finally become part of the problem; and those who look at a problem and immediately begin to search for a solution. For the person who focuses on the problem, life can seem like an uphill battle. However, if you are among the solution seekers, life can present you with many exciting opportunities for growth. The choice of how you respond to life's situations is up to you.

It's easy to become part of the problem. Anyone focusing on a number of conflicting facts and possible scenarios may see a dozen different reasons why something cannot be accomplished. It may require more effort to discipline your mind to work on ways in which the problems can be solved. What might seem to be an insurmountable obstacle for "problem" people can become an opportunity for growth for solution seekers.

A story is told about two men who were walking along a forest path late one night. It was quite dark, and the men had difficulty seeing the path. Suddenly, both men fell into a large pit, loosely covered with brush and leaves. Escape seemed impossible without outside help. Lamenting their terrible misfortune, one man sat down, buried his face in his hands, and did nothing. The other man immediately began to search for an escape route. While groping in the dark, his hand touched a long tree root hanging from the side of the wall. He quickly pulled himself out of the pit and extended his hand to assist his complaining friend out as well.

The challenges you face may not be as extreme as falling into a pit, but the decisions you make about handling the situations can be crucial in terms of success or failure—now and in the future. You may be given the opportunity to engage in gossip. Perhaps you might join others in complaining about a coworker. You may be tempted to disregard a company policy just because everyone else is doing it. In each case, you can be either part of the problem or part of the solution. Whichever role you choose can have an enormous impact on your future.

Make a conscious effort to be a solution seeker. Remember, it doesn't take courage, genius, or effort to be a problem person. Becoming a solution seeker helps you feel good about yourself and more confident about your capabilities. It can also evoke feelings of admiration and respect from those around you. They see that you are a person who knows how to get things done. Through your positive, goal-driven approach, you may even inspire them to greater levels of achievement.

A wise boss helped his colleagues to become problem solvers by keeping on his desk a sign saying, What do you suggest? When brainstorming new and better ways to accomplish a goal, he encouraged each assistant to begin with the words, "Would it be better if ...?" Do you see how this thought-provoking attitude can open doors to new possibilities?

Often, a pat on the back works better than a kick in the pants
—WILLIAM JUNEAU

In the late 1960s and early 1970s, the Texas Education Agency in the United States began a program of hiring experienced people from industry to teach vocational education. The theory was that it would be easier and faster than teaching trades to certified teachers. This program became remarkably successful, and some of these industry people brought exciting and innovative teaching methods to the students.

One such person was an experienced home builder and cabinetmaker who undertook to teach a class in construction trades. His supervisor told him that his class would be composed of underachievers and slow learners and that too much should not be expected of them. The supervisor also told him that he could not be friends with the students and still cultivate their respect; they would not bother to learn from someone who let them "get too close."

That was not this man's way of doing things. He could not be distant and formal with the students. He enforced discipline when needed, but his years of experience had taught him that people respond to positive treatment in a positive way and to negative treatment in a negative way. He knew he could find something positive about every effort the students made; just making the effort itself was a positive action. He pointed out the things the students did right and suggested ways they could improve their skills. A lot more work was accomplished by being their friend.

The last year he taught the class, nine of the twenty-seven students in the class advanced to the state finals in skills competition, and four of those received first place blue ribbons. Most of those students found good jobs after graduation. Their self-confidence had been improved by their successes in the class, and they remembered the teacher as a friend who cared.

Give credit and help to all who have helped you
—SIR JOHN TEMPLETON

When others play a meaningful role in our achievements, it is important to acknowledge their contributions. During the rehearsals for the movie *Jumbo*, Charles Lederer, an American playwright and director, watched comedian Jimmy Durante trying to spirit the elephant past the sheriff, who was trying to serve a writ of attachment. "You could have the sheriff say, 'Where are you going with that elephant?'" suggested Lederer, "and then you could have Jimmy say, 'What elephant?'" The suggestion was taken up and provided the biggest laugh in the show. Ben Hecht and Charles MacArthur, the writers, acknowledged their friend's contribution with the following note in the program: "Joke by Charles Lederer."

Here is another beautiful example of acknowledging and honoring the help we receive. It was the late 1800s and an important member of the British Parliament was hurrying through the rain and fog of the bleak Scottish countryside to deliver a crucial speech. Still miles from his destination, his carriage was forced off the road, its wheels plunging axle-deep in mud. Try as they might, the horse and driver could not move the carriage. So important was his speech that even the aristocratic Englishman, in his formal attire, gave a hand. But it was no use. The carriage would not budge.

A young Scottish farmboy happened to be driving a team of horses past the distraught parliamentarian and volunteered to help pull the carriage loose. After much effort and considerable exertion, the carriage was finally pulled free. When the boy steadfastly refused to take any money for his help or for his clothes, which were torn and dirty from the ordeal, the Englishman asked him what he wanted to be when he grew up.

"A doctor, sir. I want to be a doctor" was the reply. The gentleman was so impressed with the boy and so grateful for his kindness that he said, "Well, I want to help." And sure enough, he kept his word. Through his generosity, he made it possible for the young lad to attend the university.

More than fifty years later, Winston Churchill became dangerously ill with pneumonia while in Morocco. His life was saved by a new wonder drug called penicillin, which had been discovered a few years earlier by a Scottish-born physician, Sir Alexander Fleming.

Fleming was the farmboy who had helped the member of Parliament on that dark and rainy night in Scotland half a century before. The member of Parliament? None other than Winston Churchill's father, Randolph!

It's nice to be important, but it's more important to be nice
—SIR JOHN TEMPLETON

If we become the "playground bully," others may accede to our wishes, not because they believe in us or in our cause, but because they may be afraid to challenge us. A life lived this way is built on shaky ground. There is always someone ready and eager for us to make a mistake. Playground bullies last only until other, bigger bullies come along to take their place, or until they learn that by being nice they can achieve more of what they want in life.

What we do for others certainly comes back to us. If we are kind, generous, loving, honest, and open, others will often react the same way toward us. Our importance to others depends not on our bullying tactics but on showing through our actions that we sincerely care about them. As we weave our lives with the golden thread of caring for others, we fashion a life that is truly important.

Have you had the experience of looking at someone and seeing incredible potential in him, a possibility or a capacity he may not have known he had? When you call this to his attention, you are calling forth something lovely and beautiful, a talent or characteristic that had to exist first in you.

Based on my experience over more than half a century of studying corporations, the higher up the corporate executive ladder you interview, the greater proportion of executives are nice. I have also noted that they are more active in religious work. Maybe this is partly why they were promoted to their high posts and why they learned to be more effective executives. Perhaps they, too, realize that it's nice to be important, but it's more important to be nice.

Helpfulness, not willfulness, brings rewards
—ANONYMOUS

Are you willing or willful? Do you work well with other people's ideas and direction? Or do you demand to have your own way? When we exert our will in every situation, we may be forming a logjam that blocks the flow of good in our lives. When we allow others to express their ideas and to share in planning and direction, we open ourselves to different ideas and find new direction in the flow of life.

After trees are felled for processing into wood products, they are often floated downriver to the mill. Occasionally, logs will become stuck on rocks or some other obstruction. More logs become entangled until virtually all of them are caught in a massive logjam. Dynamite is then used to untangle the mess, remove the block, and start the logs moving downstream again. Although the dynamite removes the block, it also turns what would have been usable lumber into an unusable scattering of mulch, resulting in a tremendous waste of raw materials.

When we are willful—when we are full of our own will—we may be blocking the flow of good in our lives, just as the logjam blocks the flow of logs. What happens when we become stuck in our own willfulness? Like the lumberjack who uses dynamite to break up the logjam, life will come along with someone or some event that can blow us out of our stuck place. The results are often painful and destructive. The more we resist the flow of life, the greater the potential for an unpleasant occurrence. The more logs that are piled up in the jam, the more dynamite is necessary to get it unstuck.

When we are at variance with someone, the argument we use enables the other person to see quite well that we wish to win out. A battle of human wills often ensues. By beginning in this way, instead of making some kind of opening in his mind, we usually close the door of his heart. On the other hand, how quickly we may open the door to cooperation by gentleness, humility, and courtesy.

Too often we tend to take the facts of our lives for granted. We may learn to work within the self-imposed limitations we've experienced in our development; or, we may have developed the habit of floating from one logjam to another, allowing the forces of life to explode our world and reduce our potential for inner greatness. We have the ability to work with the forces in our lives in various ways to experience greater expression of who we are and what we're capable of being. This requires a willingness to take a new look at our current attitudes; it requires a willingness to change our mind, to think again, to make new choices, to subordinate our willfulness in favor of willingness. We can start anew from where we are right now. We can choose to work with and not against the spiritual forces of life and to experience the good that is available to us.

Willpower, which is understood to be the strength of mind that makes it capable of meeting success or failure with equanimity, is not to be confused with willfulness, which is demanding fulfillment of our personal wishes with no thought or consideration of other possibilities.

CHAPTER 5

Learning

Wisdom is born of mistakes; confront error and learn
—J. JELINEK

HERE IS A DIFFERENCE between *acquiring* knowledge and information and *possessing* wisdom. You may acquire knowledge from a university, your travels, your relationships, the books you read, and other activities in which you participate. But are you also gaining wisdom?

The Talmud asks, "Who is a wise man?" and answers, "He who learns of all men." To become wise, we must be willing to suspend our personal beliefs about something, set aside prejudices, and think with an open mind. It is important to branch out eagerly and learn in many different areas, even at the risk of being embarrassed or looking foolish. Are we able to admit that we don't yet know everything and are willing to learn? Learning is a desirable process that may include making mistakes along the road to knowledge. True wisdom acknowledges that the more we learn about a subject, the more interesting it becomes and the more there is to learn.

Many of us have heard someone say: "I learned my lesson. I'll never do that again!" But all too rarely do we hear: "That was a wonderful lesson. I'm glad it happened just the way it did, even though I was uncomfortable going through it. I now understand why I

65

experienced the pain. With this new awareness, I can change my behavior so I won't make the same mistake in the future." This person is bravely acknowledging his responsibility for creating the situation. He recognizes that he has choices, and that he *can* choose differently as long as he stays alert to each challenge, whether the situation seems to be positive or negative.

The wise person is also a courageous person. We often think of courage in terms of bravery—physical prowess and fearlessness in battle or in sports. Yet there are many forms of bravery that are not recognized by anyone but ourselves as we struggle to overcome our shortcomings. By fearlessly confronting the role each of us plays in the experiences we may have judged as mistakes in our lives, we can make future experiences fruitful and increase our wisdom. This sincere willingness to look at ourselves honestly and courageously can be the first, and perhaps most important, step we can take on the road to wisdom.

Defeat isn't bitter if you don't swallow it
—TED ENGSTROM

At one time or another in our lives, we have all experienced failure. The more often we are willing to risk trying a new approach or adopting a fresh concept, the more likely we are to experience failure, at least in the short run. It isn't easy to succeed when we first try something new and ambitious, and if we're afraid to fail, we may be quite hesitant to take risks. Yet, if we never dare to step forward, we will certainly stagnate. Growth requires a willingness to risk failure and defeat. If, as toddlers, we were afraid of failure, few of us would have learned to walk and talk. To learn to walk we had to be willing to fall down at times, scrape our knees, and bruise our shins. Confucius said, "Our greatest glory is not in never falling, but in rising every time we fall."

Everyone can improve himself regardless of his situation, place in life, or circumstances. But it is important to prove to yourself that by your own thoughts and actions you have the power to accomplish that which you make up your mind to do. Fear and hesitancy paralyze mental action and feed defeatism. They weaken both mind and body, throw dust in your eyes, and hide the mighty spiritual forces that are always with you.

The spiritual power of the universe does not know defeat or failure. How many times have you been on "rock bottom," and kind words and thoughts of encouragement spoken by a friend lifted you up and made you feel like a person again? Perhaps you kept going because someone believed in you. Well, that's as good a reason to soldier on as any. It seems that the "down times of defeat" are when we need courage the most and find it most difficult to draw from within ourselves. It is your divine birthright to express yourself as a healthy, happy, prosperous, and successful person. Yet it may seem impossible for you to express your true inner self as long as you are fearful and feel defeated instead of courageous. Real courage is a spiritual idea stemming from the mind of God. When you desire courage with all the intensity of your heart—believe in it and seek it until it becomes an awakened part of your nature—then you are able to handle difficult situations.

In the process of inventing the electric lightbulb, it was said that Thomas Edison tried and failed over a thousand times. It has been reported that someone asked Edison if he didn't grow discouraged by all his failures and consider giving up. He replied: "Those were steps on the way. In each attempt I was successful in finding a way not to create a lightbulb. I was always eager to learn, even from my mistakes."

In other words, while Edison did not always succeed, he refused to allow defeat to take up residence in his mind. There is a critical difference between saying, "I failed," and "I am a failure." To swallow defeat is to believe that what you do, or fail to do, makes you the person you are.

When we swallow defeat, our ability to function effectively is impaired from that moment on. Every great leader, athlete, explorer, thinker, inventor, and businessperson has made mistakes and experienced failure in some manner. These people, however, became great because they did not blame themselves or anyone else for their failures; instead, they learned from their mistakes how to improve their performance. They knew that failure was momentary and did not necessarily mean defeat.

You can make opposition work for you
—ANONYMOUS

Is something or someone bothering you? Is there a troublesome person or difficult situation you would like to banish from your life? How about experiences in your past? Or present? Are you facing an imminent and difficult situation that you wish would simply go away?

A story from the life of President Abraham Lincoln affords a wonderful lesson for living. During Lincoln's presidency, an appointee was always finding ways to challenge and disrupt whatever the president tried to do. If Lincoln was in favor of an issue, you could bet that this fellow would be opposed to it. When this had been going on for quite some time, a friend of Lincoln's asked him why he didn't have this person replaced by someone more agreeable. Lincoln answered by telling his friend the following tale.

Lincoln was walking down a country road one day and came upon a farmer plowing his field with a horse-drawn plow. As he drew near and was about to give a greeting, Lincoln noticed a big horsefly on the flank of the horse. As the fly was obviously biting and bothering the horse, Lincoln started to brush it off. As he raised his hand, the farmer stopped him and said: "Don't do that, friend. That horsefly is the only thing keeping this old horse moving."

If you reflect on your life, you may recall times when you couldn't see the value of some person and were tempted to brush him or her off. It takes hindsight to recognize that the very situation you may have seen as an irritating bother turned out to be a blessing in disguise. Wouldn't life be a much more enjoyable and meaningful experience if we decided to look at the difficult people and irritating situations as blessings in disguise? If we look deeply enough, we might see these experiences as situations that motivate us to grow and change for the better. Like the horsefly, they may well be what is keeping us going!

One of the most important truths we can derive from life's challenges is the following: this experience came to give me soul growth and to bless me. If we seek to avoid the experience, we deprive ourselves of the blessing contained therein. We often forget the laws of mind action and cause and effect. If we didn't need the experience for our growth, it would be unlikely to come to us. Or if it did, we wouldn't be affected or even bothered by it! We would serenely and confidently move through the situation.

As an expression of God, you are always greater than any problem, condition, experience, or situation. When you are tempted to doubt, fear, or resist what is happening, there is a tool you can effectively use. It is the simple truth statement: this came to bless me. Sometimes a situation that seems so unnecessary is essential to us and to our spiritual growth and unfolding. The Bible assures us that "in everything God works for good with those who love him" (Rom. 8:28). Think of how the seemingly worst-case scenario has often been transformed into the absolute best in the lives of those who believed this truth and accepted it into their lives.

Everything and everyone around you is your teacher
—KEN KEYES

Would you like to find the greatest teacher in the world? The one who could teach you what you most need to learn at this moment? Just look around you. Your teachers are everywhere. Your life is set up to teach you what you need to learn. Whether you recognize it or not, you possess an inner wisdom that is capable of showing you who your teachers are and what they have to teach you.

To find those teachers, look at those closest to you—your family, your friends, your coworkers. The people you spend the most time with can tell you much about yourself. How? One way is that, quite often, what we see in others is, in some way, a reflection of something within ourselves. What we most admire in another may be a quality we possess but have failed to recognize.

Conversely, what we dislike most in another may also reflect some trait within ourselves that we weren't aware was there. This can be especially true when we have very strong feelings—positive or negative—about someone. Other people can be our teachers, not necessarily because of what they themselves know or do, but rather because of the way we react to them. That is, other people can serve as mirrors to teach you about yourself.

The way people respond to us can add to our self-knowledge as well. This doesn't mean that if we aren't popular we're "bad," or that if a lot of people like us we're necessarily "good." How people respond to us is certainly their choice; yet we can use their reactions to learn something about ourselves. This is especially true when we see several people responding to us in a similar manner.

Another way we can learn from others is simply by looking at the characteristics of the people we choose to associate with. We may need to allow ourselves to be sufficiently imaginative and sympathetic to see through a crust of self-consciousness or fear to the inner person. There can be goodness waiting to be released. We may be in a position to teach as well as be taught. Again, this becomes not a matter of judging anyone as good or bad, but, rather, recognizing that there is something within ourselves that may be attracting us to these people, and them to us.

It can also be helpful to look at those activities you spend the greater part of your time pursuing. What do your time priorities tell you about yourself? Also examine yourself in other areas: How do you spend your leisure time? On what do you spend most of your money? What do you most often think about? What feelings do you experience most often? These things—indeed, everything in your life around you and within you—can teach you a great deal. We may have difficulties, sometimes a crisis, and once in a while we may have to go through some experience that seems like a tragedy. But the point to remember is that we can face what we have to face and go through it if we use our willpower to keep on keeping on. Sometimes what seems to be a most difficult experience can become one of our greatest teachers as we gain the wisdom and understanding inherent in the situation. Socrates wrote, "The Delphic oracle said I was the wisest of all the Greeks. It is because I alone, of all the Greeks, know that I know nothing." Surely these are the words of a teachable man. The truth is, you are teaching yourself, and as you use your life and the world around you as your textbook and your classroom, you can become your own greatest teacher.

We learn more by welcoming criticism than
by rendering judgment
—J. JELINEK

Like everything else in life, arguments can be managed. When someone is expressing anger toward us or seems to be overly critical, we have two basic choices: we can defend ourselves, or we can learn from the conflict. When a conflict turns defensive, lots of anger, blame, and criticism may be leveled at the other person, while you hardly listen to what the other person is saying. Nothing is learned if no one is listening.

The English judge, George Jeffreys, once pointed his cane at a man about to be tried. Jeffreys remarked, "There is a rogue at the end of my cane." The accused looked Jeffreys straight in the eye and asked, "At which end, my lord?"

Using the learning method to solve conflicts, on the other hand, encourages calmness and patience under pressure. We force ourselves to remain silent long enough to hear other people's points of view and allow them to express their feelings. If we ask questions to clarify a misunderstanding instead of summoning arguments to protect our position, we might find that what our friend is saying is not what we thought we heard. Or, we might find that the anger being expressed is the residue of an earlier argument or may be aimed at someone else and has nothing to do with us.

Sometimes the worldly press of matters may take our attention away from the spiritual side of life. During these times, it is wise to pause for a moment and reflect on the creative energy that made and sustains the whole universe and every living creature, including ourselves. When our thoughts flow in this manner, there is little room or desire for criticism or judgment of another human being.

Every moment of our lives we are molding character, and it is our character that determines our destiny. We continue to create all the conditions that now exist until we give birth to a change of thinking through an ever-growing awareness of ourselves and our connectedness with one another. Part of being human is realizing that we may not be perfect all the time. We don't have to assume that an argument is an attack on our worth as a human being. Instead, we can use it to determine if our behavior or thinking might need adjustment. Where judgment can destroy friendships, our willingness to listen to another honestly and openly helps to deepen them.

Only one thing is more important than learning from experience, and that is not learning from experience
—SIR JOHN TEMPLETON

Today can be a day filled with opportunities for you to express yourself, expand yourself, and experience the world around you. A lot of people talk about life. Some love it. Some disparage it. And a few realize that life can be what you make it because they have learned from past experiences. Lessons learned from these experiences have often contributed greatly toward seeing the possibilities in what some people call the "game of life." When we've "been there" and "done that," we can have as good of an idea of what we *don't* want as what we *do* want. Experience is certainly an excellent teacher.

A lot of emphasis is placed on winning in today's world. We've been taught that everyone loves a winner and, as the former baseball manager Leo Durocher put it, "Nice guys finish last." In professional sports, winning is everything. In business, striving for the top rung of the ladder may be a constant goal. Nations compete with other nations to win control of markets. Companies spend millions of advertising dollars to help win over the consumer. The saying "It's not whether you win or lose, it's how you play the game" may seem to some to be a shopworn shibboleth, judged by current competitive standards. However, there is great wisdom in the Chinese proverb, "Those who play the game do not see as clearly as those who watch."

While the experience of winning may be a good thing, placing an inflated value on being first may be destructive. There is often a mistaken assumption that you can be a better and happier person if you often come in first. But many who hold the top seat in their sphere of expertise prove to be unhappy and insecure on a personal level. If your self-esteem rides on your ability to outmaneuver, outwit, or outsmart someone else, you might have a great deal riding on a very shaky foundation.

Now, the experience of competition can be a positive force in our lives. On a personal level, competing with another in sports or business can provide you with an opportunity to sharpen and expand your skills. In addition, it often calls attention to areas that need further development. You can gather a tremendous amount of experience and useful information quickly either by engaging in competition or by observing others competing.

The problem lies not in competition but in our attitude toward whatever we're doing. So often we tend to measure ourselves and our self-worth by how well we do against our opponents. If we lose the game, we may believe we're losers. If we come in second, we could feel we're second-rate. It's important to remember that productive competition with another can serve as a yardstick that measures our performance, not our value as a person.

If you sincerely work toward making each performance a little better than the last one—and if you find your sense of life steadily expanding and improving because you are building on your experiences—you can emerge as a winner in more ways than one.

We can become bitter or better as a result of our experiences
—ERIC BUTTERWORTH

An article in *Abundant Living* magazine tells of an Irish uprising in 1848 in which the men were captured, tried, and convicted of treason against Her Majesty Queen Victoria. All were sentenced to death. Passionate protest from all over the world persuaded the queen to commute the death sentences. The men were banished to Australia—a place as remote and full of prisoners as Siberia was later. Years passed. In 1874 Queen Victoria learned that a Sir Charles Duffy who had been elected prime minister of Australia was the same Charles Duffy who had been banished twenty-six years earlier. She asked what had become of the other eight convicts and learned that Patrick Donahue became a brigadier general in the U.S. Army; Morris Lyene became attorney general for Australia; Michael Ireland succeeded Lyene as attorney general; Thomas McGee became minister of agriculture for Canada; Terrence McManus became a brigadier general in the U.S. Army; Thomas Meagher was elected governor of Montana; John Mitchell became a prominent New York politician, and his son, John Purroy Mitchell, became a famous mayor of New York City; and Richard O'Gorman became governor of Newfoundland!

What happens to us on the journey of life is not nearly as important as how we handle what happens. Life sometimes takes unexpected twists and turns that can throw us off course for a time. We may have experienced an unhappy childhood in a broken home or with parents who were alcoholics. We may have been considered the "black sheep," the one who just never fit in with the others. Almost anyone can find reasons for not doing as well as he thinks he should have. The key to successful living, however, is to learn from our experiences— good and bad—and go on from there. If we choose, we can try to move forward and forge the kind of life we desire to live in spite of some of the falls we may take.

Imagine for a moment that you have reached the end of your life and are reflecting on the many and varied scenarios that have comprised your world. Wouldn't you want to look back with pride, knowing you had made the best of each situation, regardless of how difficult it may have been? Isn't this better than looking back and sorrowfully wishing you had handled things differently? To guard against possible regrets, it is important to handle every experience to the best of your current ability. You may have to practice more patience; strive a little harder to accomplish your goal; reach inside yourself a little deeper to garner greater strength; and muster a little more faith in God and yourself. You may need to make a commitment to push yourself harder and further than at any time in the past. After you have given everything you feel you have to give and still seem to come up short, there is nothing to be ashamed of because you have done your best. You can experience the inner peace of those who know they gave their all. You can be a success regardless of the outcome. You can be better, not bitter, from the experience because you know you gave it your best effort.

The commitment of giving your best at all times enables you to find value in—and lend value to—every experience in life. Take what is given to you to accomplish today, and make it a most wonderful expression of your gifts and talents. Utilizing your inner resources in this manner, you can look back over the events of your life with satisfaction and peace of mind, because you will likely have no regrets.

If you think you know it all, you are less likely to learn more
—SIR JOHN TEMPLETON

As you go about your daily activities, perhaps you meet people whose lives seem tangled and for whom living seems like a hard experience. In many instances, the trouble may be that these people are caught up in the trap of personal ego; they feel that they know everything already and fail to listen. If you think you know it all, you are less likely to learn more.

Bill Johnson, well known for his overinflated ego, was constantly reminding his employees, family, and friends of his many accomplishments in life. As president of a successful business, Bill was quick to seize any opportunity to tell his workers how he single-handedly took over a company on the brink of bankruptcy and, almost overnight, turned it into a profit-making venture. To his friends, Bill constantly boasted about having the most talented and attractive children in the neighborhood. At home, Bill always had the last word. In fact, Bill was so full of himself that he had a custom-made wall plaque hung over his fireplace that read, "Bill Johnson is God." After returning from the office one evening, Bill discovered a small note placed below the plaque. It read, "One small step for Bill Johnson; one giant step for atheism!"

Perhaps the idea of humility and of approaching life humbly could work effectively in many instances. Those taking the humble approach acknowledge that their humility comes from the ultimate realization that the universe and all the creatures within it, both visible and invisible, may be manifestations of infinite creative power. The divine spirit may move in your life and make it over from within so that you see things in a new light, and love may become the spontaneous expression of a Spirit-filled soul.

In *Sand and Form*, Kahlil Gibran wrote, "I have learned silence from the talkative, tolerance from the intolerant, and kindness from the unkind; yet strangely, I am grateful to those teachers." Sometimes, if we listen to learn, the things that make us uncomfortable can provide valuable insights. We can recognize what we don't want as well as what we do want in our lives.

"Build thee more stately mansions, O my soul." How clearly the poet saw that one of the great laws of life is growth. No one is exempt from this law, and no one lacks the equipment or the ability to grow. The Bible tells us that man was created and given dominion and authority over the earth, and our charge is to demonstrate that dominion. The real dominion we need to attain is not an outer one at all; it is within ourselves. Building more stately mansions is an inner project, and the spirit within helps us build these mansions. How can we hear the guidance of the whisperings of spirit if we are too busy talking about unessential things to listen?

The art of listening can be a humbling experience. When we open ourselves to another's point of view, we may discover many new and exciting ways to look at any subject. If we examine a single leaf that has fallen from a giant tree, we can literally discover a number of ways to observe the leaf. The artist or poet may see form, color, and beauty. The biologist may see evidence of the purpose of the leaf to the tree. The atomic physicist may see trillions of atoms amazingly organized. The groundskeeper may see the leaf as littering his garden path. The caterpillar may see food for metamorphosis into a glorious butterfly. The wonders of God's creation abound—even in a simple leaf.

Our thoughts can turn to the Old Testament prophets who seemed to have such a wonderful rapport and communication with God. Back in the time of Moses, according to the scriptures, it seemed that God's voice was clearly audible. From the heights of a mountaintop, God spoke. From the fiery center of a burning bush, God spoke. Through significant dreams, God spoke—and the people listened.

We may not know whether or not God actually spoke to Moses in an audible voice or through an inner voice. In our present time, we do need to listen and hear God through the many ways in which he speaks to us. For instance, we may have heard God speaking through our quiet thoughts, through good books and expressive music, through conversations with other people, through children's activities, and through the beauty and wonder of nature. And in everything, it seems something worthwhile can be learned.

Often in our ignorance, or nonthinking, we hinder God and stop the current of divine messages. But when our lives are permeated with a lively faith and a sincere desire to learn, messages of love and guidance flow to us and through us like a beautiful river that has found smooth passage through our life-stream.

No one's education is ever complete
—SIR JOHN TEMPLETON

Anyone who believes that he has learned everything he needs to know, or all there is to learn, makes a critical error. Albert Einstein, one of the great geniuses of our age, once said: "A day without learning is a day wasted. There is so much to learn and so little time to learn it." He followed his own precept by continuing to work and study diligently until his death. Many examples of great people who never stopped learning offer inspiration for all of us.

Grandma Moses, who painted in a primitive style, took up art late in life. We might not have the opportunity to enjoy her work if she had lacked the courage to continue her education and refused to stop growing in her creativeness. Colonel Sanders, of Kentucky Fried Chicken fame, learned about the fast-food business and franchising in his sixties. Abigail Adams, American first lady, expressed the importance of learning and education in this way: "Learning is not attained by chance. It must be sought for with ardor and attended to with diligence."

"Live and learn" can be a wise motto to live by if you agree that no one's education is ever complete. It isn't by trying to squeeze the required thought out of our brain cells that we can get the knowledge we need. Rather, it is by opening up our minds, freeing, letting go, expanding, and broadening our thoughts with the implicit understanding that we may become more open to the infinite mind of

God in universal form. Who knows what realms of knowledge and learning abide therein, waiting for us to be receptive. Wherever we are and whatever we are doing, it is possible to learn something that can enrich our lives and the lives of others. It may be necessary to abandon outmoded ways of thinking and acting in order to try something new. But when we do, we often find that life becomes more exciting and fulfilling than we dreamed possible.

Could this be what Jesus meant when he spoke of hiding our light under a bushel, or, as translated by Moffatt, putting it "under a bowl"? We really cannot imprison light. If we took a glowing electric lightbulb and turned a bowl upside down over it, some of the light would still spill out from under the bowl. Even if the burning lightbulb were hermetically sealed inside the bowl, the lightbulb would still show itself by heating up the bowl and imparting some of its warmth to the surrounding air. Could this be saying to us that we can neither stifle nor suppress for very long the divine intelligence that is a part of our inherent nature?

Sometimes, we try to place the bowl of human belief over the splendor that wants to shine. Is it possible that our frustrations and discouragements may be a little leakage from the great light wanting to shine? Perhaps we need to remove a bowl or two by denying the human belief that we might be too old, have too little education, or may not be smart enough to accomplish greater things. The good news is that, even though the light of creativity and knowledge may be suppressed and hidden under the innumerable bowls of belief we may place over it, it never loses its divinity or its immense and indefatigable energy. It will try to work through the subconscious facilities instead, and we may find ourselves having interesting dreams that make a deep impression on us.

Listen to your inner promptings. Since you are a functioning human being, you may have one or more fields in which you are strong. Accentuate these strong areas of your life, and humbly claim your degree of greatness by continuing to be eager to learn.

CHAPTER 6

Examining Ourselves

The unexamined life is not worth living
—SOCRATES

HE STUDY OF human behavior is not new to our time. The ancient Greeks were probably the first to ask questions about what motivates people. The origins of psychology are often linked to the Greek philosopher Aristotle, who lived in the fifth century BCE. Aristotle built on the groundwork of Plato and Socrates. The phrase "Know thyself" is attributed to Socrates, the Greek philosopher who urged his fellow Athenians to live noble lives, to think critically and logically, and to have probing minds. He believed, along with Plato and Aristotle, that evil arises from ignorance and the failure to investigate the reasons why people behave as they do.

Most people sincerely desire to live noble and moral lives. One way to accomplish this can be through understanding the behavior of friends and associates as well as our own. Once we understand why others behave as they do, we can have more compassion and empathy for them. When we recognize our roots in the human family, we no longer feel a need to stand in judgment of others. Judgment only condemns and separates people. It places one person or group against another, whereas compassion and empathy can bring people together and promote clearer communication.

81

Socrates emphasized the Greek ideal of self-control. He believed in a divine principle, expressed through an inner voice that directs our actions along the path of morality. He taught us to explore our thinking and behavior, to reach within, and to expunge those behaviors that are unworthy of us. Honest self-analysis can help us to see if we react to people and events because we may have been socially conditioned in a certain way, or if our behavior is guided by the divine principle and inner voice within us. As important as it is to understand the behavior of others, our own behavior is the only behavior we can change. Learning the reasons behind what we do and why we do it helps us to be honest with ourselves; it builds integrity into our lives. We learn what is *real* to us, what *matters* to us. And we learn to act rather than simply react. We learn to be true to ourselves and to live our lives with dignity.

Introspection, with an emphasis on growth and change, can help us achieve a fuller and more fulfilled life. So can taking the time to understand the motives behind the actions of others. Learning to have compassion and empathy for others and for ourselves often leads to a peaceful, successful existence that is truly worth living.

What is done is done
—WILLIAM SHAKESPEARE

In examining our own lives, we might be able to spot the heavy weight of yesterday's deeds that we persist in carrying with us. We might be carrying bitterness and resentment because we may have felt betrayed by a friend. We might be carrying anger and a feeling of injustice because we lost out on something we really wanted while someone else got it. We might be carrying hurt feelings because someone we liked criticized us. But continuing to carry harsh and negative feelings from the past can be like picking up a pebble in your shoe while you are out walking. You can stop and remove the pebble, or you can continue to walk and let the pebble irritate your foot and cause pain.

The choice is yours: you can release your anger and hurt feelings, just as you can remove the pebble from your shoe.

Dr. Carl Simonton, among others, has said that the bodies that develop cancer have often been weakened by emotional or psychological factors as well as physical factors. He said, "Our body responds to the way we live, particularly our emotional reactions to life. We don't know how many cancer cells we normally develop during a lifetime, but it is probably thousands, if not millions—or even billions—in a normal lifetime without developing the disease. So our body normally has intact mechanisms for handling this very easily and automatically." An important knowledge we can gain in staying healthy is that there is a natural healing mechanism in the human body. Could a part of that mechanism be releasing, letting go, and forgiving people or situations that may have caused us pain?

When you try to continue living a normal life while carrying harsh feelings about someone else, other things in your life become affected. A small, dark cloud seems to hang overhead that warns of foul weather. The next time you feel angry or hurt, give the situation time to settle down, then go directly to the source of your anger. Explore the situation; make peace with the circumstances; and release the angry thoughts and feelings. This may oftentimes mean swallowing your pride and forgetting about who is right or wrong so that you can continue along the path of life without the extra weight of negative feelings.

In his letter to the Romans, Paul wrote, "If possible, so far as it depends upon you, live peaceably with all" (Rom. 12:18). This is sound advice. The great law of cause and effect is the avenger and is permanently active. You may not see the connection between cause and effect, but nevertheless the law of cause and effect is at work. How foolish it seems to send out vindictive, unforgiving thoughts toward a so-called enemy when we can make an effort to "live peaceably with all." We can forgive and forget injuries, hurts, and disappointments. We can have as our focus loving and harmonious thoughts toward ourselves and toward others. Nothing you or anyone else can do will erase the events of the past. Forgive, but also forget!

A soft answer turns away wrath, but a harsh word stirs up anger
—PROVERBS 15:1

Giving in to anger can rob you of good judgment and leave you regretting things said or done, once the intense emotions have subsided. A gentle and controlled approach to an angry situation can often provide an opportunity to choose your words and actions rationally and bring about a more desirable conclusion when you're faced with a potentially damaging situation. Taking charge of your emotions can allow you to assess a troubled and clouded area of misunderstanding with a clearer mind and then take the wisest course toward a resolution.

People sometimes mistakenly assume that they have no power over their emotions. In these instances, they may have ceded their power to others. "He made me so angry," someone might say. Or, "She really gets under my skin." The truth is that no one except you has the power to make you angry. If someone else assumes that power over you, you have, in some way, granted them that right! You may have reacted in anger because you felt the other person drove you to it, but the choice—to be angry or to act calmly—is yours to make.

There can be two ways to approach a situation that has triggered heated, hard-to-control feelings. You can *react* to the words and actions of others, or you can *act* from attitudes of your own choosing. The word *react* is a composite of the prefix *re-*, which means "again," and the word *act*, which means "to perform an action." In other words, to react can be to perform the actions of another. And reacting to someone else's negativity can have the potential to raise the stakes to an explosive level. To act out of understanding, on the other hand, to give a "soft answer," allows you to remain poised and calm, and creates the potential for you to forge a peaceful, happy solution.

Consider this humorous story about British professor John Burdon Sanderson Haldane. A discussion between Haldane and a friend began to take a predictable turn. The friend said with a sigh, "It's no use going on. I know what you will say next, and I know what you will do next." The distinguished professor promptly sat down on the floor, turned two back somersaults, and returned to his seat. "There," he said with a smile. "That's to prove that you're not always right!"

The next time you are faced with an angry, escalating situation, make a decision to try the "soft-answer" approach. Bring your emotions under your control, and proceed from a calmer and more peaceful state of mind. By doing so, you can remain in control of the most vital resource you possess—your mind. You can find, with practice, that the soft answer may be your best defense against harsh words.

Once a word has been spoken, it cannot be recalled
—WENTWORTH DILLON, EARL OF ROSCOMMON

There are times when we say something in anger and later wish we could recall our words. Unfortunately, once spoken, words cannot be called back. Anger is an emotion that often leads to sadness, hurt, and possibly even violence. And anger is most often vented in two ways—*physically* and through *words*. A boy, angry over what should have been a simple difference of opinion, told a close friend, "I hate you." After calming down, he deeply regretted having told his good friend that he hated him. He realized that people have a right to different viewpoints. The trouble was, even though his friend accepted his apology, something was lost in their relationship. They were no longer completely relaxed and happy in each other's company. The element of total trust no longer infused their relationship.

You can avoid this type of situation by following a very simple rule: always think before you speak!

Some metaphysical teachers believe that we literally shape our world with words. A statement spoken in spiritual consciousness may have great spiritual power. Sound (speaking the word) can change things as well as consciousness itself. Let's expand this idea a bit. Everything—from thoughts to rocks to tables and chairs, to you and me—is composed of units of energy in unique configurations of vibrations. Our scientists tell us that everything vibrates and everything has its own sounds, which are its own peculiar vibrations. Sound vibrations affect physical matter.

In the book *Physics without Mathematics,* Clarence Bennett tells of an experiment in which vibrations in metal or glass plates may produce wave patterns that can be seen with the eye. By sprinkling sand on the plates and drawing the bow of a violin across the edge, geometrical figures are formed as the plate vibrates. In this simple experiment, we see how sound vibrations affect physical matter. Could this mean that the words we speak throughout the day indirectly take physical shape in our bodies and help form our life circumstances according to their nature? Think for a moment. What happens to your face and your body when you speak in joy? In concern? In anger? In excitement? In expectancy? How do you feel when someone speaks to you in joy, concern, anger, excitement, or expectancy? A woman who once described her feelings about the angry comments of a friend said, "The words were so intense that it felt like a physical slap in the face!"

Ella Wheeler Wilcox wrote in her poem "Attainment" these words:

> Use all your hidden forces. Do not miss
> The purpose of this life, and do not wait
> For circumstances to mold or change your fate!

Get into the habit of thinking before you speak. You'll never regret it.

Speak positive affirmations during your prayer time to identify with the Spirit.

Aim for the highest relations with yourself and others.

Refrain from gossip. Speak only words of truth.

Learn to observe yourself with detachment. Be aware of your words.

You choose the path you want to walk down
—SIR JOHN TEMPLETON

As spiritual beings, we were designed to be filled with love and trust. People seem increasingly aware of their responsibility to each other as members of the human family. Physicists and scientists are conducting experiments in an attempt to prove that we are united; that each living soul is interlinked with others; that we are indeed part of the whole; and that what each of us does affects others. More and more people are coming to believe that a power greater than themselves is in charge.

Sophie is a recent convert to a belief in spiritual progress. She experienced a dysfunctional childhood, and much of her thinking was very negative. As long as she continued to hold on to old ideas, her journey to spiritual maturity seemed difficult and slow. One day, she was moaning, as was her habit, about a headache. She was rehearsing the headache's progress, how it would probably develop into a migraine by the evening, and how she would miss work the next day—which she really couldn't afford to do. A friend overheard her and suggested that she just might be enjoying her misery. "Why don't you take an aspirin and a hot drink and lie down? Stop holding on to what you don't want. Start believing the headache can go away, and look forward to a wonderful day at work tomorrow—or do you *prefer* being miserable?"

The truth of her friend's words struck Sophie. She followed her friend's advice, and her headache was gone when she awakened from a nap. It was then that Sophie started doing some serious self-examination. She could comprehend how she often used sickness as a way of getting attention and vowed to begin reprogramming her thinking process.

Like Sophie, we, too, can begin to become masters of our world instead of its victims. Rather than allow ourselves to be consumed by our egos, we need to remember that each of us is a cocreator in life. When we abide in this truth, we can rise above doubts, fears, and negativity and allow the indwelling Divinity in each of us to guide us to better solutions.

You may be living in trying times and faced with problems or situations over which you may feel you have no control. You may be confronted—as many people are—with taxes that seem like an onerous burden, rising costs of supplies that may make financial management challenging. You may feel like an innocent bystander in a world of international conflicts, a society replete with injustices. You may even feel there can be little you can do to change any of this. Yet you do have a choice!

Ella Wheeler Wilcox sat by the East River in New York City years ago reflecting on the fact that people coming from the same home environment may turn out so differently. Inspired by some sailing vessels pulling up the river to their docks, she wrote the following poem:

> One ship drives east, and the other drives west,
> With the self-same winds that blow.
> 'Tis the set of the sails and not the gales,
> Which tells us which way to go.

Aldous Huxley said, "Experience is not what happens to you; it is what you do with what happens to you." We can choose how we handle anything that comes into our lives. We can choose love or hate. We can worry about the situation, or we can pray about it. We can struggle, or we can meet the experience with nonresistance. We can accept the experience as a crushing blow of defeat, or we can lift our eyes and move toward victory. An old Asian axiom says, "You may not be able to keep the birds from flying over your head, but you can keep them from building nests in your hair!"

When we rule our minds in a positive way, we choose the path we want to walk down. We are no longer driven by ego. Instead, we become masters of our world and our destiny, and create a life that is happy, joyous, and free.

Destructive language tends to produce destructive results
—SIR JOHN TEMPLETON

When David's parents were divorced, the settlement provided that he would live with his mother. Because tightened financial circumstances forced them to move to another city, David had to attend a new school and make new friends. The changes were traumatic for him. He resented the children whose parents were still married, and he often got into fights with little or no provocation. In his bitterness, he developed the habit of being overly critical of others. He rarely had a kind word to say about anyone.

One day a classmate, who was aware of David's situation, approached him. "My parents are divorced, too," he said gently. "I know what you're going through. But you have to let go of your anger and bitterness. You're really hard on people, and it only hurts you. If you can't say something good, it's better not to say anything at all."

In his pain, David found it difficult at first to appreciate the boy's advice. But since things only seemed to be getting worse, he became more cautious about what he said to others. He often refrained from speaking, whereas before he would have quickly said something sarcastic and cutting. He began to see how insensitively he responded to those around him. He realized that he was not alone in his particular situation. Many of the other children had also experienced difficult family breakups, and David began to find ways to encourage them and help them deal with their own pain and confusion. By the end of the school term, David made a complete turnaround in his attitude and gained the respect of many whom he had alienated in his earlier anger.

Any one of us may experience stressful times at home, at school, or in our work. When things are not going well, it is often tempting to criticize others. We may think finding fault with someone else can help us feel better about ourselves or our condition. Or maybe it could be simply that misery loves company!

In those "down" moments, it may be best to remain silent if we cannot say things that are helpful and kind. Besides causing unnecessary pain and suffering for those around us, our negative words frequently compound our own problems.

In his book *When Bad Things Happen to Good People*, Rabbi Harold Kushner wrote about perspective. He said:

> God has created a world in which many more good things than bad things happen. We find life's disasters upsetting not only because they are painful, but because they are exceptional. Most people wake up on most days feeling good. Most illnesses are curable. Most airplanes take off and land safely. . . . The accident, the robbery, the inoperable tumor are life-shattering exceptions, but they are very rare exceptions. When you have been hurt by life, it may be hard to keep that in mind. When you are standing very close to a large object, all you can see is the object. Only by stepping back from it can you also see the rest of the setting around it. When we are stunned by some tragedy, we can only see and feel the tragedy. Only with time and distance can we see the tragedy in the context of a whole life and a whole world.

If we could keep this perspective in mind when situations are disruptive or disturbing and learn to "hold our tongue" until the bigger picture becomes more clear, perhaps a lot of destructive language could be avoided. In various areas of life, people who are burdened with problems can cast a deadening influence on themselves and others. They stress the negative rather than the positive. It is important to learn that inventive thinking can result from a constant search for solutions.

The time-honored adage "If you can't say something good, then don't say anything at all" can be a benchmark for the words you speak throughout the day. If you feel discouraged about something, talk to a friend or a counselor. Everyone has dark moments. But be careful not to lash out and hurt others when you're not feeling good about yourself because they, too, may need words of understanding and support. Always be sensitive in what you say to others. Try to remember that the bad moments will pass, and, if you refrain from lashing out with your tongue, when they do pass, you will have no unnecessary wounds to heal.

There are more possibilities in the universe than one can imagine
—ANONYMOUS

From the time of our birth, we have been taught to think in terms of limits, boundaries, and restrictions. Fences surround our property, speed limits slow us down, and some say there are even limits to our endurance. It has been proven, however, that all limits are surpassed as humanity progresses. Astronomers pushed back the earlier belief in a dome-shaped firmament covering the earth and gave us knowledge of galaxies millions of light-years away. Gerontologists assure us that a life span of one hundred years is conceivable in the near future. Athletic records are broken time and again. So much is happening that pushes back boundaries of heretofore seeming limitation.

It may be difficult for people born in the twentieth and twenty-first centuries to imagine the limited concept of the cosmos that was prevalent when the scriptures of the major religions were written. This thought raises a question: do scriptures need reinterpreting to accommodate our expanded notion of the universe?

Teilhard de Chardin called for a new theology that would incorporate the modern scientific discoveries of the "immensity of space, which imbues our accustomed way of looking at things with a strain of Universalism," and the progressive "duration of time which . . . introduces . . . the idea of a possible unlimited Progress Futurism." Because of these two concepts—universalism and futurism—Teilhard believed we now possess a higher and more organic understanding of the cosmos, which could serve as a basis for new spiritual understandings.

Life is consciousness. There is no place in the world that is truly empty, without substance or energy. Wherever we look, we see some form of life, of growth, or vitality. All around us is the matter from which we build and create. Philosopher and writer George Santayana offers a provocative perspective: "The universe, as far as we can observe it, is a wonderful and immense engine. . . . If we dramatize its life and conceive its spirit, we are filled with wonder, terror and amusement, so magnificent is that spirit."

If we turn from the physical world and look within our minds for an empty space, we quickly realize that the mind is constantly active—filled with ideas and thoughts. The great mystics taught that to still the mind is to realize an unseen power and activity far greater than ourselves. This speaks of a great truth of another law of life: there is no limit in the universe. Look around at the many objects that have been made by humans. Now, look beyond those things and see before you the vastness of the resources from which those objects are created: the greatest of these resources is the mind. Our minds are filled with ideas and thoughts that show us how to build or create the things our imagination can conceive.

You make yourself and others suffer just as much when
you take offense as when you give offense
—KEN KEYES

Have you ever walked into a room where everyone stopped talking and you were certain they were talking about you? Or perhaps you looked over at a group of people sitting together and they started whispering? You may have been convinced they were saying something about your clothes or your manners. Whether we choose to react or respond to these situations can bring either suffering to those involved or peace and understanding.

If we react in a thin-skinned manner, the slightest remark could bring pain to the core of our being. We might see offenses where none were intended and possibly become paranoid in our thinking. Our hurt feelings may cause us to feel we're justified in lashing out at our perceived accusers. If our reaction to the situation is to become quiet and introspective, we might sulk alone and nurse our self-pity. If we allow ourselves to become immersed in miserable isolation, we may fail to see that we are not the only ones suffering.

The person who knows his own worth makes an effort to respond to situations in ways that can bring harmony and peace to his relationships. He demonstrates the ability to accept criticism for what it may be worth. Instead of allowing himself to be overcome by negative feelings, he often pauses to review what may have been said and look for the seeds of truth. When he finds those seeds, he can then apply them to the situation at hand and choose to behave in ways that support the highest and best good, based on his perception, for those involved. Paranoia does not become a problem, because his self-image remains strong.

A woman shared a story that when her son called the family from Vietnam, the call had to be relayed through an amateur radio station in Hawaii. The operator asked if they had ever talked by radio before, and they told him "No." "Well," the operator said, "you have to say what you want to say, then say 'Over,' and then listen. You see, you can't both talk at the same time."

When we talk to God, we may come to a point where we need to say "Over," and then listen. By the same token, in communicating with others, it is important to learn to say "Over," and listen. As we keep our lines of communication open between ourselves and God and between ourselves and other people, we can communicate through our true self—the self that is loving, caring, understanding, helpful, progressive, and creative. On this great journey through life, our relationships can be rewarding, for we can choose how we wish to respond to any given situation.

Remember, no one can make you feel inferior without your consent
—ELEANOR ROOSEVELT

You are under no obligation to let the world decide how you are going to feel about yourself. You have the right and the opportunity to discern the events in your life and judge yourself. Criticism may take on many forms, the majority of which seem petty and trivial. And criticism, whether directed toward us or coming from us, may be a deterrent to progress and may lead us into discord and trouble. By feeling confident and enhancing the positive qualities in others, we may actually be revealing our own fine qualities.

Many of us may have been raised to cede to others a great deal of control over our feelings. But, as we grow, it's important to learn that how we feel about ourselves, in spite of the opinions of others, can be an essential element in a happy life. If you allow others to determine your self-esteem, you may find yourself at the mercy of their opinions. Your happiness could then depend on many conditions over which you have no healthy inner control.

How you feel about yourself can determine, to a large extent, your experience of life. You cannot afford to surrender control of your feelings to the whims of others. If you know people who seem to be going through life constantly miserable for no apparent reason, it is likely that they have relinquished power over their feelings. This state of powerlessness often creates a high level of tension and anxiety.

You can feel good about yourself and your life, despite what others think. No one knows you or your capabilities as well as you do. Therefore, it is important for you to be in charge of how you feel about yourself.

Be open enough to learn from others, but make a commitment to stay in control of your feelings about yourself and your estimate of your worth. If you find that you have put someone else in charge of your self-esteem, begin making a simple statement like the following to set yourself free: "Today, I feel good about myself despite what others say, think, or do. I am the master of my feelings and hold that authority in my life today!" Self-knowledge may be difficult to obtain because the tendency to self-protection may seem so great. But it is in looking squarely at our own feelings and possible shortcomings that we may be able to see the work that needs to be done to bring about transformation in our lives. Once the decision is made about a "weak spot"—whether it be a "short-fuse" temper, feelings of unworthiness, feelings of being inferior, or whatever—we can engage ourselves in thinking about the opposite quality. For instance, if you desire to curb feelings of inferiority, think about the desirability of a pleasant disposition and feeling confident of the spirit within you. You can give your thoughts and feelings a new direction.

When you live from the center of your own being, life can become much more productive and joyful at the circumference.

Nothing is interesting if you are not interested
—SIR JOHN TEMPLETON

Two people can wake up in the same neighborhood, on the same day, to the same conditions, and yet have a vastly different day depending on who is doing the seeing. One person may have a positive attitude and awaken with the thought, "Good morning, God!" The other may dwell in pessimistic shadows and greet the day with "Good God, morning!" Same words, but a vastly different emphasis.

The concept of choice can be of utmost importance when we talk about perception. It is important to understand that we may be making a choice to see the proverbial glass half full or half empty.

An Eastern legend tells of a fair maiden who was offered a rare gift by the king of the land. The king presented her with a bag of pearls and promised her she could keep the largest, most perfect pearl she could find in the bag. However, he set down these conditions: she must choose one pearl only; she must remove one pearl at a time from the bag and either accept it or reject it; and she could not pick up a pearl for another look once it had been rejected.

So joyously the maiden began taking the pearls, one at a time, from the bag. In the process, she saw and held many large and perfect pearls. But she was looking for the one gem that would be just a little larger and a little more perfect. So she passed up many special treasures.

As she delved more deeply into the bag, the pearls became smaller and of poorer quality. Occasionally, she found pebbles instead of pearls. Now, inasmuch as she could not go back to the pearls she had formerly discarded, she had to keep on looking. The pearls continued to become smaller and less valuable. Even the pebbles became more common. When the maiden reached the bottom of the bag, she sadly went away as empty-handed as when she received the bag from the king.

The lesson of this legend may also remind us of ourselves, as we may sometimes rush through life seeking to get a better job, a bigger house, a better mate, a more glamorous social life, or whatever, and we miss the great pearls of abundance all around us every day.

We may be searching for the kingdom of heaven, which is right within us all the time, yet often we fail to recognize it. Then we sit down, dreading to go on because of our concern that things may get worse tomorrow. Either way—the rushing around or the sitting down and waiting—can produce the same results. Nothing much happens! This is why we often hear the phrase from philosophers and teachers, "Now is the most important moment of your life." We cannot go back even two seconds, nor can we leap forward two seconds. We live in the eternal moment of now, and our interest in life and its offerings exist in this moment. *Now* is the time of choice and blessing. The present day becomes the pearl of great price.

When anger reigns, negative consequences occur
—CHARLES D. LELLY

The high school students lifted their heads from their books when they heard Tracy in the hall yelling at Mr. Moorehead, the assistant principal. Tracy had been accused of stealing an expensive art book, and she was extremely upset over the false accusation. Ms. Taylor, the art teacher, believed Tracy had stolen the book because she was the last person seen reading it. Tracy, stung by the teacher's accusation, screamed at her that she'd put the book back on the shelf, but Ms. Taylor refused to believe her. The more Ms. Taylor refused to believe her, the more Tracy lost control. She began to curse at the older woman.

"I won't stand for this abuse," Ms. Taylor said, picking up the telephone to call Mr. Moorehead. "You'll stay for detention all this week after school."

Tracy had a record of getting into trouble at school. But this time, she had done nothing wrong.

"You're in deep trouble, young lady," Mr. Moorehead said quietly. "No one talks to me or any of the teachers this way and gets away with it."

The question to ask in this situation would be: how could Tracy have avoided needless trouble? Although anger may be a natural reaction when you're treated unfairly, it only makes matters worse to act out your anger. Remaining as calm as possible provides an avenue to examine the options that may be open to us. If Tracy had remained calm, she might have remembered that a very quiet, studious boy who was sitting in the back of the room could have been a witness. By talking calmly and rationally with Ms. Taylor and Mr. Moorehead, she may have had a better chance of convincing them of her innocence. Also, by maintaining her calm, Tracy could have heard Ms. Taylor's words more clearly. The art teacher told her she was very upset because so many art books were disappearing.

Although it wasn't right for Ms. Taylor to accuse Tracy, a little understanding on Tracy's part might have helped ease the situation.

Anger is a strong emotion that can have powerful detrimental effects on ourselves and others. When we can direct our angry feelings into positive actions, we're no longer needlessly wasting our energy. If Tracy had remained calm, she could have checked at the library to see if the book was there, or she might have asked the studious boy or other art students if they had seen the book.

Angry words and actions serve no useful purpose because they tend to set up a chain of negative reactions that often result in a communication breakdown. Not that it's easy to remain levelheaded when we're falsely accused, or even when we may have made a mistake. But it makes an already bad situation worse when we don't. Once anger takes over, common sense and reasonableness often fly out the window. Hurt feelings often ensue, and seeds may be planted that sprout into negative consequences.

President Abraham Lincoln's secretary of war, Edwin Stanton, had some trouble with a major general who accused him, in abusive terms, of favoritism. Stanton complained to Lincoln, who suggested that he write the officer a sharp letter. Stanton did so, and showed the strongly worded missive to the president, who applauded its powerful language. "What are you going to do with it?" he asked. Surprised at the question, Stanton said, "Send it." Lincoln shook his head. "You don't want to send that letter," he said. "Put it in the stove. That's what I do when I have written a letter while I am angry. It's a good letter, and you had a good time writing it and feel better. Now, burn it, and write another one."

Because anger is both an emotion and often a coping response, it falls into a special category, which Nicholas R. M. Martin, author of *An Operator's Manual for Successful Living*, calls "secondary emotions." He states that most of us feel more comfortable with anger than with the underlying feelings it masks, and we are often quicker to express that anger than the "softer" feelings closer to the heart.

He mentions four standard feelings that tend to precede anger: fear, hurt, frustration, and injustice. Although the list of possible underlying feelings may be much longer, Martin feels these four are the most common and could be called the "four pillars that hold up the roof of anger."

Furthermore, because we tend to get back what we send out, the expression of anger usually invites a counterattack or defensiveness in return. Here is a partial list of the typical consequences of the choice to become angry:

- Investigating feelings of "distance" between you and others
- Promoting negative feelings in others that may be difficult to overcome
- Covering up your true feelings and wishes and preventing others from being open and honest with you
- Inviting retaliation and/or defensiveness
- Establishing a roadblock that can hinder getting to the bottom of the situation and reaching a solution
- Ending friendships

There is certainly a time to speak directly and honestly. But before you speak in anger, pause for a moment and ask yourself if another tool would serve the purpose just as well or better. If there's a fly in your ointment, you can do the following: shoot it (hostility); hammer it into nothingness (anger); plead with it (helplessness); run away from it (fear); moan and groan (hurt or self-pity); go forward indignantly (injustice); or carefully carry it outside (kindness and love). Any one of the above may get the job done, but with what consequences for yourself and any others who may be involved?

Planning Your Life's Journey

Failing to plan is planning to fail
—BENJAMIN FRANKLIN

F YOU DECIDE TO drive from Maine to California, one of the first things you will probably do is study a road map. You will see that there's a choice of routes you may take to reach your destination. If you're in a hurry, you may choose the route that will get you there the fastest. You can then estimate how long the trip will take and plan a more accurate arrival time.

What holds true for a trip holds equally true for the accomplishment of any goal. Without a road map, your mind may wander aimlessly and be ineffective in reaching out for solutions. By formulating a plan to achieve your goals, in much the same way as you would use a road map, and by being systematic and studying the various alternatives, you focus the direction of your thoughts and find that you can reach almost any reasonable goal.

Now, the big question is, How can I discern the personal path that will bring me the fulfillment of my divine plan? The answer to it is another intriguing question: what is the best thing I can do for myself and for all concerned in the particular circumstances of my life with respect to the spiritual ideal? The spiritual ideal refers to purpose, intent, desire, motivation, incentive, and the "spirit in which you do anything."

Many people know what they want out of life, but few turn their dreams into a carefully planned, successful journey. They often depend on lucky breaks or the help of others. When they fail, they may often say of those more successful, "They just happen to know the right people" or "They get all the breaks." They fail to realize that planning for success has no more to do with luck or knowing the right people than does planning carefully for a cross-country trip. It's true that when you start moving toward your goal, you'll meet people who can help you advance. But you'll know that you earned those breaks because you had a goal and a plan in place to help you achieve that goal.

To develop a workable plan of action, mentally visualize the things you want to accomplish. Jot them down across a sheet of paper, and then list the steps necessary to accomplish your plan. Long-term objectives, of course, may involve more steps and more elaborate planning, but the principle remains the same. When you know what you want to achieve, create a plan to reach that goal. Once you have a basic plan, devote some time often to adjusting it as you gather new information. Then follow through with the plan until you achieve your objectives.

Stephen Covey, author of *The Seven Habits of Highly Effective People*, recommends that you "begin [planning] with the end in mind." The best planning encompasses what you want to accomplish and where you want to end up. Whether it is a special project or a simple daily routine, begin by setting a goal that takes into account the steps needed to reach it. If your goal is composed of many levels, you might want to prioritize them. Make a list, giving them a rating of A, B, or C. Then tackle the A's first. Professional planners have shown that tasks written down are much more likely to be completed.

The following guidelines may help you to achieve your goal:

1. Think of your goal not as some vague and nebulous idea but in clear and specific terms.
2. Outline your goal in writing, in detail.

3. Keep your goal in the forefront of your mind by reviewing it almost every day.

4. Learn everything you can that relates to your goal.

5. Be willing to work as hard as you can toward achieving your goal when the opportunity comes along.

6. Give the universe an opportunity to help you achieve your goal by affirming, "This or something better!"

7. Stay open to receive all possibilities for achieving your goal.

If you do not know what you want to achieve with your life, you may not achieve much
—SIR JOHN TEMPLETON

Those who set no goals in their lives drift aimlessly through the average three score and ten years, often complaining that "life's not fair." They also may say, to paraphrase the Rolling Stones, "I can't always get what I want." On the contrary, however, in keeping with an important law of life, they are receiving in proportion to what they are prepared to give. Many of us are quite clear about what we *don't* want in our lives, but how many of us are prepared to do the inner work that can lead us to what we *do* want? Once we know what we want, we can move into a position to establish goals and work toward achieving them.

You may have experienced this situation yourself with your friends when discussing which movie to go to. "Well, I don't want to see *Benji Goes to the Seaside*, and I've already seen *Rambo 9* so I don't want to see that again." It's only when you start talking about what you *do* want to see that you end up in the theater with a tub of popcorn in your hands.

By setting goals, you give yourself the opportunity to develop more of your potential. Hold a vision of your goal in mind, and the more you work toward this goal, the closer it will come to reality or manifestation. It can also be quite helpful to write your goals in a journal so you have a nearby daily reminder. Making a vision board by cutting out pictures from magazines and making a collage of the things you would like to see successfully fulfilled is a manner of establishing goals. And this goes beyond material goals to such areas of life as emotions, family, and relationships.

As a quiet young man, publisher Robert Bernstein had a job at New York's radio station WNEW. Albert Leventhal, head of sales of the publishing house of Simon & Schuster, liked the looks of the tall, red-headed, engaging Bernstein and enticed him into publishing. Bernstein turned out to be a phenomenon of energy. Once Leventhal happened to enter the office at the early hour of 7:30 and found his protégé already busy at work. Bernstein looked up at his employer, saw his questioning look, and said, "I'm ambitious. What's your excuse for being here at this unearthly hour?"

Locked within the human superconsciousness are the answers to our questions and the secret to the mysteries we may encounter. But in order to tap into and activate this reservoir, we must decide the avenue we wish to follow. Making a decision about what we want to achieve can be like putting a bit in a horse's mouth. The bit is probably the smallest part of the harness of a horse, but it is the most important. With this bit, we can control the movements of the horse. With a mere tug on the bit, we can get the horse to move his whole body in any direction we wish it to go. Without the guidance of a goal, we may flounder without direction and fail to achieve very much.

If you are facing in the right direction, all you need to do is keep walking
—BUDDHIST PROVERB

Have you ever had a cherished goal that appeared to be just out of reach? Maybe it seemed years away from fulfillment and the direction to travel unclear. For some of us, our present direction might lead to a new vocation or to money for a child's education. Whatever waits for you at the end of your path, however, the only way to get there is to keep your eyes on your goal. Something exotic may entice you to choose a diversion or an easier path, but the surest path—although perhaps not the easiest—is the one that leads directly to your goal with the fewest distractions and false starts.

If you plan to go from point A to point B in the woods and you prepare yourself for the journey by studying the trail and bringing along a compass, you can keep from getting lost. As the Buddhist proverb says, "If you are facing in the right direction, all you need to do is keep on walking!"

Conditions today are vastly different from those of even fifty years ago. Thus, the needs of the individual and the human family are different from those of ages past. We live in a time of tremendous change. We think and feel in progressive capacities as we have evolved from the ox cart, through the horse and buggy, the automobile, the airplane, supersonic jets, and into the age of space travel. We've come a long way from a pale tallow candle to lamps, gas, electricity, and quantum advances into the age of electronics. The children of today live with, understand, and use items that even the greatest minds of the past knew nothing about! Best-selling author and Harvard Business School professor Rosabeth Moss Kanter likens the constant changes happening today to the croquet game in *Alice in Wonderland*—a game in which "nothing remains stable for very long, because everything is alive and changing." The reality of life is that you cannot live in the past or in the future. You can only live in the present moment, and the direction in which you are facing is vitally important.

Open your mind to light and truth. There never need be a time when you are at a loss for ideas, inspiration, or guidance. Believe in yourself. Believe in your ability to cope with difficulties. Look at how you have grown through the experiences of your life. Think of the insight and understanding each situation brought. Exercise your ability to rejoice in the positive events that have happened. Continue to walk in the direction of greater illumination. Let joy be your compass!

Focus on where you want to go instead of where you have been
—SIR JOHN TEMPLETON

In his book *Helping Heaven Happen*, Dr. Donald Curtis presents a short dialogue that could well describe the situation in which many people find themselves. It goes like this:

"How is everything going?"

"Well, I've got bad news and I've got good news. I'll give you the bad news first. We're lost."

"We're lost? And what's the good news?"

"We're making very good time!"

From this conversation, these people do not seem to know where they are going. Instead of formulating a plan and following it, they run around in circles, gaining speed and momentum, but going nowhere. They are like a rudderless ship.

And with no focus or definite direction, how can their goals be achieved? An old axiom from the Qur'an says, "If you don't know where you're going, any road will get you there." When you want to achieve a goal, first have a mental picture or vision of it. Be sure your goal is genuine. Do not let yourself get caught up in spurious appearances or illusions of the outer world. Keep on track. Doing something about your goal comes next if you are to translate your vision into reality in your world.

Keeping your eye on the vision becomes necessary throughout the process. Focus on where you want to go, instead of where you have been. So much valuable time can be wasted in getting bogged down in past experiences or mistakes that have no relevance to the present goal. It is good to learn from past experiences and then continue forward. As you set your priorities, your objectives, and your direction in life, think positively and optimistically. And be aware of others who may come after you.

A story comes to us from long ago of a king who organized a great race within his kingdom. All the young men of the kingdom participated. A bag of gold was to be given to the winner, and the finish line was within the courtyard of the king's palace. The race was run, and the runners were surprised to find a great pile of rocks and stones in the middle of the road leading to the palace. However, they managed to scramble over it, or run around it, and eventually to come into the courtyard.

Finally, all the runners had crossed the finish line except one. Still the king did not call the race off. Everyone waited. After a while the last runner came through the gate. He lifted a bleeding hand and said, "Oh, king, I am sorry to be so late. But you see, I found a large pile of rocks and stones in the road, and it took me a while to remove them. I wounded myself in the process." Then the runner lifted the other hand in which he held a bag. "But, great king, I found this bag of gold beneath the pile of rocks and stones!"

The king responded, "My son, you have won the race, for the one who runs best makes the way safer for those who follow."

We have a choice. We can live in the past and be miserable and unhappy, or we can pick ourselves up and move ahead in life. When we choose to focus on the future, we can find the energy and ability to remove any "rocks" that may appear to be hindering our progress. If you take stock of yourself and find that you may be spending time frequently reliving unhappy experiences of the past, make the decision to rid yourself of the ties that bind you to a former way of life.

Where would we be as a human race—scientifically, technically, economically, medically, culturally, or environmentally—if those fine minds who made many unprecedented discoveries had looked backward and dwelled in the past instead of visioning growth and new horizons and setting goals to reach them? The evolution of human knowledge is accelerating enormously. More than half of the scientists who ever lived are alive today. More than half the discoveries in the natural sciences have been made in this century. More than half the goods produced in the history of the earth have been produced since 1800. More than half the books ever written were written in the last fifty years.

What does this mean to us now? Choose this day to move ahead into life. Focus on where you want to go. Look forward to new horizons. As we read in Maya Angelou's work *All God's Children Need Traveling Shoes*, the future is "plump with promise." Open your visioning to new possibilities. Experience the peace that passes understanding and the joy of abundant living!

Progress requires change
—SIR JOHN TEMPLETON

From one viewpoint, everything in life may seem unstable. Changes can take place so rapidly that it may seem as if nothing in the world could be looked upon as permanent. Friends may come and go. Possessions may be here today and gone tomorrow. The home of our childhood may be razed for a new office building. The babe in arms grows into an adult. Relationships begin and end. People die.

Yet looking at the universe from another viewpoint, everything is alive and growing. Everything is in joyous motion. New combinations appear. New beauty touches our souls. New opportunities spring up. Adventures may be ours for the adventuring!

When the billowing waves of change come rolling into our lives—and it has been said that "change is the one constant in life"—it may be upsetting to us if our heart is too attached to material things or we are too wedded to an erroneous concept of permanence. And if there is little or no understanding of how to handle change, it can seem heartbreaking. How do we deal with the pain of loss that seems to touch everyone's life at some point? If we are open and receptive to God's presence in every change, we ride safely on the crest of the wave.

When a seed falls or is planted in the darkness of the earth, the seed's outer shell must break so that new life can emerge. Jesus said, "Unless a kernel of wheat falls to the ground and dies, it remains only a single seed. But if it dies, it produces many seeds" (John 12:24, NIV). When our outer shells break in pain, when our hearts seem broken, it is important to learn the lesson that Jesus set out to teach us.

Whenever we lose something we may, in some way, gain something else at the same time.

The prospect of making changes may be greeted more cordially if we remember that the journey of life is forward and progressive. And as you grow and progress, changes come.

Have you considered that to say, "This is not the time for change," could be the equivalent of saying, "This is not the time for new blessings to come into my life"? It is important to continually grow physically, mentally, and spiritually. Because changes inevitably come about in our lives, we should be prepared to handle them courageously and triumphantly. Have faith in your own soul's capacity, realizing that there is present within you the fullness of God's love, wisdom, and intelligence to draw upon. By making an inner preparation for change, you can gear yourself up for the idea of change.

The next time you feel some shell breaking in your heart, feel it fully and deeply, and take comfort in knowing that living with and through pain can help you become a more understanding and compassionate person toward yourself and others. Adversity can be a rich and educational gift. Adversity can be a milestone in your mental and spiritual growth. Find it in your heart to welcome change and rejoice in the opportunities for soul growth and development.

No man is free who is not master of himself
—EPICTETUS

The Greek philosopher and slave Epictetus declared this truth in the first century CE. Of course, if you were a slave, then as now, freedom to control your own destiny would very likely be the foremost thought in your mind. While it may be true that the owner, the slave master, stands between the slave and his freedom, Epictetus understood that true freedom results not merely from escaping the slave master but also from becoming master of yourself.

There are many paths—and a wide diversity of philosophies and practices—that lead to self-mastery, as countless books written on this subject can attest. Yet a common theme runs through each of them. In Christian teaching, it is stated this way: "The kingdom of God is within you." Freedom, happiness, peace of mind—all that we seek and more—lies within us.

Self-mastery begins the moment you realize that you make your own prison and that you're the only person who can set yourself free. What is freedom? Is it the right to do what we want without restriction? Not really, for even in the freest of all societies, laws are needed to ensure freedom for everyone. Perhaps true freedom is not the freedom to *do* but rather the freedom to *become* all that we can be.

How do you earn the right to play a musical instrument or to create a work of art? It isn't a right given to you by someone else, but only comes once you master the skills necessary to create music or art. How do you attain the freedom to live a happy, creative life? Can anyone else grant you that freedom? No, that freedom also results from mastering the attitudes and skills needed to create a happy life.

When you conquer those twin enemies—your own fear and ignorance—you are on your way to true freedom. Fear and ignorance can be tough slave masters, and we remain enslaved as long as we give them living space in our hearts and minds. By overcoming thoughts of fear and by knowing the truth, we can become truly free.

A good way to overcome fear is to face squarely whatever makes us afraid. Avoiding fear-provoking situations does not resolve them. Like the mouse that roared, often the things that cause us the greatest anxiety can be much less threatening than we imagined. Whenever life challenges you with something unknown and you find yourself afraid, face and analyze your fear and watch it diminish.

Promise yourself to do your part, and try to be so strong in self-mastery that almost nothing can disturb your peace of mind. Try to talk health, happiness, and prosperity to most every person you meet; to look at the sunny side of life and make your optimism come true. Try to think only the best, and to expect only the best; to be too large for worry, too noble for anger, too strong for fear, and too happy to permit the presence of troubling thoughts.

Freedom can be ours when we recognize that we create our own prisons and that we can set ourselves free at any time. By facing our fears, we can learn to relinquish them and begin to take full responsibility for the usefulness of our lives. That is true self-mastery and true freedom.

Whatever you have, you must either use or lose
—HENRY FORD

In the United States, in 1956, Harland Sanders was an out-of-work sixty-six-year-old. Colonel Sanders's principal asset was his method of frying chicken. Loading up his automobile with a fifty-pound can of seasoning and his beloved pressure cooker, he took to the road. As he visited various restaurants, he said to the owners, "Let me cook chicken for you and your staff. If you like the way it tastes, I'll sell you my seasoning, teach you how to cook the chicken, and you pay me a four-cent royalty on every chicken you sell." He was so successful with his marketing idea that in his promotional travels, which averaged 250,000 miles annually, he wore out eight suits a year! Colonel Sanders acted on an idea that provided a useful service.

The gifts of the inner being may just as easily be lost if they are squandered. Confidence is a good example. Think of the confidence you feel when an idea comes to you that holds real potential for success, usefulness, and satisfaction. Develop the idea and act on it! A fruition of some sort can be realized, whether or not it may be exactly what you had in mind in the beginning

Progress and growth are impossible if you always do things the way you've always done things
—WAYNE DYER

Change is both good and necessary. Our evolution as a people and a planet depends on change. It is important to find new and better ways of doing things in our individual lives as well. Just because we've always done things a certain way doesn't mean that way is the only way. We can experience change in our lives by beginning with little things. We can take a new route to work or order a different item on the menu. As we consciously choose to see life in a different light, as we expand our minds to learn new things, growth can certainly come. In order for us to see life with fresh eyes, we must keep our minds open to new and different experiences.

Each individual human being has the capacity to grow and become both useful and happy. For this growth to take place, it is important to allow the natural process of change to occur. There is a saying that "life is change, and change is life." In other words, change is all around us. It is when we resist change that progress and growth are often stunted. By forging ahead and looking for new and better ways of living and perhaps discovering unseen resources, we can bring about progress and growth for ourselves and for others.

W. G. Montgomery writes in *Your Hidden Treasure* about two brothers who landed in New York in the year 1845. The older brother had learned the trade of making sauerkraut back in his native Germany. Hearing of possible fortunes to be made in America, he set off for California, where land was cheap. His goal was to grow cabbage, make the cabbage into sauerkraut, and begin a business. His venture was successful, and eventually he bought additional land, planted more cabbage, made more money, and was content.

The younger brother, meanwhile, remained in New York, working during the day and attending school at night. Taking a course in geology and metallurgy, he learned about the rocks and soils with which various minerals are associated. A few years passed and one day, he set out for California by stagecoach to visit his brother. Along the way he kept his eyes open to see what others had not seen.

Upon his arrival, the older brother took him into his cabbage patch to show what good crops he grew. But the younger brother wasn't interested in cabbage; he was staring at something else. He began picking up handfuls of the sandy soil, pressing it through his fingers, throwing it down, and picking up more.

Walking over to a nearby shallow stream, the young man stooped over and grabbed a handful of quartz and sand from the bottom of the stream and pointed to a dull, yellow piece. "Do you know what this is?" he asked his brother. The cabbage king shook his head, "No."

"That's a gold nugget," said the younger brother with excitement in his voice. "You've been growing your cabbage on a gold mine!" and so he had. One of the richest gold mines in California was found in that cabbage patch. While growing cabbage is a worthwhile enterprise, the cabbage can become quite costly when grown on a gold mine.

Our human mind can be just as rich in unseen resources as that cabbage patch was rich in the unseen gold in the ground where the cabbage grew. Again, it is important to be open to new possibilities, to better ways of doing things, to change. Like the butterfly going through its metamorphosis, we may find we can no longer stay behind self-made walls of protection. Something within us struggles to be free, to break the bonds of stagnation and soar into a new dimension. Perhaps you desire to find out who you really are in this new day. You may be feeling greater development in your spiritual awareness. Your consciousness may be moving and stretching and re-creating itself anew. You may feel that you are entering a realm of new and increased good in and for your life.

When your mind is lifted high, you refuse to give up or allow defeat to thwart righteous ambitions. Dare to step out in faith. Refuse to be content to be a caterpillar!

CHAPTER 8

Making Every Moment Count

Lost time is never found again
—BENJAMIN FRANKLIN

HEN THE MOMENTS that make up our lives go unappreciated, we may find our capacity to experience and enjoy diminished. It is *our* own life that is passing away as slippery and elusive as mercury.

To understand time is to be aware of how it operates in our lives, for time is a subjective experience—different for everyone. We've all experienced how each minute seems to stretch interminably when we're unhappy or when the task at hand is unpleasant; yet we're also aware of how fast time races by when we're engaged in a creative and useful project. Many people have also had those moments of total absorption when the clock's minute and hour hands seem frozen—with reality compressed into the experience of *now*.

A magazine article on making good use of time stated: "If you had a bank that credited your account each morning with U.S. currency in the amount of $86,400, and every evening cancelled whatever part of the amount you failed to use, what would you do? Of course, you would draw out every cent of the deposit!"

Well, time is just such a bank. Every morning it credits you with 86,400 seconds. Every night it writes off as lost whatever of those seconds you have failed to invest to good purpose. It carries no balance forward to the next day. It allows no overdrafts. Each day it opens a new account with you. Each night it burns the record for the day.

If you fail to use the day's deposit, the loss is yours. There is no going back. There is no drawing against tomorrow. You must live in the present—on today's deposit. Invest it so as to get the most in health, happiness, and service.

Time, like money, can be valuable precisely because it *is* limited—we are all allotted a finite amount. Even if our time on earth were unlimited, we would still need to use it well in order for it to retain its value. Only by putting the amount of time we have to good use can we find success and satisfaction in our lives. Time is like the cement that turns over and over in a concrete mixer. The cement exists only as a potential until the operator opens the chute and lets the mixture pour into a form, where it can harden into something useful. Time wasted is the concrete that never gets poured, or that gets poured from the chute but finds no form to contain it. We can prosper if we learn to shape our lives within increments of time. Through efficient use of time, we are better able to take stock of ourselves and express our inner genius in tangible ways that can help others and bring joy and satisfaction to our lives. In learning time-management skills, we discover strategies for developing new responses that give us more hours in every day.

One of the best strategies for giving form to our time is to establish long-term and short-term goals for ourselves. What do we hope to accomplish? What steps need to be taken today to fulfill tomorrow's goal? Each day, make a list. Use every minute because if you don't, you'll lose it. And the time lost today is gone forever.

A task takes as long as there is time to do it
—PARKINSON'S LAW

A deadline frames untamed impressions, thoughts, and feelings so your ideas take shape as an attainable goal. Many people find it difficult to effectively begin a project until they can see an end to it. A goal without some kind of deadline is a goal most likely not attained. A deadline may also serve as an inspiration to complete a project. Objectives not accomplished can lead to frustration and a sense of failure. A deadline or target date can help you know when your goal may be attained.

Without a deadline, you could exhaust yourself, galloping around in an open, often bleak, desert of amorphous thoughts and non-productive activity. A deadline, properly developed, can actually be a lifeline—like a lasso that can save you from wandering the plains of an endeavor that may seem to be without a beginning or an end. As a lifeline, a deadline draws you into alignment with your purpose and allows you to tame your time, talent, and resources, and apply them where they may be most useful.

A deadline also invites you to concentrate your energies on those interests that have greater value to you. Just as a spoonful of honey can sweeten a cup of tea more readily than it would a lake, your efforts need to be concentrated in the direction of your priorities in order to be more effective.

Time-management experts say the best deadlines are the ones you choose for yourself. Setting reasonable deadlines often results in a more effective use of your time. However, when other people impose deadlines on you, you may sometimes waste much valuable time in resisting and resenting them. When you are tempted to feel that others' deadlines are arbitrary or unfair, you can choose them for yourself anyway. As you meet the challenge of doing the best you can with what you have, your vigorous cooperation can reward you with a sense of great vitality and a feeling of tremendous accomplishment.

What would you like to achieve in your lifetime? How do you visualize making a difference in this world? Whatever large or small ambition you may have, begin today to create goals that suit your purpose, and set deadlines or target dates for those goals. Remember, deadlines can be lifelines that define your success.

Worry achieves nothing and wastes valuable time
—SIR JOHN TEMPLETON

A talented young woman thought seriously about becoming a doctor. She considered how wonderful it would be to make people feel better. She would be given the opportunity to heal the sick and help save lives. She fantasized about the substantial income she could earn by following her deepest desire.

Then she began to worry. She worried about the length of time it would take to become a doctor. She worried about the cost of her studies. She even worried about worrying so much. Because of her vacillating between desire and doubt, the young woman never took the entrance exams for the school to which she applied. As a result, she failed to achieve her principal goal in life and exemplified the old adage, "Worry is like a rocking chair that gives you something to do, but doesn't get you anywhere."

Many of us know the enjoyment of the soothing activity of rocking in a rocking chair. A frightened child may be comforted by a gentle, rocking motion. A physically injured person may often rock back and forth to temper sensations of pain. Rocking not only soothes the body, it can also be as comforting to the spirit as watching the ocean rise and fall in the rhythm of the waves. However, rocking leaves us in the present place; it doesn't move us forward.

In some ways, worrying is the same as rocking. Worrying can become a familiar behavior and, in this sense, a comfortable one that might trick us into believing that we may be doing something to solve a problem. Once worrying becomes a habit, we may no longer be conscious of choosing to do it. It becomes automatic. Yet worrying wastes valuable time that could be spent in finding ways to approach a challenge creatively. Worry can occupy a place better given to rest and relaxation; and rest and relaxation often allow us to approach a challenge with refreshed and revitalized energies. There can be numerous ways to look at, experience, and overcome obstacles. One of the most destructive and self-defeating ways to meet a challenge is to worry about it.

To free yourself from worry, accept responsibility for your own thoughts and actions. In his book *Your Erroneous Zones*, Dr. Wayne Dyer writes, "The tragedy of being guilty and worrying is that we immobilize ourselves in the present moment." If, by contrast, we take responsibility for our thoughts and feelings, we can refuse to allow worry to interfere with our success.

A husband and wife were having a discussion about a domestic situation. The husband spent long hours worrying about how they would meet the month's financial obligations. The wife, having listened to his discouraging remarks for a couple of days, called him to sit with her at the kitchen table. She laid the bills on the table, picked up a pencil and a piece of paper, and said: "Now you give me one good reason how worrying can help pay these bills, and I'll sit here and worry with you for the rest of the day. Otherwise, let's look at possible ways we can increase our income to meet our financial responsibilities."

We can decide in the present moment to release ourselves from worry and choose more positive life options, more creative and freeing attitudes, more enlightened states of mind and healthier beliefs. You are a growing and unfolding creation. You can accept your wonderful capacity for constructive actions. Most things people worry about tend not to happen. Worry can be one way to approach life, but taking responsibility for yourself is a better way. Worry often stems from fear, but self-responsibility and self-respect move from an attitude of faith in God, faith in the goodness of life, faith in the universe, and faith in our own potential.

If the young woman who wanted to become a doctor had used the time she spent worrying to study for her entrance exams and concentrate on a positive attitude, she may have taken a positive action, no matter how minor. You may rest for a while when necessary, then get up and move forward by placing one foot in front of the other, one step at a time.

Never put off until tomorrow what you can do today

—LORD CHESTERFIELD

Did you ever experience a problem so difficult and complex that you didn't know how to begin to solve it? Have you faced an examination that involved so much material you didn't know where to begin to study for it? Most people have found themselves in such situations and have often felt overwhelmed.

There are many reasons not to delay action. Problems can grow more serious and complex when they're not addressed promptly. Minor difficulties treated in a positive, active manner generally do not become major issues. For example, a minor cut properly treated usually heals quickly. But if left untreated and exposed to additional adverse conditions, it may become infected and require serious medical attention. Thus, a minor inconvenience may turn into a major problem.

In the same way, loans of money that are not repaid on a timely basis can grow into major debts when interest on such loans accumulates. Doing what is possible today to make life better can translate into a more orderly and productive tomorrow. The key is careful assessment of what needs to be done immediately, and what can be put off for a time.

Steady effort is more productive than sudden, frenzied activity. Orderly progression toward a goal prevents the tangle of problems that so often occurs when too many small areas needing attention suddenly come together. Doing the best you can do on a daily basis often frees up more energy for further progress in the future. Steady effort can move a person comfortably toward a goal, with energy left to handle unforeseen difficulties.

If you were to ship a fragile vase in a carefully packed, sturdy box directly to a friend, most likely the vase would arrive in good condition. If, instead, the vase were poorly packed in a thin-walled box and delayed at many stations along the way, it would most likely arrive in a damaged condition. This analogy is also true of problems or difficulties. The longer you ignore them and the more poorly they are handled, the bigger the problems become.

Elizabeth Blackwell, the first woman doctor in the United States, started her practice in New York in 1851. Not only was she unable to find patients, but no one would even rent her a room once she mentioned that she was a doctor. After weeks of trudging the streets, she finally rented rooms from a landlady who asked no questions about what Elizabeth planned to do with the rooms.

Quaker women, who had been receptive to the goal of equal rights, became Elizabeth's first patients. But no hospital would allow her on its staff. Finally, with financial help from her Quaker friends, Elizabeth opened her own clinic in one of New York's worst slums in March 1853. Elizabeth hung out a sign announcing that all patients would be treated free. Yet, for the first few weeks, no one showed up. Then one day a woman in such agony that she didn't care who treated her staggered up the steps and collapsed in Elizabeth's arms.

When the woman was treated and recovered, she told all her friends about the wonderful woman doctor on Seventh Street. The dispensary was soon going well and eventually expanded into the New York Infirmary for Women and Children—now the large and thriving New York Downtown Hospital in Lower Manhattan.

Each of us moves toward major goals by steps in a process. Usually these steps are small ones. Whenever we put off taking the necessary steps, progress may grind to a standstill or recede even further into the future. By following Lord Chesterfield's advice and not putting off until tomorrow what can be done sensibly today, we can achieve an orderly, harmonious, steady movement toward whatever goal we have set for ourselves.

CHAPTER 9

Practicing Forgiveness

To be forgiven, we must first forgive
—SIR JOHN TEMPLETON

OY MASTERS, founder of the Foundation of Human Understanding, writes in his book *How Your Mind Can Keep You Well*, that we ought to be grateful when others offend us. They are doing us a favor, he suggests, because when we forgive those who have offended us, it erases some of the self-destructive effects of offenses we may have caused others.

The person who cannot forgive may become physically, mentally, emotionally, or spiritually ill, as the following story so convincingly demonstrates. Kathy had hated her father all her life and felt justified in her extreme feelings. He abandoned her mother, Kathy, and six other children. Each time her mother became pregnant, her father disappeared until the new baby arrived. When he returned, the sad process would repeat itself. While the father was home, he physically abused everyone, occasionally beating his wife with a horse whip. She and the children were terrified of him. None of them knew when he would lose his temper and turn violent. Kathy sometimes hid under the table or bed in fear, and many people agreed that she was justified in hating her father.

However, Kathy's chronic state of anger damaged her own life more than anyone else's. Like her father, Kathy would lash out at others with only the slightest provocation. Her actions cost Kathy job after job and many strained and unhappy relationships.

Hatred and bitterness finally eroded her health. She suffered from headaches, stomach problems, and eventually developed arthritis. By her twenty-fifth birthday, Kathy looked middle-aged.

She knew she would be better off if only she could learn to forgive her father, but she just couldn't do it. Kathy's inner guidance kept reminding her that "to be forgiven, you must forgive." So she started the forgiveness process with a statement that went something like this, "I forgive you, you sorry so-and-so."

At first it was difficult, and Kathy felt dishonest because she didn't feel at all forgiving. But as she persisted, the statement became softer. Soon she was able to drop the "you sorry so-and-so." As she came to understand how her father could have acted so violently, she began to feel pity for him, then compassion, and, finally, real love.

When Kathy learned to forgive her father, she began to forgive and actually love herself, gaining a sense of inner peace. Eventually, her physical problems cleared up, and her life became transformed for the better.

When we feel we have been wronged, however, just knowing the importance of forgiveness does not make the situation easier. Circumstances cannot be changed, but it is possible to change the patterns of our thoughts about the situation.

Pause to examine your thought patterns from time to time. As Henry H. Buckley said: "Keep your thoughts right—for as you think, so you are. Thoughts are things; therefore, think only the things that will make the world better and you unashamed." For some, it may be necessary to learn how to forgive. Presbyterian minister Theodore Cuyler Speers emphasized this idea when he said, "How to forgive is something we have to learn, not as a duty or an obligation, but as an experience akin to the experience of love; it must come into being spontaneously."

Forgiving uplifts the forgiver

—SIR JOHN TEMPLETON

Most of us understand giving, but some of us may still be confused about the meaning of forgiveness. Some people may go through life in a groveling mode, mistakenly believing they have to receive forgiveness from others. Forgiveness offers more than a reprieve granted to us by another person.

Forgiveness is about loving oneself enough to be honest, open-minded, and willing to move forward in life. It is about learning to be grateful, not only for our own mistakes but for all our experiences, even if they are painful. Forgiveness can be about knowing that, although we experience pain, we don't have to suffer. The faith expressed through giving thanks for our challenges can help dissolve the appearance of negative circumstances as we look for the good in every situation. We learn not to resist the changes that truly come to bless us.

It may not be easy to let go of old ideas, even though we recognize that they may be self-defeating. Sometimes we struggle to hold on to the familiar. Growth, however, is not intended to be a struggle but rather a surrender to the higher good. When you forgive yourself, you stop doing the hurtful thing. You make a deep and conscious commitment to live in accordance with universal law. Your mind changes from a material to a spiritual base. When an error is discovered and there is a willingness to correct it, under the law of forgiveness, we can erase the mistake as easily as a child erases false figures in an arithmetic exercise. The moment we correct our error, we align ourselves in harmony with the truth of being, and the law wipes out our transgressions. Self-forgiving is uplifting, but total forgiving is even more uplifting.

Through giving and forgiving, the old ego-structures that have been built up over a lifetime start to crumble. When that wall comes down, we are free to build healthy structures in our minds. And when the mind is strong and healthy, then our world reflects strength and health. As we give thanks and forgive, we are uplifted.

To err is human, to forgive is divine
—ALEXANDER POPE

Imagine a majestic mountain, its granite peaks towering thousands of feet into the sky. Nothing would seem to be more invincible than this giant fortress of rock. Yet, in time, it is possible that certain forces can reduce this mountain to tiny pebbles. Ironically, the forces that wield such power are among the softest, most yielding elements of nature—water and air. The blowing of winds and the gentle flowing streams can ultimately conquer the mightiest of mountains. The power of the gentle approach can be illustrated by a statement from the *Tao Te Ching*, the sacred writings of the Chinese religion of Taoism: "What is of all things most yielding can overcome that which is the most hard." And is not the spiritual power of forgiveness a loving, gentle approach that can soften the hardest of situations?

When forgiveness is genuine and complete, it goes to the depths of the situation. Hatreds, resentments, even mild dislikes can be dissolved by the power of forgiveness.

Do you currently blame someone for a wrong you may believe has been done to you? Do you hold any resentments toward someone for your present situation? Is there a part of you that says, "If only so-and-so had not done such-and-such to me, I would be happier and more successful"? In one way or another, we often try to find a scapegoat for a lack we feel in our lives. Have you heard yourself say, "I will never forget the way she or he treated me." And you didn't forget! It may be difficult to keep such thoughts and feelings from recurring. But it can be done. Assistance is at hand when you truly begin to understand and know that God's law of love and justice adjusts all matters for those who trust it.

When Leonardo da Vinci was painting the *Last Supper* on the walls of Santa Maria delle Grazie, a church in Milan, the story goes that da Vinci got into an argument with a man while he was working on the face of Jesus. The artist became so upset that a violent confrontation erupted, during which da Vinci threatened bodily harm to the man and chased him away. When da Vinci returned to work on the fresco, he was so filled with hatred and resentment that the flow of inspiration dried up. Try as he might, da Vinci couldn't paint the face of Jesus. Repeatedly, he attempted to apply subtle brushstrokes to the wet plaster, only to be unhappy with the results. Finally, on realizing that his anger was depriving him of the peace of mind necessary to be creative, the great artist laid aside his brushes and went in search of the man with whom he had quarreled to apologize and ask for forgiveness. After much persuasion, da Vinci convinced the man of his pure intent, and the situation was resolved. With a peace-filled and loving heart, da Vinci returned to his work, and the magnificent face of the Savior that flowed from his brushes became a mystical moment captured by the great artist. It is said that even now, in spite of the pathetic condition of the walls of the ruined church, the *Last Supper* remains one of the great art treasures of the world.

We need to be aware of the price we pay for holding grudges and resentments. We need to understand that we are the ones who suffer from this lack of forgiveness. It takes a lot of energy, which could be much better spent, to hold onto a grudge. We may feel temporarily justified in our attitude, but in the long run what does it really matter? A tremendous cost in sickness of mind and body affects those who cling to feelings of unforgiveness.

Complete and total forgiveness can be a sure way to health and happiness and to new energy and enthusiasm. It is a sign that we are taking responsibility for our lives. Once we realize that we're in the driver's seat, we can move swiftly and surely to accept our greater good.

To be wronged is nothing unless you continue to remember it
—CONFUCIUS

Codependency and *dysfunction* are two important words in today's psychological vocabulary. Support groups are everywhere for every problem—Sexaholics Anonymous, Workaholics Anonymous, Neurotics Anonymous, Victims Anonymous, Overeaters Anonymous, and Alcoholics Anonymous, to name just a few. It isn't unusual for one person to be in several recovery programs at the same time.

Individually, most of these groups are indeed worthwhile. At the same time, it is vital to address the commonsense approach expressed by Confucius, "To be wronged is nothing unless you continue to remember it." This advice may be more important than the recovery craze. If we can let our past remain in the past, we are not compelled to endlessly reenact it.

On occasion, it can be a healing experience to recall and face traumatic experiences. This type of remembering can enable us to see past events for what they were and release them, instead of dreading some future time when we may be faced with hurting or embarrassing revelations.

Forgiveness can be a powerful healing agent. Forgiveness is a process of giving up the false for the true, erasing error from mind and body and life. Forgive yourself. Forgive others. Forgive everything. Forgiveness sometimes involves a flight of imagination—being able to understand the influences that may have shaped your oppressor's behavior. If we seek to understand, to the best of our ability, where another person may be coming from, observe what situations may be prevalent in his life, and put forth the effort to "walk a mile in his shoes," we may be less quick to take offense at what may be directed toward us. Once you can comprehend the dynamics behind the abuse, you may be more ready to forgive. An old African proverb says, "He who forgives ends the quarrel." Are you willing to be the instigator of such a positive action?

Understand that forgiving does not mean excusing. But dwelling on past slights or offenses contracts us rather than expands us. If you want to become a fully functional person, whole and free in every way, you must release the pain from the past, reframe the experience, and renew your allegiance to life. This thought, feeling, and action can take you back to your true purpose of living, and you can walk through the gateway to freedom from past miseries. Are you prepared and willing to get on with the purpose of your life, to "let go and let God" handle everything else? Can you learn to love every person on earth without exception?

Holding onto grievances is a decision to suffer
—GERALD JAMPOLSKY

For many years, an old farmer plowed around a rock in one of his fields. As a result, he grew morbid over it, for he had broken a cultivator and two plows, as well as lost a lot of valuable land in the rock's vicinity. One day, he made up his mind that he would dig it out and be done with it. When he put his crowbar under the rock, he found it was less than a foot thick and that he could loosen it with a trifling effort and carry it away in his wagon. He smiled to think how all through the years the rock had haunted him. As he mulled over the experience with the rock, he began to see other areas in his life where he was holding onto old thoughts and feelings that were like rocks in the middle of the field of his mind. One by one, he began to take these past experiences, reflect on them, and follow through with whatever appropriate action was necessary to remove them—in other words, to "loosen them and let them go." With each releasing and forgiving of an old grievance, he felt his spirit lighten, his mind become more clear, and his heart fill with joy and delight in each new day.

Some of us may choose to hold onto old and painful thoughts as though they were treasures. We may sometimes seem to cherish memories of imagined or real slights and forget the good that people have done for us, the good health with which we may be blessed, and the many successes we have enjoyed along the way.

Although we may have experienced some difficult times and painful situations, it is unnecessary to remain locked in negative thoughts, nor is it beneficial to our peace of mind to react in a negative way to daily events. The way in which we choose to interpret what happens to us has a great deal to do with how the important moments in our lives may be stored in our memory through the unfolding years. We alone have control over our thoughts, although many of us may have forgotten how to exercise that control.

Try to hold this simple truth in mind: yesterday is gone. No matter what happened in the past, it's over. We cannot go back. Tomorrow may never come, so the present is the moment we have. Let us strive to make the best, most positive use of every precious moment, each special day. The ill feelings and negative thoughts we may have had in the past were of no value to us then and have not increased in worth since. The choice is ours; we can hold onto negative thoughts, or we can put some "altitude in our attitude." The Dalai Lama spoke of the power of forgiveness in his book *Freedom in Exile: The Autobiography of the Dalai Lama* with these words: "Learning to forgive is much more useful than merely picking up a stone and throwing it at the object of one's anger, the more so when the provocation is extreme. For it is under the greatest adversity that there exists the greatest potential for doing good, both for oneself and others."

A mind that is occupied by positive thoughts blossoms like a beautiful garden, free of the weeds of negativity. Whether your mind dwells on a beautiful garden or a weed patch is up to you. You can choose to overlook and forgive the shortcomings of others, or you can keep a mental ledger listing all the unkind things people may have said or done to you.

After all, you are the one who suffers most by holding onto grievances. If you can't overlook and forgive the faults of others, how can you forgive your own? Any hardship—actual or imagined—can be undone, transformed, and healed to reveal a shining star of awareness where once there may have loomed a dark night of despair. One of the most powerful ways to accomplish this transformation into light is through the process of forgiveness. There is a bumper sticker that proclaims, "Misery is optional." And so it is. It doesn't matter what you have chosen in the past; your present choices are the ones that matter. "Hatred stirs up trouble; love overlooks the wrongs that others do" (Prov. 10:12, CEV).

Forgiveness benefits both the giver and the receiver
—SIR JOHN TEMPLETON

Who has not at one time or another held a grudge? Perhaps we may have felt hurt by something someone said. It is possible to mentally erase a negative experience like erasing a blackboard and drawing a new life for yourself. How? Through the power of forgiveness.

In any athletic race, the athletes are careful to carry no more weight than absolutely necessary. In the race of life, it is equally important for us not to weigh ourselves down by clinging to the mistakes we may have made in the past, or by grudges or negative thoughts. We can release these burdens and let them go. As an African proverb states, "He who forgives ends the quarrel."

Let's look for a moment at the meaning of forgiveness and some of its benefits. *Forgiveness* means "for giving." *For* "in favor of "; *giving* "to give." That is, in favor of giving. Forgiveness is a process of giving up that which is false for that which is true. It can be giving positive energies for something that may have been less than positive. For example, giving love in response to less than loving actions. When we forgive, we release unproductive thoughts and attitudes from our mind so we can partake more fully of the ever-renewing life and vitality God has prepared for us.

After you have forgiven the transgression and released any judgment of the situation or the person, then forget it. The value of forgetting is, again, in the word—to be in favor of getting, of receiving. Replacing a negative memory with a positive one can bring about healing. Let the old image fade. Take whatever steps you may be able to take to heal the situation.

Forgiveness plays such a vital role in our lives. When true forgiveness takes place, no scars are left, no hurts, no thoughts of revenge, only healing. Forgiveness is a healing power. And forgiveness can bring out the greatness in you.

CHAPTER 10

Embracing Humility

Humility leads to prayer as well as progress
and brings you in tune with the Infinite
—SIR JOHN TEMPLETON

UMILITY IS THE KEY to progress. Without it we may become too self-satisfied with past glories to launch boldly into the challenges ahead. Without humility we may not be wide-eyed and open-minded enough to discover new areas for research. If we are not as humble as children, we may be unable to admit mistakes, to seek advice, to try again. I use the word *humility* here to mean understanding that God infinitely exceeds anything anyone has ever said of him, and that he is infinitely beyond human comprehension and understanding. As we realize this and become more humble, we reduce the stumbling blocks placed in our paths by our own egos.

Think, for a moment, about an analogy. When a man is born into the world, he is like a piece of charcoal. It is soft and amorphous, so when rays of sunlight fall upon it, it reflects nothing. Then, in the crucible it is subjected to such intense pressure and heat that the charcoal is transformed into a diamond. The natural diamond is appraised by the master craftsman; its inner design is determined, and the stone is then cut with many facets to become a precious and radiant jewel. Now when the sun's rays fall upon it, the colors of the rainbow are reflected, creating a magnificent symphony of beauty and radiance. So it is with a man between the time he is born into the material world, where he is "cut and chipped" by life's experiences and the choices he makes, and then born again into heaven where the humility his soul has achieved begins to reflect the divine light of God. Maybe this was God's purpose for creating the crucible called earth.

One of the major lessons to learn while on earth is that building our heaven is up to us. Emanuel Swedenborg wrote that we will not be in heaven until heaven is in us. So how may we begin to build that heaven within? True humility can lead us into a prayerful attitude, and prayer can bring us in tune with the Infinite. There is a real mystical power in prayer, and it works. Through your prayer times and your attunement with God, you are increasing your own spiritual light. You are building a better expression of life in every way and you are attracting exactly what you are building—more light. There is a larger power you are touching. There is a larger life you are building. Prayer can make difficult tasks easier, can consecrate every effort to a more noble use, and produce successful results. The prayer life is a life of humility and gratitude and is made sacred by the intimacy of the soul with its Creator.

The person who relies on wisdom or beauty or skill or money tends to shut God out. But the person who is humble and grateful for these God-given blessings opens the door to a kind of heaven on earth here and now. It is important to free ourselves of self-will and surrender to God's will. Can you see how letting go of ego-centeredness can help you become a clear channel for God's love and wisdom to flow through, just as sunlight pours through an open window?

In humility we have an opportunity to learn from one another, for it enables us to open to each other and see things from the other person's point of view. We may also share our views with the other person freely. It is by humility that we avoid the sins of pride and intolerance and avoid religious strife. Muhammad, the Prophet of Islam, stated, "Whoever has in his heart even so much as a rice grain of pride cannot enter into paradise." Humility opens the door to the realms of the spirit, and to research and progress in religion. Humility is the gateway to knowledge.

Humility opens the door to progress
—SIR JOHN TEMPLETON

Humility is a gateway to greater understanding. Just as thanksgiving opens the door to spiritual growth, humility opens the door to greater knowledge and open-mindedness. It is difficult for a person to learn anything more if he is certain he knows everything already. When we begin to comprehend how little we know, then we begin to seek and to learn. Unless we recognize our ignorance, why should we broaden our horizon and investigate the world?

To be successful, each of us must build our own soul in the image of the Creator. This means it is important to appreciate, honor, and respect other people. Endeavoring to express our faith in all situations, whether at home, at work, or with friends, can often lead to greater growth. Even with our vast technologies, how little we know and how eager we need to be to learn!

Egotism is a stumbling block that inhibits future progress. The broad-minded person expands beyond the limiting self and sees truth in a variety of incarnations: in theosophy, in science, in philosophy. And to those in whom love dwells, the whole world is but one family in various manifestations. The humble person is ready and willing to admit and welcome these various manifestations.

What are the practical applications of a sense of humility and an appreciation of God's infinite powers? There are many, including love of God, love of your work, love of others, self-appreciation, patience, steadfastness, and the ability to see more clearly. This last ability is crucial because things are not always as they seem. Sometimes phenomena that may appear "real" to us are actually hoaxes perpetrated by those taking advantage of our lack of knowledge and limited senses.

For example, until about five hundred years ago it was assumed that lying in bed was a relatively motionless experience. However, Copernicus's discovery that the Earth and the planets move around the Sun implied that the Earth rotates, and therefore a person sleeping in bed moves eastward at 1,000 miles an hour! The sleeper also flies 1,080 miles a minute in another direction because of the Earth's revolution around the Sun. In humility we should be able to admit that many things may be unknown to us presently. By becoming humble, we can learn more and make greater progress.

Bishop Gerald Kennedy commented:

> The greater a man is, the more humble he is as he remembers the faith, the dream, the hope, that made his life possible. If any man is tempted to pride because of his accomplishments, let him remember what he has received from all those people of the past. It was their faith that set the direction of his life, and the best he can strive for is to become the fulfillment of their father.

And Proverbs 11:2 (CEV) states, "Too much pride can put you to shame. It's wiser to be humble." Humility, however, can open the door to progress and make you a benefactor.

Each passing day, scientists discover increasing wonders of the universe. Many of them stand in awe of the complexity, the diversity, and the exquisite organization of the universe. Oftentimes, they experience a sense of humility as well.

Humility, like darkness, reveals the heavenly light
—HENRY DAVID THOREAU

If you walk outside on a clear, dark night and look up into the sky, you can see thousands of stars. Did you ever consider that if it were not for the darkness of space, the starlight would never be revealed to us on Earth?

We tend to think of anything dark or black as bad and perhaps not as valuable as white or light. Or, we may perceive black as nothing at all, since it has no color. Scientifically, it is the absence of light and could be called an illusion or invisible. Going to a movie can remind you of how important it is for the theater to be dark, for it is the darkness that allows the movie to be seen most clearly.

Perhaps the heavenly light within each one of us—our divine purpose or potential—also has a dark background against which it becomes illumined. This is not a destructive or negative darkness, but rather a necessary foundation of strength. Could this darkness perhaps be what is called *humility*—our ability to admit that we may not know everything or be all things to all people?

Humility is not self-deprecation. To believe that you have no worth, or were created somehow flawed or incompetent, can be foolish. Humility represents wisdom. It is knowing you were created with special talents and abilities to share with the world; but it can also be an understanding that you are one of many souls created by God, and each has an important role to play in life. Humility is knowing you are smart, but not all-knowing. It is accepting that you have personal power, but are not omnipotent. If we don't believe we're alive with inner potential, we may not be progressive in our lives. But if we are aware of the tremendous potential within and the value of our self-worth, we can understand that the true reality abides in God. When we reach this stage of maturity and moral development, we can become consistently more productive and useful. We may also become more outgoing. We can feel a surge of joy when others experience good fortune. The desire to accomplish something of lasting benefit can reside at the forefront of our thoughts and bring us closer to success.

The humble attitude is a flexible attitude. Just as the tree and the building must sway with the wind, our agility in dealing with whatever life throws our way can become our strength. Inherent in humility resides an open and receptive mind. We don't know all the answers to life, and sometimes we don't even know the right questions to ask. Humility can be a strength that serves us well; it leaves us more open to learn from others and helps us refrain from seeing issues and people only in black and white.

The opposite of humility is arrogance—the belief that we are wiser or better than others. Arrogance promotes separation rather than community. It looms like a brick wall between us and those from whom we could learn. An example could be Virginia Smith, a young woman who was about to graduate from college with honors. She held a high opinion of herself and lofty visions of greatness. As Virginia descended from the podium in her cap and gown, she carried her diploma . . . and an air of intellectual smugness. From out of the crowd of onlookers, an old woman stepped to Virginia's side. We can call her Wisdom of the World. She spoke casually to the young graduate, "Well, who have we here?"

"You evidently don't know me," said the young woman in an arrogant tone. "I am Virginia Cordelia Smith, AB."

"Well, my young friend," said Wisdom of the World with a chuckle, "come with me and I will teach you the rest of your alphabet!"

This young woman undoubtedly contained a bright light to shine on the world. She had great potential for doing good, but she had yet to understand how much of life would be a mystery to her.

Great heroes are humble
—ST. FRANCIS

Most great people are humble. Those among the most respected who have ever lived acknowledge that their greatness came, not from themselves, but from a higher power working through them. The true meaning of humility is knowing that the personal self is a vehicle for a higher power. Jesus of Nazareth said, "I do not speak on my own authority, but the Father who dwells in me does his works" (John 14:10). Other great spiritual leaders have recognized this; true genius has a deep sense of personal humility. First Imam of the Shia branch of Islam, fourth caliph, said, "Hide the good you do, and make known the good done to you"; and Ben Sira, the great Hebrew scholar, commented, "The greater you are, the more you must practice humility."

Sir Isaac Newton, one of the world's greatest scientific explorers, made the following statement near the end of his life: "I seem to have been only like a boy, playing on the seashore . . . while the great ocean of truth lay all undiscovered before me." Another great scientist, Albert Einstein, was also known for his childlike simplicity. With all his achievements in the world, he maintained a strong sense of humility. Dr. Walter Russell, a genius in many fields, echoed Jesus's teaching when he said: "Until one learns to lose oneself, he cannot find himself. The personal ego must be dissolved and replaced by the universal ego."

What is this universal ego and what's the difference between that and personal ego? To begin with, personal ego is what most of us identify as our "self." It's who we believe ourselves to be. It contains the modes of expression we give to our current opinions of ourselves. The personal ego identifies with our appearance, our achievements, and our possessions. It is this self that can be inclined to compete with others and may feel hurt or angry if it doesn't get what it wants. The human ego-self wants to feel important, to be right, to be in control. The human ego also causes people to try to solve problems by human effort alone without seeking God's wisdom. Sound familiar?

Some people would say, "You've just described human nature." Perhaps this may be a description of the most familiar part of human nature. Yet there is another part, a "higher self," that exists in each of us as a spark of the Divine. Unfortunately, most of the time this higher self remains hidden by the personal ego just described. We often can't see this universal or "higher" self because we are blinded by our identification with the personal. It may be likened to trying to see the stars during the day. They are present in the universe but obscured by the light of the sun. Only when the sun goes down do we see these heavenly lights.

The true, universal self within us is an individualized center of God consciousness. As we become more willing to release the personal ego, we open the door to greater communication with God. The one who relies on his own wisdom, beauty, skill, or money seldom relies on God. But the one who is humble and grateful for all such God-given blessings opens the door to heaven on earth here and now. Although God's principles are spirit and cannot be seen, they are more real than tangible things. Who today does not have faith in cosmic rays and radio waves, even though they are invisible? For each of us to grow in spirituality, it is important to free ourselves of self-will and seek God's will. When we avoid ego-centeredness, we open the way to becoming clear channels for God's love and wisdom to flow through us.

To express greatness in our lives, we should learn to be humble. In becoming humble, we can discover that humility rewards itself. To acknowledge humbly that we know only a little of God's truth does not make us agnostic. If a medical doctor can admit with an open mind that he does not understand all diseases, symptoms, and cures, surely we can be humble by admitting that we each have more to learn about God.

CHAPTER 11

Overcoming Fear

Thoughts of doubt and fear are pathways to failure
—BRIAN ADAMS

HE TWIN MONSTERS of doubt and fear frequently play a leading role when we don't achieve a goal. When allowed to fester in our minds, these two negative forces can multiply and overrun a person's ability to enjoy a situation or to see positive strategies that can help overcome temporary difficulties.

For example, a student who is mentally or physically fatigued, poorly nourished, or emotionally upset may give doubt and fear fertile ground in which to take root. A student who seriously doubts his ability to perform on a test may, in fact, perform poorly. Tension created by a growing sense of insecurity can mentally erase the facts a person needs to remember.

This holds true in the animal kingdom as well. A horse about to take a hurdle sometimes balks short of the jump if it senses doubt or fear in its rider. The situation that the rider fears most—failure to complete the jump—can be the end result. Doubt and fear are like thieves who rob the precious moment of its rightful dominion and joy. They bring about manifestations of disease, lack, and inharmonious relationships.

In 1914, a doctor advised Selig Grossinger to take a vacation from the

141

fast pace on the Lower East Side of New York City. After three weeks in the mountains, Grossinger returned to the city rested, strengthened, restored to clear thinking, and determined to buy a small farm in the Catskill Mountains for his family. The rock-strewn farm that the Grossingers purchased had no electricity or indoor plumbing and did not provide an income. So they decided to take in boarders who sought good food, fresh air, and quiet surroundings. The Grossingers were such good hosts that, in spite of the farm's primitiveness, they soon had more guests than they could handle. Within five years, the family was able to buy a larger, more modern place nearby, which became the world-famous resort hotel Grossinger's. The family was so busy following the adventure of a dream, they allowed no possibility for doubt or fear to mar their vision.

Thoughts are pathways and positive thoughts are upward pathways. When clogged by doubt and fear, our thoughts are often of failure and defeat. When the pathways are well chosen and fortified with positive thoughts and expectations, the monsters are usually defeated. In a positive mind, doubt and fear are not allowed to be present to sabotage ultimate success.

The light of understanding dissolves the phantom of fear
—ELLIE HAROLD

There once was a woman who became terribly upset when she returned home from a trip to find that her beloved cat was missing. She spent the day searching the neighborhood, calling her cat by name, and asking the neighbors if they had seen her beloved pet. Between heaving sobs, all she could repeatedly say was, "I know she's out there starving somewhere. Or else dogs have killed her. She can't protect herself; she's a house cat. She has no front claws." In her mind, the woman visualized a variety of horrible things that could have happened to her cat. Twilight finally drew her away from the search, and the grieving woman went into her house and began to unpack from the trip. As she walked to a closet to hang up a dress, deep from within the closet came the cry of her hiding cat. The poor woman nearly fainted with relief.

By allowing her thoughts to run wild and unchecked, the woman created a worst-case scenario. When we let fear overwhelm us, the worst possibilities often flash before our minds. Perhaps it's an instant replay of some disaster from the evening news, personalized to involve our children, or our parents, or a nightmare from our childhood. Thoughts stained by fear cannot perceive reality accurately. It's like trying to study objects through a clouded lens. Little may be seen clearly for what it is. Vision is reduced to diffused and shadowy images. Sometimes we may feel paralyzed by our fear. Other times we may react defensively because doom seems so imminent. Like the woman who thought her cat had been destroyed by dogs, only to find it safely hiding in her closet, we often put ourselves and others through a lot of anguish before we discover that the facts do not support our worst fears.

Fear is also FEAR (*F*alse *E*vidence *A*ppearing *R*eal)—a famous acronym that sheds the light of understanding on those phantoms of fear. There are at least two false premises regarding fear. First is the belief that things are as·they appear to be. Increasingly, scientists are discovering evidence to the contrary. For example, what seems to be solid matter is, in fact, composed of patterns of subatomic units of energy. Second, fearful individuals assume that they lack the resources to handle a tragic situation. The truth is, courage belongs not only to heroes and heroines but can also be developed within you as you meet life's challenges. As Eleanor Roosevelt wrote, "You gain strength, courage, and confidence by every experience in which you really stop to look fear in the face."

The shadow of ignorance is fear
—J. JELINEK

Fear is one of the greatest challenges we face today, as individuals and as a society. Fear holds us back from the fullest expression of ourselves; it prevents us from loving ourselves and others. Unreasoning, irrational fear can lock us in an invisible prison. Yet fear may also have uses that can serve us. Some fear may be necessary for self-preservation. An instinctive awareness of danger can alert us to potential harm and help us mobilize the resources we need to keep ourselves from injury.

Many times we fear things that cannot hurt us. We may turn a natural anxiety we feel in an uncomfortable emotional situation into a state of fear and panic. When this happens, we become unable to live fully. We may cower in the face of possible humiliation and forgo making a creative contribution. Fear of rejection may prevent us from working for the things we really need. We may refuse to commit ourselves because of the risk of failure. It is important to distinguish between fears that can assist us and those that may hurt or hinder us.

Franklin Delano Roosevelt wrote, in his message to Congress on January 6, 1941, these immortal words:

> We look forward to a world founded upon four essential human freedoms. The first is freedom of speech and expression—everywhere in the world. The second is the freedom of every person to worship God in his own way—everywhere in the world. The third is freedom from want . . . everywhere in the world. The fourth is freedom from fear . . . anywhere in the world.

It is better to light a single candle than to curse the darkness
—MOTTO OF THE CHRISTOPHERS

Darkness is one of the first things most people fear. Darkness holds the unknown and the undefinable. When we wake in the middle of the night from a nightmare, we are in the darkness. We may stay there, paralyzed by fear, and do nothing but curse our situation. Or, we may reach for a nearby lamp and switch it on, thus freeing ourselves from the terror. Problems affect us much as the darkness does. When we are faced with tough situations, we may become too scared to make a move and curse our situation, rather than make the effort to do something about it.

Is there anything to be gained by cursing the darkness? Or the situation? Not really. Nothing has changed. The darkness or the fear remains, totally unaffected by our outburst. But when our perception of the darkness changes, or we acknowledge that a problem exists, then we can begin to make some headway. We have been told that a problem cannot be solved at the level it began. It is necessary to move to a higher level of consciousness. Isn't this like turning on the light? We move the focus of our thoughts from the difficulties of the situation and begin to look for a solution. We become *pro*active instead of *re*active!

Any scientist can tell you that formulating the proper definition of any problem is the biggest single step toward solving it. Understanding is a strong foundation of progress, and a little old-fashioned introspection is good for what ails you! A lot of people are living in the abject depressive atmosphere of the darkness of fear. In the early stages of the evolution of humanity, fear was positive and productive. It was needed to guide the instinctive intelligence of the lower forms of nature into the correct use of themselves and their environment so they could preserve themselves as long as possible. For the people of that time, fear played a positive role.

In the present day, however, fear—which is in our lower physical consciousness and is a part of our instinctive nature—is the basis for many of the mistakes we make. One who is riddled by fear finds it difficult to concentrate his mind in order to think straight. In a state of fear, which is also the result of the emotional nature trying to rid itself of some threat, we can become almost helpless—until we decide to turn on the light and dispel the darkness!

The divine nature of our soul is the very opposite of anxiety or fear of anything. It is creative, it is positive, and it shows us certain kinds of knowledge and wisdom and power or inspiration without which we may sink back into the depths of darkness and fear.

There can be times when we may need others' help. Certainly, if we curse the darkness, others will realize that we are faced with a problem. Yet unless they see us trying to solve the problem, they may be unaware that we could use their support and assistance.

Until we make an active effort to solve our problems, they may not go away. Even the smallest effort can bring us closer to solving the problem and overcoming a difficult situation. In attempting one possible solution, we may realize different and better solutions.

Thus, cursing the darkness is to no avail. It does nothing but magnify the problem. It pushes away from us others who may have the power to help. Only by putting forth the effort to do something about a problem can we expect to solve it. To curse the darkness may be a first reaction, but hopefully it will not be our last.

CHAPTER 12

Demonstrating Courage

*You cannot discover new oceans until you have the courage
to lose sight of the shore*

—ANONYMOUS

HE EAGLES that live in the canyons of the state of
Colorado in the United States use a special kind of
stick with which to build their nests. A female eagle
can sometimes fly two hundred miles in a single day
in order to find a branch from an ironwood tree.
Not only are the ironwood sticks as strong as their name suggests, but
they also have thorns that allow them to lock together so the nest can
sit securely on a ledge high up in the canyon. After building the nest,
the eagle pads it with layer upon layer of leaves, feathers, and grass
to protect future offspring from the sharp thorns of the ironwood.

In her preparations, the female eagle goes to great lengths to promote the survival of the birds she will hatch. This interest in their
survival extends well beyond their birth, although the expression of
that interest changes. As the young eagles grow, they begin to fight for
space in the nest. The chicks' demands for food eventually become so
onerous the mother eagle is unable to fulfill their needs. She instinctively knows that in order to survive, her brood is going to have to
leave the nest.

To encourage the young eagles to fend for themselves, the mother
pulls the padding out of the nest so the thorns of the ironwood

147

branches prick the young birds. As their living conditions become more painful, they are forced to climb up on the edge of the nest. The mother eagle then coaxes the young eagles off the edge. As they begin to plummet to the bottom of the canyon, they wildly flap their wings to break their fall, and end up doing what is the most natural thing in the world for an eagle—they fly!

As human beings, we may often find ourselves in a similar situation. When our lives can no longer provide us with the growth we desire and change must take place, we may need to leave safety and familiarity behind and journey into unknown territory. Just as the baby eagles are reluctant to leave the nest, we may also resist change.

Many times unpleasant conditions in our lives signal us that we are ready to move on and experience new areas of our potential. While our fear of the unknown might temporarily increase our tolerance of an uncomfortable situation, life's circumstances may likely get thorny enough that, like the growing eagles, we'll be coaxed into moving on. We can trust life and move ahead into new experiences with confidence because, in a wonderful way, we live in a friendly universe—a universe designed to support us and our activities. Dr. Irving Oyle recognized this when he commented, "The universe is not opposed to our best interest."

Have you ever said to yourself, "I've wanted to do something like this, but never quite had the courage?" Take a look at the urge within your being that may be prompting you to step forward. When the time comes to venture out and accept new challenges, remember that everyone has an innate ability not only to survive but to prosper. We are designed, by God, with the possibility to achieve high levels of success and to enjoy fulfillment and satisfaction in life. This means we do not have to settle for less than we're capable of, unless that is our choice.

The following quote taken from the *Association for Humanistic Psychology Newsletter* was written by an eighty-five-year-old woman. Take a moment and reflect on the wisdom shared through her observations:

If I had my life to live over, I'd dare to make more mistakes next time. I'd relax. I'd limber up. I would be sillier than I've been this trip. I would take fewer things seriously. I would take more chances. I would take more trips. I would climb more mountains and swim more rivers. I would eat more ice cream and less beans. I would perhaps have more actual troubles, but I'd have fewer imaginary ones! . . .

I've been one of those persons who never goes anywhere without a thermometer, a hot water bottle, a raincoat, and a parachute! If I had to do it again, I would travel lighter than I have. . . .

If I had my life to live over, I would start barefoot earlier in the spring and stay that way later in the fall. I would go to more dances. I would ride more merry-go-rounds. I would pick more daisies.

So often, we have within our grasp a whole new way of life and fail to explore it. Why? Could one reason be that we may not be secure enough in who and what we are to release the pioneering spirit? An interesting thing is that we do have our life to live over. Every day life comes for us to live a new experience. Over and over, around the calendar, twenty-four new hours present themselves to us. Perhaps we could ask ourselves, regardless of our age, "Have I really lived all my years, or has each year been one day lived over and over again?"

Within each of us are resources that can be realized only when we climb to the edge of the nest, slip off into the air—and fly!

If nothing is ventured, nothing is gained
—SIR JOHN HEYWOOD

The spirit of adventure is a deeply human trait and one that has helped us develop over thousands of years of recorded history. It is the potential you have within you to leave the world a better place than you found it. Not that you have to; few are likely to notice if you do nothing with your life. You can be one of those who plays it safe, who ventures nothing. However, when you choose to leave what seems safe and familiar and voyage into uncharted waters of intellect and creativity, you become one who can make a difference.

The courage to venture forth in life paves the way for many a success. Alex Haley was raised from infancy by his grandmother because his mother had passed away and his father, a student in another state, was unable to care for him. As an adult, Haley served twenty years in the Coast Guard, then left to pursue a career as a freelance writer in New York. The years after Haley left the Coast Guard were not easy, personally or financially. He endured overwhelming poverty. Yet Haley had a burning desire to become a successful and self-supporting writer. He committed himself to writing the saga of his family's genealogy. Despite the hardship and lack of material resources, Haley spent twelve years writing *Roots*. Finally, seventeen years after he left the Coast Guard, *Roots* was published. The book was translated into thirty-seven languages and became the basis for two incredibly successful television miniseries.

In the 1992 Summer Olympics, American sprinter Gail Devers, the clear leader in the hundred-meter hurdles, tripped over the last barrier. She agonizingly pulled herself to her knees and crawled the last five meters, finishing fifth—but finishing.

We are like travelers continuing on a journey begun so long ago by our ancestors. To the brave of heart and the inquisitive of mind, the journey can offer an infinite variety.

Today's frontiers may no longer be the uncharted earthly lands that challenged our ancestors; yet the territories of the human mind and heart and soul can be even more awesome in their mystery. The exploration of the power of love may be one of the next great challenges.

Those who seldom make mistakes seldom make discoveries
—SIR JOHN TEMPLETON

In the Gospel of Matthew 25:14–30, Jesus tells the story of a man who left money with three servants before setting out on a journey. To one servant he gave five talents (approximately $5,000 today); to another he gave two talents; and to the third servant, he gave only one talent. Upon returning from his journey, he called in each of the three for an accounting of how they had used their portion of the money. The servant who received five talents had doubled that amount through investments, as had the man who had been given two talents. But the servant who had been given one talent, afraid of making a poor investment, had buried his portion in the ground. The two servants who doubled the man's money were rewarded handsomely, while the third servant was penalized.

How many times have you missed out on an opportunity because, like the fearful servant, you were afraid of making a mistake? How many times have you limited yourself because you were afraid you might appear foolish in the eyes of your peers? Self-imposed limitations based on fear can be very difficult to break. The sooner you learn to cope constructively with such fears, the better off you'll be.

Life can be as interesting and stimulating as the discoveries we allow ourselves to make. Staying within known parameters of thought and action may prevent mistakes, but they can also prevent your life from becoming rich and exciting. Exploring frontiers of thought, feeling, and action means you have to put yourself in places you may never have been before. In such places it might be easy to make mistakes. But mistakes are negative only when they inhibit further growth. If you become fearful of testing out a new thought or trying a new approach to a stubborn problem because you're afraid of making a mistake, you may be making the biggest mistake of all. While it may be foolish to plunge into situations with no forethought, it may be equally foolish and futile to be afraid to venture into unknown territory. If you're committed to growth, you can learn that each new situation finds you better able to cope. Your guidance may come either intuitively or through someone else, but it will come.

While mistakes can cause stress and pain, they may also provide you with an excellent resource for learning what not to do the next time. Often you learn more from your mistakes than from formal instruction on the correct way to proceed. Trial and error, which allows you to measure the impact of your misguided actions, is often a great teacher.

Tim Hansel talks about the importance of overcoming circumstances and seeming mistakes in his book *You Gotta Keep Dancing*. He describes how John Bunyan wrote *Pilgrim's Progress* from jail. Florence Nightingale, too ill to move from her bed, reorganized the hospitals of England. Semiparalyzed and under the constant menace of apoplexy, Louis Pasteur was tireless in his attack on disease. These people were dauntless in their efforts to do the most with what they had.

Whether you fully realize it or not, you are like the men in the parable. You have been given many "talents" that can take you as far as you want to go in life. Don't make the mistake of burying them for fear of making a mistake. You don't want to look back over your life one day with regret that you did not pursue an opportunity because you were afraid of making a blunder. Instead, develop your talents wisely, confidently, to the best of your understanding and with self-trust, and you are likely to enjoy a profitable and exciting life!

You fear what you do not understand
—ANONYMOUS

Before the fall of the Berlin Wall and the demise of the Soviet Union, there had been a live simultaneous broadcast between San Francisco and Leningrad. Audiences in both cities were able to see the programs presented. One of the most dramatic moments came near the end of the broadcast when the reality of the situation dawned on both audiences and they began to wave to each other. People who had been on opposite sides of a Cold War for more than a generation suddenly became aware that people on the other side were just like them. This new level of understanding increased the potential for peace in the world.

During World War II, Allied soldiers referred to the Germans as "jerrys." During the Korean and Vietnam conflicts, the Red Chinese, North Koreans, and Vietnamese were called "gooks." These names dehumanized the enemy and created a sense of superiority and loathing (which is a form of fear) in the troops that had to fight them. If the name-callers had understood that the troops on the other side were also fighting for what they believed in, killing them would have become an infinitely more difficult task. An old Moorish proverb brings to mind a great truth: "He who is afraid of a thing gives it power over him."

We all have fears of different sizes and shapes, and it is important to learn what they are and face them directly. Courage overcomes the feeling of helplessness and encourages us to think clearly and take action in any given situation. When we increase our understanding of ourselves and others, fear and hatred are much less likely to take root. When the audience in San Francisco understood that the people in Leningrad also had hopes and aspirations, fear and misunderstanding began to evaporate. When the audience in Leningrad understood that the people in San Francisco looked like them, laughed like them, and had a similar vision of the future, the world took a giant step closer toward realizing peace and brotherhood.

If we choose to remain in fear, then one fear leads to another fear, which can only lead to additional fears. If we live in a fearful state, there is always something to be afraid of. Most fears are educated into us and can be educated out! Fear may be a lack of the awareness of the presence of God as a real force in our lives. With the realization of God's active presence in our lives, many aspects of fear may disappear. Like a snowball dropped into a pail of hot water, fear dissipates, and its energy is transmuted into positive faith.

Take the example of recovering alcoholics. During the course of the disease, these people increasingly come to deny they have a problem with alcohol. Most of them have to hit bottom—some literally have to wake up in the gutter—before they can look up and see that the solution lies in recovery. The anxieties that were the cause of their drinking had to come to light so they could face and defeat them.

But you don't have to hit bottom to look up. You can begin right now to understand that life without fear works out for the best. You can begin now to understand that people on "the other side" of the world are just like you and me—they only want to be free to be happy and useful. You can go forth without fear in the direction of success, harmony, health, prosperity, and usefulness.

You never really lose until you stop trying
—MIKE DITKA, FOOTBALL COACH

Surely there are times when each of us feels that we need more strength and courage to get things done. We feel inadequate to meet some new challenge that appears in our lives, or we feel tired of coping with the old ones.

An Olympic swimmer strains every muscle to push himself over the finish line a fraction of an inch in front of his competitors. A computer technician may work far into the night puzzling out the final solution to a complex problem. An artist may painstakingly make changes in the detail of a flower in a painting. As different as their goals may appear, something within seems to beckon each one to strive for the vision of excellence until the goal is achieved.

John Hockenberry, an American journalist, has been paralyzed from the waist down since he was nineteen, but he has covered news stories all over the world in his wheelchair. Ernest Hemingway rewrote the ending of his book *A Farewell to Arms* no less than thirty-nine times before he was finally satisfied with it! When we begin to feel discouraged, perhaps that is the time to take a deep breath and a long look at where we may be placing our faith. If we are willing to keep our eye on our goals, continue to see ourselves achieving them, and do the necessary work along that line, we can ultimately claim our good.

CHAPTER 13

Sharing Love

It is better to love than to be loved
—ST. FRANCIS

HERE'S A SWEET spirit moving through people—the sweet spirit of love and compassion. The poet Carl Sandberg described this movement as follows: "Not always shall you be what you are now. You are going toward something great. I am on the way with you and, therefore, I love you." The sacred scriptures of the Holy Bible, in Paul's letter to the Corinthians, portrays this sweet spirit in another way. He said, "Faith, hope, love abide, these three; but the greatest of these is love" (1 Cor. 13:13). Love—the great potential that is within you!

Consider the sun for a moment. It is a self-sustaining unit that generates energy from internal thermonuclear reactions. The energy released in these reactions is so great that the sun could shine for millions of years with little change in its size or brightness.

Love is like the sun. It sustains itself. It needs neither thanks nor reward to radiate its powerful and healing energy. Love is always present, although at times it may seem to be hidden from view. Even when the clouds of human emotions hide it, love is present just as the sun is present when clouds hide it from the earth.

As we release the energy of our love, a chain reaction takes place similar to the thermonuclear reactions within the sun that change hydrogen into helium. The energy of love flows within us, changing and enlarging us. Love can open hearts that may have once been closed by bitterness, and love has the power to replace that bitterness with acceptance and joy. Hate no longer erodes our soul, and caring and compassion replace apathy. Changes are evident in our lives as we begin to love ourselves and see ourselves as models of love.

Love's energy is a healing balm. When we allow love to express itself through us as our basic nature, it automatically radiates out to every aspect of our lives. Just as photosynthesis is the process by which the sun and plants together make food, a similar process takes place within us as we allow the energy of love to transform our lives.

Once the spark is kindled within and begins to burn brightly, we can't stop it from flowing from us to others. Some may not come close enough to feel the warmth of our love. Others may bask in the glow of our energy. Because we *are* love, it doesn't matter if we receive thanks or recognition. Like the durability of the sun, love gives and gives with no diminution of its supply. As Iris Murdoch, the Irish writer, stated, "We can only learn to love by loving." Our lives become brighter the more we express love. We can shine like the sun and we can radiate love for everyone—without exception!

Love given is love received
—SIR JOHN TEMPLETON

Oddly, when it comes to love, people search for, run after, and try to earn, get, grasp, and hold onto something that is as naturally theirs as the air they breathe. Many of us think it all depends on having the right person see us in just the right light, so that person will feel the right way about us and love us. That raises the pressure on us to try to be just what that person wants, trying to please, trying to be good enough to deserve her love. Having to look just right, say the right things, do the right things. Nothing makes people more emotionally crippled, dependent, self-pitying, bitter, and cynical than thinking that someone else must give them love.

Each of us instinctively wants to experience love because love is the true nature of every soul. The power, force, and energy of love reside within us as our very life's blood. And it is vital to express that love! The world-renowned opera singer Luciano Pavarotti said:

> You never know what little bundle of encouragements art-
> ists carry around with them, what little pats on the back
> from what hands, what newspaper clipping, what word of
> hope from what teacher. I suppose that the so-called faith
> in ourselves is the foundation of our talent, but I am sure
> these encouragements are the mortar that hold it together.

An ancient story describes how the greatest gift of life was hidden. When the gods were creating the human race, they wondered where to hide this most precious and powerful treasure so it would not be misused or mistreated by the universe: Shall we hide it atop the high-est mountain? Shall we bury it deep within the earth? Shall we entomb it at the bottom of the deepest ocean? Or shall we conceal it in the heart of the thickest, darkest forest? After much pondering, they finally decided to implant the gift within human beings themselves, for surely they would not think to look there. And just to make cer-tain, the gods designed human eyes to look only outward, not inward.

Now the secret is yours. You can look within to find this treasure and experience it in every facet of your life. A sure way to experience love is to give love. There is no one without love to give. You need not search for the right people on which to lavish your love.

Love holds mind and body together. It is an attractive force that draws good to us in proportion to the depth and strength of our real-ization and understanding of love. When we live in love, and make a conscious choice to express and to experience love, we participate in a powerful force that is active in our lives and our world.

Start with whoever is around you—men, women, girls, boys, old people, young people, yourself. Express your love as a natural attitude and demeanor of goodwill, kindliness, support, caring, and benevolence, as well as a willingness to do what you can to be helpful and make things a little better for someone. Giving love consciously—through thoughts, words, and deeds—can help you to become your own force field of love.

A loving person lives in a loving world
—KEN KEYES

Two students, Bill and Mike, moved to new towns with their parents. Bill disliked his new community from the first day. He felt the new school was inferior to the one he had attended in his former hometown. His new classmates seemed boring and unfriendly. "I wish we hadn't moved here," Bill told his parents. "This is a cold, dull place, and I'll never fit in."

Mike was far more fortunate. He discovered that his new school was not only excellent academically but provided many interesting activities and challenges. "I can't believe how many new friends I made today," he told his family at the dinner table after his first day at school. "I feel as though some of the students have been my friends forever."

Before you pity Bill for not moving to a town as warm and friendly as the one Mike moved to, you should know that they both moved to the same town, the same neighborhood, and they attend the same school!

Why did two young people respond to a similar situation so differently? Bill tends to expect the worst in life, whereas Mike is outgoing and friendly. Mike went to the new school with a smile on his face and an open and positive outlook. Mike is a loving person who lives in a loving world.

The loving person can feel hurt, can experience sorrow, can be angry at someone for some reason. These are human emotions. Life, after all, offers its share of disappointments, troubles, worries, and sorrows for each of us. But the loving person refuses to allow negative emotions to dominate her life. The loving person can forgive another who may have hurt her. The loving person goes for a long walk or becomes involved in an activity that takes her mind off the feelings of anger or frustration that may be threatening her peace of mind. The loving person clears the air by talking with the person with whom she may be angry, and then perhaps offers a hug or a handshake in reconciliation. Regardless of the degrees of stress or confusion she must undergo, her world continues to be a loving world.

Try a smile instead of a scowl. Expect the best and not the worst. Do your utmost to be understanding and to care for the people in your life. The "Bills" of this world often find things to complain about throughout their lives. The "Mikes," on the other hand, not only look for the best but help to create that best through their own attitudes and integrity. The loving person, from youth to old age, lives in a loving world and leads a full and happy life, finding the strength to face problems and tragedies because of the loving world he inhabits.

Love conquers all things
—VIRGIL

Many fables and fairy tales depict stories of a mythical monster called a dragon. This large, winged, reptilian creature is often described as guarding a mysterious castle or lair, spewing his fiery breath and attempting to destroy white knights, fair maidens, and complete villages. It always seems to be in a roaring rage. The main character in these fables and stories is often a brave knight in shining armor who makes many complicated attempts to vanquish the dragon. In reading these adventures, have you ever wondered why very few people made an effort to tame the dragon with love, understanding, and compassion?

Whether or not we like to admit it, we, too, have our inner dragons. When intense anger "rears its head" in our lives; when we are overcome by sadness and grief over a major loss; when our world seems to drop from beneath our feet, we face our personal dragons. Few of us travel the road of life without suffering occasional feelings of anger, sadness, and grief. The big question is, What do we do with these "beasts" when they attack us? Sometimes we have to wrestle with a paper tiger, or a dragon, for a while before we realize that it is a fraud.

Being compassionate might mean taking your anger out on a pillow instead of your best friend, or going for a run in the park instead of letting your feelings smolder and fester inside. Being understanding can mean knowing you have a right to *all* your feelings—even the negative ones—and that you're not a bad person for feeling the way you do. Being loving can indicate a willingness to forgive yourself for unacceptable actions and continuing on with your life.

You can be a conscious (and unconscious!) *loving* influence in the lives of others as you simply move throughout your day. You may feel that others do not pay a lot of attention to what you say or do, or you may feel that other people do not necessarily think of you except when they are with you. But the loving things you think, say, and do can have a real effect on others. Someone may be comforted by the memory of your loving words. Friends may face a difficult experience with greater faith and fortitude because they may have seen you stand strong in your faith in a similar situation. A family member, coworker, or fellow student may express greater potential because you lovingly recognized and commented on the possibilities you saw in him.

Love is a powerful, creative force that can dissolve misunderstandings. Mother Teresa said:

Spread love everywhere you go—first of all in your own house. Give love to your children, to your wife or husband, to a next-door neighbor. . . . Let no one ever come to you without leaving better and happier. Be the living expression of God's kindness; kindness in your face, kindness in your eyes, kindness in your smile, kindness in your warm greeting.

So the next time you feel a dragon breathing down your neck, pause and think about the following possibilities:

1. What is the dragon trying to say to me?
2. Observe and acknowledge the presence of your feelings.
3. Take the dragon (anger, fear, grief, or whatever) to a place where it can't hurt you or anyone else, and let it blow off steam.

You may want to talk about your feelings with a trusted friend or a counselor. Sometimes a "listening ear" may be sufficient for you to find a new perspective. These emotional feelings could be delivering a message you need to hear. They could be saying, for example, "I don't want to do this any more." Or "I don't like the way this feels." Once the dragon learns it can trust you to love it, you may not need to fear it again.

There is an old saying that "he who lives with acceptance, friendship, and love will find those very qualities everywhere he looks." Lovingly search and find!

There is no difficulty that enough love will not conquer
—EMMET FOX

On his seventh birthday, Simon Evans adopted Sam, an eighteen-month-old gray cat, from the animal pound. Sam had been very badly treated for most of his life. This became obvious once Simon got him home. Sam acted skittish and frightened, and he spent most of his time hiding behind the dishwasher.

Simon was very wise for his age and persisted with his new friend, being very gentle and loving. Gradually, Simon's unconditional love began to pay dividends. Sam stayed out from behind the dishwasher for longer periods. He was still jumpy and nervous, and he would eat only with Simon guarding his back. But as the weeks progressed, the boy's love turned the little feline into a more trusting and responsive creature.

Constant, unconditional love can communicate itself to even the most badly abused among us. Love is one power that can eventually cut through the obstacles. Students in a class taught by a friendly and warm teacher—one who is understanding and patient—respond far more positively than those in a class taught by a tyrant. The students' grades are better, and laughter, joy, and a willingness to learn suffuse the classroom. The same constancy of love and caring can work in almost every area of human relationships—between a supervisor and a worker, an executive and a manager, a politician and constituents, or wherever there is a relationship.

Loving, kind, nurturing behavior is considered our natural state. We were born with these innate and positive social and moral gifts, but over the years we may have developed many defense mechanisms that block our true selves. Love, of the type offered by Simon to Sam, can be a great healer. Pure and unconditional love is what Teilhard de Chardin had in mind when he wrote: "Someday, after we have mastered the winds, the waves, the tides and gravity, we shall harness for God the energies of love, and then, for a second time in history, man will have discovered fire."

The only way to have a friend is to be a friend
—RALPH WALDO EMERSON

A friend has been described as a gift we give ourselves, another part of ourselves, a mirror reflection. Friendship not only involves us, it begins with us. The attractive force of friendship has its source within our actions. What does a friend do? How does a friend act? What does a friend require of another friend? The answers to all these questions revolve around the word *love*. A friend loves!

Reaching out to another with love means reaching within to find the love we want reflected back to us. When we love ourselves, when we are a friend to ourselves, we are in a position to attract a friend to us. As our own best friend, we have that gift to give to another.

What friends have in common is each other's best interest. Friends seek to coexist, complement, and grow toward the greater good with each other. One example of such a friendship was the relationship between Ruth Eisenberg and Margaret Patrick, pianists who played to audiences in Canada and the United States. Because of the effect of strokes, one woman played the piano with her right hand and the other with her left. Together they produced the mutually harmonious music they both loved because each woman was willing to share the best of herself.

Love gives of itself. Once we feel solid in self-friendship, we are in a position to offer the gift of friendship to another.

Love has the patience to endure the fault we cannot cure
—J. JELINEK

Because the word *love* is often used loosely to describe a variety of feelings and relationships, it is easy to become confused about love's real meaning. Beyond defining love as a romantic feeling for someone of the opposite sex, it's possible to think of love in much broader terms: the basic feeling of goodwill for others, concern for their health and well-being, and the desire to have only good come to them. This includes our parents, siblings, friends, everyone!

Love is the ideal and the dream of every one of us. In the Creator's love were our souls conceived and in love lies our destiny. We are fulfilled when we are in the state of love, and bereft without it. Love becomes the purpose of our lives. Although there have been billions of words written about love in its many incarnations, none of them can fully capture the essence of love.

Love at its highest level demands nothing in return. It loves simply for the sake of loving. It is not concerned with *what* or *who* it loves, nor is it concerned with whether or not that love is returned. Like the sun, its joy is in the shining forth of its nature.

Love is an inner quality that sees good everywhere and in everyone. It insists that all is good, and by refusing to see anything but good, it tends to elicit that quality in other people and other things. Love takes no notice of faults, imagined or otherwise. Love is considered the great harmonizer and healer in life.

Several years ago, a businessman pointed out the tremendous power of unconditional love, especially in dealing with troublesome people. When an important appointment was coming up, he retired to his office, closed the door, and became still and quiet. He filled his mind with a mental picture of the people he was to meet with and blessed every one of them with an affirmation of love. Here is his affirmation:

I am a radiating center of universal love, mighty to attract
my good, and with the ability to radiate good to others,
especially, [the name of the clients].

This affirmation generated a powerful energy force field to which both he and his client became attuned. He remarked that it wasn't enough merely to verbalize the words. It was important to *feel* what you were saying; to feel the power of universal, unconditional love, pulsing through you and your words, with your whole heart, mind, soul, and strength. Love expressed in this manner can overcome many barriers. Every single atom in the universe responds and yields its deepest secrets to unconditional love.

From an early Christian manuscript comes a beautiful admonition:

Nor can that endure which has not its foundation upon
love. For love alone diminishes not, but shines with its own
light; makes an end of discord, softens the fires of hate,
restores peace in the world, and brings together the sun-

dered, redresses wrong, aids all and injures none; and who
so invokes its aid will have no fear of future ill, but shall
find safety and have everlasting peace.

In human relationships we sometimes forget that true love is given
freely with no strings attached. Love is gentle, yet undoubtedly one
of the strongest tools we have. Let love suffuse you with the patience
to handle every situation.

CHAPTER 14

Giving and Receiving

*Whatever you wish that men would do to you,
do so to them (The Golden Rule)*
—MATTHEW 7:12 AND LUKE 6:31

F YOU KNEW of one specific thing you could do that would bring you happiness, poise, courage, success, and contentment, would you do it? Of course. Yet such a tool is available right now. The Golden Rule can help you achieve these things if you only practice what it says.

Jesus gave his own wording to the Golden Rule, and it is expressed in various forms in every major religion. Similar codes of conduct are found in the literature of Hinduism, Buddhism, Islam, and in the writings of Aristotle, Plato, and Seneca. In Jewish literature, the negative expression of the Golden Rule appears as, "What you hate, do not do to anyone."

Think for a moment about Jesus. Jesus started his career as a carpenter. He knew the importance of good tools. Later on, when he began to teach principles of living, he used words as tools to communicate his ideas. He "hammered home" the idea that it is merely common sense to treat others the way you wish to be treated yourself. If you don't want to be cheated, don't cheat. If you don't want to be lied to, don't lie to others.

169

To build a fine structure, you need solid building materials. You certainly would not use a rotten piece of wood to build your house. If you used lumber that had been warped by the weather, the foundation might not be secure and the walls might not stand straight. The building would lack structural integrity. Likewise, as a builder of your own life, you need good attitudes to create your house of living. If you act in ways that are abusive to others, you may find yourself abused. Others may not trust your integrity.

Kindness, caring, and consideration have often been described as "love in action." Each day offers many opportunities for anyone to perform some little kindness for another and to be caring and considerate, understanding and supportive. Yet many of us are so busy, harried, and sometimes worried about situations in our own lives that we fail to see the blessed opportunity to embody love in action. Begin to bring about a change for the good by shifting your awareness outside yourself to others. Surely someone whose life you touch today can use the gift of your kindness. Surely your sincere caring would be appreciated by someone in your world. The Golden Rule offers a pattern, or a plan, that we can read and follow and build on to usher all kinds of good things into our lives. To treat others as we wish to be treated is a plan that works wonderfully.

By giving you grow
—SIR JOHN TEMPLETON

After serving for more than eighteen years in the U.S. Army, Sam was dishonorably discharged for drinking and fighting. Depressed and unable even to imagine himself holding a steady job, he soon exhausted the little money he had managed to save during his army career and became a "street person."

"Living on the streets was worse than Vietnam," Sam recalls. "At least in Vietnam you usually knew who your enemy was. On the streets, you never knew who might knock you out and steal your shoes right off your feet!"

Early one afternoon, while waiting for lunch to be served at a church-run center, Sam answered a call for volunteers to help move some furniture and roll up a rug that needed replacing. It was the first time he had done anything for anyone but himself in quite some time. It felt good.

As he was leaving the building after lunch, Sam noticed a heavy growth of moss on the roof that threatened to damage the shingles. He volunteered to remove it. "You're welcome to help, but you know we can't pay you," the supervisor said. Sam went ahead with the work anyway, again experiencing an unexpected good feeling.

Sam developed the habit of offering his services whenever he heard of a job he thought he could do. It wasn't long before the center needed a volunteer typist. Sam had learned to type in the army and offered his services if someone would help him purchase a pair of reading glasses. Money was found to pay for the glasses, and Sam became an enthusiastic office volunteer.

Soon after he began working in the office, Sam moved from the streets to a spare bedroom in the home of one of his coworkers. Then, without his asking for it, the manager of the center offered Sam a small salary and increased his responsibilities in the office. Another coworker offered Sam a good used automobile for a reasonable price, with payments he could easily afford.

Sam believes that the positive changes in his life started when the people at the center began to believe in him. Others believed in Sam, it's true, but it seems clear that Sam was the one who took the first step. With his first gift of willing service, Sam began to establish himself in the creative, prospering flow of abundant life. He began to see himself in a new light.

We can all experience a reward like Sam's, almost regardless of our circumstances. No matter how well or how poorly our lives seem to be going, we can become part of a greater flow of good and increase our awareness by doing something more than we have to do—by giving of ourselves. One of the keys to prosperity is realizing that true prosperity doesn't come from *getting* more—it comes from *giving* more! We can prosper by emphasizing what we are giving rather than by concentrating on what we are getting.

When we merely try to hold on to what is given or entrusted to us, life may seem to take away even that. But when we choose to *use* what life has given us, the return of abundance may include friendship, companionship, financial blessings, homes, transportation, and security in wonderful ways. The universe holds nothing back from the one who lovingly and sincerely gives.

As we become aware of our potential for giving, there is no limit to the good we can receive. Giving can naturally lead to actions that are positive experiences for all concerned. Think of some ways you can use your mind, your energy, and your time. Are you using the hours of the day in the best and most creative ways? Is there something constructive that you would like to do that could add to the good of the world? Remember that little things can mean a lot. Plant one seed and it can yield many fruits. This is how nature operates, and we are a part of nature. Look around you from the perspective of determining opportunities to express your talents and abilities. Find some way in which you may give, and then do it with a loving heart.

You cannot be lonely if you help the lonely
—SIR JOHN TEMPLETON

"Alone, alone, all, all alone; Alone on a wide, wide sea." Have you ever felt the kind of loneliness expressed by the poet Samuel Taylor Coleridge? Have you ever looked at a picture of a deserted beach in winter or caught a glimpse of the bleak emptiness of a city street at five o'clock in the morning and shivered as you identified with the feeling of isolation that suffused the scene? What is this thing called loneliness? Is it simply being alone? No. As one writer observed, "Cannot the heart in the midst of crowds feel alone?" On the other hand, cannot a person be alone and still feel a sense of closeness with loved ones?

The feeling of loneliness is not the same as being alone. Loneliness is described as a state of mind, a deficiency of the spirit; and it can be corrected by overcoming that sense of deficiency. Loneliness cannot be overcome by getting something; it must be remedied by giving something.

Few people remember the days when bartering undergirded the economy. A farmer could offer sacks of grain to the town doctor for setting a broken arm. Chickens might be given to the blacksmith and his family or potatoes to the village midwife for assistance in the delivery of a child.

An old friend often reminisced about his childhood days when his mother, Sarah, became very skillful at making tantalizingly delicious dishes from frequent gifts of cabbage, rutabagas, and yams. His father was a minister, and the family of the town parson was held in high regard in southern Mississippi. A visit to the reverend and his wife in their modest frame cottage was a rare treat indeed. The moment a knock was heard at the door, Sarah bustled with a flourish to greet her guests with hugs, kisses, and warm words of welcome. Always dressed in the traditional black clerical suit with starched white collar, the reverend followed Sarah to extend a warm hand and twinkling smile, saying, "The Lord blesses you, come in." Their gentle manner was the same whether their visitor was a cherished relative, a pauper needing a meal, or the town's mayor.

As time laid to rest Sarah's husband, she elected to move to a port city in another state to be closer to her son and daughter. As was her custom for over fifty years, she arose daily before dawn, dressed meticulously with cloak and a tiny veil, and walked to church. She polished and prepared all the vessels and linens necessary for the priest to offer the sacrament. She tended to every menial task needed by the church personnel. Upon finishing, she went out, walking to the hospital to visit and cheer those who were ill. Afterwards, one by one, she visited the homes of the shut-ins, sharing her joy and kindness and what might be needed of her slender pension.

When news came that Sarah had left this life, a touching story was told. That day she had made her service offering at the church, as usual. Returning home, she gathered a few items of hand-washed laundry from the clothesline and laid her wrap over the back of the sofa. When she was found, she was resting with her eyes closed, in her favorite lounge chair and with a gentle, sweet smile on her lips. The tiny net veil was still in place. Spending a few hours in the presence of this special lady conveyed the essence of more gratitude and joy than any sermon or lecture. To Sarah, loneliness was an ill to be tended to and abolished. She used every waking moment to instill, or perpetuate, a bit of happiness in someone's life.

Mother Teresa reported in some of her television interviews that she finds the greatest poverty and desolation among the wealthy of the world today. She noted that there is a stark need for missions to offer love and nurturing to the barren of heart.

Opportunities are limitless when you seek to fill a need in humanity. Surprisingly, within three blocks of your own home, you might find desperation and helplessness. Often those in greatest pain are unable to discern for themselves the source of their anguish. Hunger, shelter, and the need for gainful productivity are easily recognized. Emotional pain and inner desolation, however, may require more gentle effort and sensitivity. Looking within yourself, you may find valuable assets, special resources, and talents that can be shared. When thoughts are turned outward in search of usefulness, loneliness often disappears.

Beginning with one effort, such as spending an unselfish hour with someone less fortunate, can produce a miracle for the giver and the receiver. If these two should remember another friend in need and go together to help that friend, three or more agents of caring are now set in motion. This positive force multiplies in energy, which moves joy, love, and sustenance into the world to dispel sorrow and lack. Sharing these priceless gifts of caring, encouragement, appreciation, and praise fills our day with rich purpose.

Thoughts can crystallize into habit, and habit solidifies into circumstance
—ANONYMOUS

A gentleman we'll call Mr. Smith was the richest man in the small town in Tennessee, where he had lived all of his life. He was not rich in money. He and his wife lived comfortably but carefully on social security and a small pension check. The wealth Mr. Smith enjoyed was quite different from the financial kind.

The days did not seem long enough for him to do the many things he enjoyed. He began each day by filling the bird feeders and the bird-bath. A neighbor once asked him why he bought so much birdseed when he was living on a fixed income. He commented that he was well paid for the birdseed. The birds sat on the white picket fence, the porch rail, tree limbs, and bushes, and they chirped, giving the Smiths a world filled with music. In this way, Mr. Smith received much more than he gave. His positive thoughts of loving life crystallized into the habit of enjoying each day's activities and solidified into the beauty and sound in his world.

Each weekday morning, Mr. Smith walked two blocks to the handsome old Victorian house that housed SARC—The Seaton Association for Retarded Citizens—where he worked with the children. They were unable to attend regular school, but the center assisted each of the children in reaching their potential. Although Mr. Smith was not a trained teacher, there was much he could do. With endless patience he helped little ones learn to tie a shoe or eat with a fork and spoon. Friends tried to tell the retired man that with his talent for this work he could certainly find a part-time, paid position. But Mr. Smith was paid a huge salary for his work with these youngsters—a tearful "thank-you" from a mother and father, a bear hug from a tot overjoyed at successfully doing something on his own, or a "God bless you" from one of the paid workers. Mr. Smith gave much to the children, but he received abundant personal blessings in return.

While Mr. Smith was at the center, Mrs. Smith worked in the chamber of commerce office, which helped the business and professional people in town. Money was not plentiful, so the office had only two employees, the director and the office manager/secretary. Mrs. Smith gladly helped with mailings, copying, telephoning, filling the counter rack with town maps and postcards and other free literature. She even watered the plants. Mrs. Smith loved the office, because she was right in the middle of what was going on in town. She gave a lot of herself in that office, but she received so much back that it literally filled her heart with joy.

The couple also gave time to their children and their grandchildren, and the Smiths' lifestyle was so inspirational it was reflected in their children. Their son was an accountant, who spent every Saturday morning at a senior center in his city helping seniors handle their finances at no charge. His wife was a volunteer at the grade school their son attended. And their little boy was raising a puppy for the Seeing Eye–dog group. Their daughter assisted five mornings a week at the town's small hospital. Her husband, an insurance executive, was a member of the finance board at his church and worked many hours in this role. Their children were members of a youth group that visited a nursing home on Saturday mornings, listening, writing letters, combing residents' hair, taking someone for a ride outside in a wheelchair. They gave and they gave. And received and received!

Every thought we allow into our mind can affect the thoughts, feelings, and actions we express. If we hold negative thoughts, our actions are likely going to be negative. In turn, negative habits might develop, and negative results may be returned to us. On the other hand, positive thoughts aid in developing positive habits and positive results, and life can become a happy, motivating adventure in which we see ourselves and others in the true light of what we really are—a wonderful, magical, mysterious expression of life. As long as our thoughts remain positive and are grounded in accomplishing the goal in front of us, the progress we make on the path of life will be steady and rewarding.

Agape given grows; agape hoarded dwindles
—SIR JOHN TEMPLETON

No other word in our language has been given so many definitions or been written about in such depth in poetry, theater, novels, and philosophical and theological texts as *love*. Regardless of how it is defined or what is written about it, surely the most important thing about love is what we do with it.

The Greeks developed several definitions of love. *Eros* is romantic love, the kind that puts butterflies in your stomach. *Storge* is the type of love that we feel for members of our family; it is the love of security. *Phileo,* or comradeship, is the type of love we feel for our friends. The most important love, however, is *agape*.

Agape is the unselfish love that gives of itself and expects nothing in return. It is the love that grows as you give it to others. Miraculously, the more *agape* you give, the more you have to give. It is the love that great spiritual teachers, such as Jesus, Buddha, Muhammad, Lao Tzu, Confucius, and others taught us to practice.

The writer C. S. Lewis likened *agape* to the tools it takes to grow an abundant garden. We always have a choice. We can let the garden of our lives grow wild and unattended until it fills with weeds, or we can take up the proper tools and tend to our garden until we create a place of unimaginable loveliness—full of flowers and all the vegetables we need. One of the most important tools can be our willingness to extend our love to others.

When we discover the miracle of love, we cannot stop ourselves from giving—nor do we want to stop. Love only increases when it is given and dwindles when we attempt to conserve it.

Agape is the unconditional love God gives us, regardless of what we look like, how much money we have, how smart we are, even how unloving our actions may sometimes be. God loves us unconditionally, and that is what we should try to do as well. When we practice *agape*, it becomes easier to love our enemies, to tolerate those who annoy us, and to find something to appreciate in every person we meet.

To develop *agape* we, too, should practice expressing sincere love until it becomes second nature—as natural to us as breathing. When it does, love may flow out of us and into us as easily as air flows in and out of our lungs when we inhale and exhale. *Agape* is a deliberate choice, one you can make right now. It does not depend on how you feel, but on loving *regardless* of how you feel. It resembles an exercise program. When you start a program like walking, running, or lifting weights, you don't immediately sign up for a marathon or reach for the heaviest weight. You exercise every day, and, as you do, you are able to walk farther, run faster, or lift heavier weights.

The rewards of consistent exercise include feeling good about your accomplishments and improving your ability. The rewards of practicing *agape* include feeling good about others as well as about yourself—two components to living a happy life.

Tithing often brings prosperity and honor
—SIR JOHN TEMPLETON

Nearly all civilizations have practiced some form of philanthropy. Many ancient civilizations levied a tithe, or tax, for the poor. The Egyptians and Greeks gave money to establish libraries and universities. By encouraging members to tithe, medieval churches supported hospitals and orphanages.

The word *tithe* is from the Anglo-Saxon word *teotha*, which means "a tenth part." To tithe means to donate one-tenth of a person's income. In the Bible, tithing supported the religious order given in Numbers 18:26–27 (NIV), "When you receive from the Israelites the tithe I give you as your inheritance, you must present a tenth of that tithe as the LORD's offering. Your offering will be reckoned to you as grain from the threshing floor or juice from the winepress."

Many people believe that by tithing they appease their God and secure their place in heaven. Inside of King's College Chapel in Cambridge, England, are these words of William Wordsworth, "Give all thou canst; high Heaven rejects the lore of nicely calculated less or more." The underlying belief is that if we give our bountiful share of this life's abundance, then we will receive all we are due on earth and in heaven.

Benjamin Franklin is remembered not only for his statesmanship but also for his tithing. In his will, Franklin left $5,000 each in trust for two hundred years to Boston and Philadelphia for philanthropic purposes, a sizable amount of money at that time. Franklin also established America's first city hospital, the Pennsylvania Hospital for the Unfortunate.

Andrew Carnegie used a large share of his fortune to establish many cultural, educational, and scientific institutions. He believed that "surplus wealth is a sacred trust which its possessor is bound to administer in his lifetime for the good of the community." In 1901, Carnegie's fortune was estimated to be $500 million, of which he donated $350 million to a variety of causes. His generosity established 2,500 public libraries throughout the world, paid for the construction for the famed Carnegie Hall in New York City, and created Carnegie-Mellon University in Pittsburgh and the Carnegie Institution of Washington to encourage research in biological and physical sciences.

Tithing often brings prosperity and honor because it is an important aspect of the law of giving and receiving, which is an integral part of the law of cause and effect—"As you give forth, so shall you receive."

A lot of people right now are seeking economic healing. One of the quickest ways to relieve economic stress and effect economic healing is to tithe—or give. Not only is tithing a prospering activity, it is also a healing activity. Tithing establishes a consistent method of giving and for stewarding the bounty in one's life. This consistency can help the mind to build in awareness toward supply, abundance, and further giving. In my lifetime of observing many hundreds of families, almost without exception, the family that tithes for more than ten years becomes both prosperous and happy. This is the one investment suitable for everyone.

Those who do good do well
—SIR JOHN TEMPLETON

Scripture says, "Freely ye have received, freely give." (Matt. 10:8, KJV). Over and over we hear that giving enables us to receive. The purpose for which we give is vital. To give with secret hope of reward is in direct opposition to the law of love. When we give from a heart of love that simply must give because it loves, we are expressing unconditional love. True giving, with no strings attached, manifests love. Through true giving we express our love to others, and when we give in this manner we gain in understanding.

In the Holy Land, there are two seas—the Sea of Galilee and the Dead Sea. The Sea of Galilee has both an inlet and an outlet. The water that circulates through it is fresh and sweet, and marine life, both flora and fauna, abound in its depths. The Sea of Galilee is fertile and productive; and by giving of the fruits of its being, it supports the entire surrounding land and the multitudes who rely on it for nourishment and refreshment. The water of life circulates through the Sea of Galilee and flows on into the Dead Sea, which exemplifies a direct contrast to the Sea of Galilee.

The water of the Dead Sea is brackish and dead. It is stagnant because, even though it has an inlet that receives the fresh water of the River Jordan, which flows through the Sea of Galilee, the Dead Sea has no outlet. It only receives; it does not give. Therefore, it cannot flourish. The surrounding desert area is also sterile and lifeless.

The businessman who seeks to give the most to his customers will gain more customers and do well in his profession and in prosperity. The activity of giving is part of the law of cause and effect. Giving (the cause) prompts circulation (the effect). It is the returning energy of circulation that brings our increased abundance. In helping others, we help ourselves, for whatever mood we send out completes the circle and returns to us.

Says Muhammad:

"Every good act is charity. Your smiling in your brother's face is charity; an exhortation of your fellowman to virtuous deeds is equal to almsgiving; your putting a wanderer in the right road is charity; your assisting the blind is charity; your removing stones, and thorns, and other obstructions from the road is charity; your giving water to the thirsty is charity. A man's true wealth hereafter is the good he does in this world to his fellowman. When he dies, people will say, "What property has he left behind him?" but the angels will ask, "What good deeds has he sent before him?"

Giving and receiving have to do with every area of life, not just money and other tangible or material goods. In a much larger sense, giving has to do with our health, happiness, and overall well-being. Does your being not sing when you give from the love within your mind and heart? Is there not a spring in your step and a light in your eyes when you have helped another—just from the sheer pleasure of helping? Perhaps especially if you did your good deed anonymously? In the Talmud we are told:

There are ten strong things. Iron is strong, but fire melts it. Fire is strong, but water quenches it. Water is strong, but the clouds evaporate it. Clouds are strong, but wind drives them away. Man is strong, but fears cast him down. Fear is strong, but wine allays it. Wine is strong, but sleep overcomes it. Sleep is strong, but death is stronger, but loving-kindness survives death.

Ruth Stafford Peale defines giving in this manner: "Giving is using what you have, both time and resources, for the benefit of others, without regard to the consequences to yourself. This giving is uniquely human and, most certainly, spiritually motivated." Mrs. Peale identifies three areas of giving: charity, philanthropy, and volunteerism. Charity is giving away a portion of what you have for the benefit of others. Philanthropy involves the giving of private or corporate wealth to projects or individuals. And volunteerism is the giving of time to charitable causes and involves working with essential tasks such as teaching illiterate adults to read, mentoring a juvenile offender, assisting in relief agencies, or nursing AIDS babies.

Ask not what you can expect from life; ask what life expects from you
—VIKTOR FRANKL

What are we going to get out of life? This can understandably be a question of fundamental importance to us. We begin with certain basic needs and desires. It is important to have a comfortable home, plenty of food, a meaningful and well-paying job, comfort, companionship, and joy. However, many of us have not fully realized a simple, basic principle: for our receiving to take place, we must first give. Giving and receiving are two aspects of the same law of life.

President John F. Kennedy advised Americans, "Ask not what your country can do for you; ask what you can do for your country." This is an expression of the law of giving and receiving, and it applies to everyone in our world. For example, if we seek a certain type of employment and there are no jobs available in that area, we might see if there is some volunteer position to be found in our area of interest. Rather than demanding of life that we receive the job we want, we ask if there is anything we can give. Through volunteering, we gain experience and contacts, and, oftentimes, the job we've been seeking eventually becomes ours.

Every time an opportunity comes your way that allows you to give, welcome that opportunity with open arms. It may be heaven's call to fulfill your highest destiny. And the attitude of the giver may be more important than the gift itself. Life's gifts that we continually benefit from are, in themselves, a good reason to develop and maintain an attitude of gratitude. Many of us want love and companionship, but it is a law of life that we must first be loving and friendly if we would attract to us the love and companionship we desire. We give and then we receive.

The law of giving and receiving also asks us to be good receivers. As we give of ourselves, our time and resources, our positive attitudes and loving thoughts and actions, it is also important to be able to receive the gifts of others in a gracious way, to say, "Thank you, I accept your thoughtful gift."

The law of giving and receiving is basic to a life of successful and graceful living. If we are feeling a lack in some area, our first thought should be, "What can I give? What do I have to give?" If we remain open and receptive, we will know how we may give. The more we give, the more we receive.

We receive freely when we give freely
—ANONYMOUS

Chris Hartley is in the fishing business. He is a man with his own boat who lives in some of the best fishing territory in the world. The clear, turquoise-green waters of the Bahamas teem with many varieties of fish, and charter boats abound that take visitors on fishing trips out of Nassau. However, Chris doesn't fish from his boat, and neither does he allow others to fish from it. Furthermore, he will not eat fish that anyone else has caught. You might think such a fisherman would have a hard time running a successful business, but Chris is thriving in his endeavor. He has a different kind of tourist fishing business, based on the universal principle that as you give freely, you also receive freely, and his enterprise profits by using this principle.

Chris loves to be underwater and seems to be in his element there. Capitalizing on his affinity for the sea, he procured a boat and some equipment, which allowed him to establish "Hartley's Underwater Wonderland," a business that takes tourists on boat excursions to a nearby coral reef. There, wearing scuba gear, the tourists can walk along the seafloor fifteen feet below the surface, while Chris introduces them to the magnificent flora and fauna of the sea world.

A white-striped fish swims up to Chris, who pets "Harry the Grouper" as he would a cat or dog. Harry then swims to each of the underwater guests, allows himself to be touched by them, and poses for photographs that Chris later sells to the tourists. One year Chris dressed Harry up with a Santa Claus hat, snapped his picture, and made a unique Christmas card souvenir.

If you're wondering why Harry performs so well for Chris, it's because of Chris's practice of giving and receiving—one of the laws of life that he lives by. When Chris began his business, he realized that a tame fish around the coral reef would be a great attraction for tourists. But most fish were afraid of people; a basic instinct for survival made them stay away. Chris realized that he would have to give the fish an assurance that they wouldn't be killed and that he was coming to them as a friend.

Chris began to bring food to the fish—food for them to eat, not bait on the end of a hooked line. Although Chris had no guarantee the fish would respond, they did by flocking around the coral reef every time his boat appeared. Receiving Chris's loving attention and food freely, the fish responded with their friendship, and Chris has benefited tremendously by sharing that friendship with his customers.

In 2 Corinthians 9:6 we read, "He who sows sparingly will also reap sparingly; and he who sows bountifully will also reap bountifully." Throughout the sacred scriptures of the world, we are reminded often of the importance of the great law of giving and receiving. In fact, one of the basic laws of prosperity states: give and you will receive. Sow and you will reap. Like attracts like.

This is important to remember. Even though prosperity may stand on our doorstep, we may not necessarily invite it into our lives. Why not? Because we may need to do something first. We should claim it; we should accept it with thanksgiving; and then we use this prosperity in the highest and best manner to help others. A good example of why a person may not achieve an objective of prosperity comes from a magazine cartoon some years ago. Here's the scenario: a man is imploring God, "Please let me win the lottery!" From the clouds above comes a booming voice, presumably God, declaring, "At least buy a ticket!" Therein lies the problem. Too often people may desire prosperity but may not be willing to pay the price. What is the price? It is sharing, giving, loving, and caring. Prosperity needs an inflow and an outflow, just as any body of water does if it is to remain fresh and clean. Otherwise, stagnation often results.

Perhaps you've been led to believe that in order to have profit in an enterprise, someone must lose—that for you to win at life there must be a loser. What Chris Hartley demonstrates is that you rarely lose by giving, whether it's food for fish or love for friends. For in giving freely without guarantee of return, you may set into motion a great momentum of goodness. When we give, everyone is a winner.

No person was ever honored for what he received.
Honor has been the reward for what he gave
—CALVIN COOLIDGE

In the Gospel according to Luke, Jesus said, "Give, and it will be given to you; good measure, pressed down, shaken together, running over, will be put into your lap. For the measure you give will be the measure you get back" (Luke 6:38). Jesus states a fundamental law of life that has been recognized by most great spiritual leaders as well as by many truly successful men and women.

If you love the work you do, you are going to put all of yourself into it, giving freely of your energy and your talents. When you give of yourself, when you work for the joy of achievement, when you share your bounty with others, the gift of appreciation—tangible or intangible—becomes a part of your daily life. Tangible appreciation could be a monetary return or a gift from someone for work accomplished.

Intangible appreciation could be gratitude from others for what you have done and a good reputation. On the other hand, if you're working for the paycheck, willing only to do what you believe you're getting paid to do and no more, chances are you'll grow to despise your job.

Bob was such a man. For eight hours a day, five days a week, year after year, he pulled down a salary while putting forth as little effort as possible. He always seemed to be tired and discontented, and he blamed his job for many of his problems.

One thing Bob loved to do, however, was watch his daughter play softball. When he was offered the chance to coach her Little League team, he eagerly accepted. Although coaching the girls took a great deal of time and commitment, Bob didn't mind. He said the hours he spent with the team were energizing. The girls ended up taking a first-place trophy, and Bob received an outpouring of praise from the parents who were amazed by his commitment.

Fortunately, the story doesn't end there. At the prompting of his concerned wife, Bob decided to seek spiritual counseling about the problem in his professional life. The counselor suggested that he begin to embrace his job with the same enthusiasm that he was pouring into coaching the girl's softball team. He reluctantly agreed to give it a try.

To his surprise, Bob began noticing things at work he could do to make the day more personally fulfilling. He began to take an interest in the lives of his fellow employees. He challenged himself to improve the ways in which he was doing his job. He began to pretend he was actually the owner of the plant instead of just another cog in the machine. He began to make suggestions to his superiors on how things could be run more efficiently in his department. And, to his great surprise, he found himself thinking about ways to improve his work after hours! Each day now he awoke with a sense of enthusiasm instead of dull despair. Bob learned the valuable lesson of honestly and sincerely giving of yourself in whatever you do.

Giving is similar to financial investing. If you invest carelessly and without any effort or research, you are likely to fail in the long run. On the other hand, when you wisely invest your energies, interests, and abilities, you are more likely to succeed.

Remember that merely putting your time into something doesn't mean you're giving yourself to it. There are various levels or degrees of giving. Dedicate your attention, your interest, your love, your imagination, your creativity to the task at hand, and you can transform an undesirable condition into something that gives back to you. This is a law of life that can work for you in the same way it worked for Bob and for millions of other people who have discovered it. Think less about what you can get and more about what you can give, and your life will take on a luster you haven't yet dreamed possible.

As you are active in blessing others, they find their burdens easier to bear
—SIR JOHN TEMPLETON

When we desire to be a blessing to others, we find that there are many ways in which we can bless others. We can give material goods to others, and we can also offer them the benefit of our experience. People who have faced and overcome challenges with alcohol and drugs often involve themselves in helping others who are experiencing similar difficulties. They understand the value of overcoming the problem. In every area of human experience, we may find those precious ones who are able and willing to be a blessing to others.

A well-known building contractor begins his day with a prayer like this:

Father, you are the Master Architect. Let me never "hammer and saw" so loudly that You can't get through to discuss Your blueprints with me. My business is Your business. Work through me to build good houses and a good life. Help me be a blessing to all I meet.

Many people find that they receive more benefit from *being* a blessing than from being blessed. Oftentimes, being a blessing requires nothing more than a word of encouragement and hope to someone who may be experiencing situations that bring discouragement and despair.

E. Stanley Jones tells of seeing a little frail flower growing in the vast ruins of ancient Babylon. He wondered how a little flower, so frail that he could crush it in his fingers, could have survived while a vast empire founded on military power had perished. As he contemplated the mystery before him, he realized that it was because the flower followed the ways of nature's gentleness, but the nation perished by its militaristic doctrine. He concluded that love is the answer; light is a continuing need; and each one of us can serve as a channel of blessing.

The air we breathe is necessary to keep us alive, but we must continually exhale so we can inhale fresh air back into our lungs. God gives us his love, which we can keep in action by breathing it out to others, thus making room in our hearts for a fresh supply of love. Muhammad, the Prophet of Islam, wrote as follows: "No man is a true believer unless he desireth for his brother that which he desireth for himself." We must share our gifts to provide opportunity for increase in our lives. For example, when knowledge is shared, it increases for those concerned. When we share with others our substance and our blessings, they can increase for us and for others as the loaves and fishes increased for Jesus and the multitudes. When we share garden seed with nature by sowing it in the ground, the unfolding harvest brings increase. When we speak kind words, kindness is multiplied in our lives.

The law of blessedness may indicate that a real part of our lives' work may be to help other's burdens become easier to bear. Have we not each experienced—at some time in our lives—a problem situation, a personal challenge, or possibly confusion? And perhaps we were the recipient of caring and compassion from another. As we humble ourselves to the multitude of expressions of the Spirit that sing to us each moment, as we come to appreciate and love the inner richness of our lives, we may become the blessing that adds the "flavor" to our lives. What a wonderful awareness to know that as we open ourselves to rich blessings, those blessings flow through the channel of our love to bless and help others. Let's pause and give thanks for being blessed and for the opportunity to be a blessing.

The more love we give, the more love we have left
—SIR JOHN TEMPLETON

A woman tells a story about the time when her daughter announced that she no longer believed in Santa Claus and flatly refused to leave milk and cookies out for this nocturnal visitor on Christmas Eve. Upset at abandoning a four-year tradition, the child's father tried bribing and cajoling her. Nothing worked. As the evening eased into night, imagine the mother's surprise when the daughter walked into the living room carrying a bowl of oatmeal. Her father helped her put the bowl under the tree, next to eight others just like it. "What on earth are you doing?" the mother asked. "I thought you didn't believe in Santa."

"She doesn't," the father replied, beaming. "But the reindeer—they're a different story!"

A humorous little story, but one that tells of a child's love for animals. The little girl was giving from an inexhaustible heart of love, and such is the way of love. The more love we give, the more love we have left. Would it not seem wise, then, to let love pour forth from us in all our thoughts, words, and actions? To let love be the bond between ourselves and each person who touches our lives daily? To let love be the forgiving force whenever forgiveness may be needed? To ask love to strip from our consciousness every vestige of selfishness, bitterness, revengefulness, and unhappiness? To allow the harmonizing power of love to restore our bodies, renew our minds, and lift us to ever-higher levels of understanding and compassion? Oh, what love can do when we give it the opportunity!

From the Midrash comes this story of love in action that has been given an opportunity: Rabbi Joshua ben Ibn dreamed that his neighbor in paradise would be Nanas, the butcher. He visited this Nanas to inquire what good deeds he was performing to deserve such a high place in paradise. The butcher replied, "I know not, but I have an aged father and mother who are helpless, and I give them food and drink, and wash and dress them daily."

The rabbi then said: "I will be happy to have thee as my neighbor in paradise."

To allow a full and free flow of love from the heart into life is a secret of rich and satisfying living. Sincere love can overcome every obstacle, from the smallest irritation to the largest problem we may encounter. One reason: as we grow in the consciousness of love, we come to realize that love takes no account of the seeming shortcomings of others. Too often we react to the moods of others, letting their words and actions influence our own. When others may snap at us or are irritable, love can help us see beyond appearances, and to understand that their mood may be the result of a dissatisfaction within themselves. It is not necessary to react to their mood, nor do we need to allow that kind of energy to filter into our own actions. Whenever we feel out of sorts with the world around us, we may need only to look within for love to pour out. Giving forth all the love we feel capable of giving at the time may help set a disorder right. And we find we still have plenty of love left.

Giving more love can be a turning point for the soul. Turning points are the blessed moments when the hardships of life's adversity give way to awakening to the presence of God. It can be the dark hour of crisis that bears the golden dawning of the richness of Spirit. Sometimes we may need to discipline ourselves with "tough love" to break a habit that may be working against our highest interests. But letting go of these blockages can open wide the doorway to greater giving of our love.

A spiritual teacher once asked a class, "What did you come to earth for?"

One student, feeling he had the right answer, rose and said, "Love!"

"Oh, really?" responded the teacher in the tone of voice that indicated the student was about to be taught a lesson. "Is there anyone you love more than anyone else?"

The student thought for a moment and responded, "Yes."

To which the teacher answered, "Then you haven't lived up to your potential yet. For your work is not complete until you experience the joy of loving all as you love the one you love most."

This all-encompassing ideal of love can compel a person to look more deeply to the inner self to attempt to discover what love really is, and what it means to truly love someone in an unconditional manner. How many times have you spoken the words *I love you* and really felt the reverence those sacred words deserve? How wide is the path of love you tread? Can it encompass all those around you? How aware are you of the love returning from others that may be prompted by the love you are giving? Pour out love in thought, in word, and in action. Try to think love, speak love, feel love, and become immersed in it, until all else in your life and world is absorbed and melted into giving love.

CHAPTER 15

Giving Thanks

An attitude of gratitude creates blessings
—SIR JOHN TEMPLETON

O YOU AWAKEN every morning with a song of praise on your lips? Do you feel full of appreciation for life as you live it every day? Or do you have to think long and hard before finding anything to be grateful for?

Consider your response to these questions carefully, for they could be crucial to a life of usefulness and joy. It is a law of life, and an inexorable principle, that if we develop an attitude of gratitude, our happiness will increase. The very reasons for being thankful begin to multiply.

"But how does this positive approach really work?" you may ask. The only way to prove it to yourself is to give it a try and see what happens. Whether you know it or not, you have multitudes of reasons to break out in a wonderful song of praise at this very moment!

Wherever you focus your attention and belief becomes your experience. So direct your attention to the way you would like to see yourself. Give thanks for the realization that you are becoming that person. Give thanks for all the abundance you're presently enjoying, and give thanks for the abundance of every good thing that's on its way to you. As you count your blessings and become increasingly aware of how truly blessed you are, you can begin to develop an attitude of

193

gratitude. Your life will be blessed in ways you never thought were possible. Practice waking up each day with an inherent expectation of good and with a wonderful feeling of thanksgiving for life itself. Your days will be filled with exciting adventures.

You may already realize the wisdom of an attitude of gratitude. If so, it may only be a small step for you to begin to open yourself to greater appreciation and greater abundance. As you become a good steward of the abundance that is yours right now, an increasing attitude of gratitude will bring greater blessings to you and, then through you, to our world.

Thanksgiving leads to having more to give thanks for
—SIR JOHN TEMPLETON

The grateful mind is more than simply a response to the condition of things in life; it is a celebration of an ever-present spiritual reality. This attitude of gratitude can open the door to the increased flow of abundance in your life. However, a deeper and seldom considered interpretation of thanksgiving can focus on what you have to give thanks *from*.

Thanksgiving is a creative force that, if lived on a continuous basis and not just for one day each year, can create more good in your life. Perhaps we could call this way of life "thanksliving." Thanksliving is based on the premise that living a life of appreciation and gratefulness leads to having more to be thankful for. We have the ability to create blessings in our lives through the power of mind action and the choices we make. Let's look at some ways we can choose to practice thanksliving.

First, let's take a look at our lives, find the good that is already there, and praise this good. An old adage states that "where your attention goes, your energy flows." This means we tend to attract that to which we give our attention. A good idea can get even better as its possibilities for greater good are explored. The more good you can see and praise, the more you direct creative energy to positive results. Even in situations that at first appear difficult or unpleasant, see all the good you can and bless the good you can see! Praise the good and watch it multiply.

A second way to experience thanksliving is to give thanks ahead of time for whatever good you desire in your life. Feel as if you have *already* received this good. One law of life can be stated in these words: "Thoughts held in mind will reproduce in the outer world after their own kind." In other words, you help create your outer life according to the way you have created your inner life—with thoughts, beliefs, and attitudes. If what you desire is a more prosperous lifestyle, start feeling and acting like a grateful and prosperous person today. Your attitude tends to draw prosperity to you like a magnet.

A third way to experience thanksliving—perhaps the most difficult, yet the most powerful of all—is to give thanks for your problems and challenges. As you face your situations and overcome them, you grow in strength, wisdom, and compassion. One of the best ways to learn mathematics is to be given a problem to solve. One of the best ways to prepare for an athletic event is to practice with a strong, competitive opponent. Sometimes people feel the weight of circumstances and lose sight of the precious nature of the many and various gifts of life. Adversity, when overcome, strengthens you. So you are giving thanks, not for the problem itself, but for the strength and knowledge that result from the experience. Giving thanks for this growth ahead of time helps you to *grow* through—not just *go* through—any challenges that arise.

It is more blessed to give than to receive
—ACTS 20:35

Many of the world's most successful and influential people seek and experience a greater reward in the giving of their wealth than in getting it. They understand the law of life that giving leads to more giving and greater personal rewards. Many a successful person can tell you that he first thought out his moves in his inner consciousness because he understands that the door to success opens from within. As Robert Dedman, a businessman who contributed more than $100 million to education and other causes before his death, remarked in a 1986 interview in *Town & Country* magazine, "The more you give, the more you live."

There is certainly nothing wrong with getting ahead or being in a position where you can be a positive influence on those around you. But it is through giving, not getting, that you can exert a truly positive force for good.

If you want to be happy, strive to make someone else happy. Give happiness. If you want to have more love in your life, strive to be a more loving person. Give love. If you want to be successful, help others to succeed. It's not difficult to see how much better and richer your life can be when you become a source of encouragement, inspiration, and friendship to others. Giving can make you a magnet for success, because good attracts good.

Almost everyone prefers the company of givers over takers. Takers leave you feeling depleted. You may be reluctant to become their friend. Givers, on the other hand, are a pleasure to be with because they help to establish an environment that blesses and enriches relationships. A taker often becomes someone to avoid, but a giver is always welcomed.

It is important to remember that the Creator is our true source, and there are many channels through which God's good can flow. We can easily forget where our ideas come from, and, when we do, we are likely to experience lack of some kind. Instead of habitually asking what you can get from the various people and situations in your life, ask what you can give to them. The more you give to life, the more you get back. This is a universal law that can go a long way toward creating for you an inner life that is well balanced, prosperous, happy, and fulfilled. Dr. Harry Koch said, "If you are giving while you are living, you are knowing where it's going."

In his book *Your Life—Understanding the Universal Laws*, author Bruce McArthur tells a story of increase. He states:

> My wife has a greenhouse and a green thumb. She plants several tiny seeds. In a few months we are eating huge, delicious, fresh, ripe tomatoes. She sowed only several tiny seeds. She was patient. She gave love, care, consideration, food, water. She reaps not just a few seeds, but wonderful, nourishing, beautiful fruit and hundreds of new seeds. The miracle in this law is one of abundance and joy and beauty, wherein you reap not only what you sow, but far, far more—multiplied many times—when the right kind of seed is nurtured with the spirit of love and cooperation. The harvest is abundance! We reap abundantly in our gardens and in our lives according to the seeds we sow.

Giving is sowing seeds of caring and love. The more you give, the more you receive.

It is better to praise than to criticize
—SIR JOHN TEMPLETON

Praise is a powerful tool. Remember that the spoken word is like a seed. It must grow. To find contentment in the heart and a sense of fulfillment in the mind, we need to praise and affirm life and the goodness of living.

Praise can be the mental attitude that stimulates, quickens, whirls into action, and establishes in character the ideals of which it is the vehicle. Through an inherent law of mind action, you increase whatever you praise. You may praise a fearful heart into peace and trust, sickness into radiant health, a problem into the perfect solution.

Give praise. Be thankful. If you attune your mind to the infinite presence of God each day and acknowledge that presence in your life, you can give forth love instead of malice; you can see good in everything around you; you can count your blessings until they number into the thousands; and you can have the peace knowing that your world is in tune with the Infinite.

Through the ages, the wise and thoughtful among us have said that there is good in everything and everyone if we just take the time to look for it. A Chinese proverb states, "In our actions we should accord with the will of Heaven; in our words we should accord with the hearts of men." We have experienced how wonderful it feels to receive praise and gratitude from others. It is equally wonderful to give praise. Children who are praised and encouraged do better in school and in play than those whose accomplishments are ignored. Let's approach every situation with the exciting truth that there is something wonderful awaiting us. As we learn to praise ourselves and our world, we begin to blossom in ways that are wonderful to behold.

Count your blessings and you will have an attitude of gratitude
—SIR JOHN TEMPLETON

It was only a few days until Christmas, and Jennifer Noble, a British citizen, was feeling low. This was the first holiday season since her divorce, and she was living in the United States, thousands of miles away from her home and family. She had married an American eight years earlier, and for the past two years, they lived in the Midwest while he studied for a new career. Following the divorce, Jennifer made a decision to remain in the United States. But most of her friends had moved on, and, although she made new friends and was successful in rebuilding her life, on this particular day Jennifer felt sorry for herself.

In order to shake off the blues and increase her feeling of well-being, Jennifer decided to help others less fortunate than herself. She went to the local Salvation Army shelter and began to assist with the Christmas dinner preparations. She also bought a few inexpensive toys for the children who were there. The light in the children's eyes when they were given the toys touched Jennifer's heart, and the laughter and holiday cheer among those who were preparing the dinner brought a warm feeling of camaraderie. Her holiday unfolded with special warmth and sparkle because Jennifer decided to give of herself.

Actively acknowledging our good creates more good. When we are grateful for the blessings we already have, our very gratitude attracts extra good to us. Gratitude can be a powerful magnet that draws to us friends, love, peace, health, and material good. Those who are grateful experience the wonderful balance of being both givers and receivers. Gratitude nurtures within us a positive, joy-filled consciousness and unifies us with life's flow, which gives birth to inner fulfillment.

Many of the world's great figures have been faced with problems so large that, at first, they seemed insurmountable. What would have happened if Beethoven had wallowed in self-pity because of his deafness? The world would not have benefited from the legacy of his profoundly beautiful music. What would our transportation system be like today if the Wright brothers had given up after their first test flight?

When looking at the glass that symbolizes our life, we can view it as half full or half empty. The choice is ours. The person who sees the glass as half empty may bemoan his lot. But the person who cultivates an attitude of gratitude will more readily see the glass as half-full, and this positive outlook is self-perpetuating. When we feel gratitude for our experiences, it becomes easier to see the good all around us.

Thanksgiving, not complaining, attracts people to you
—SIR JOHN TEMPLETON

It was the four-year-old's birthday. Around the room were strewn heaps of wrapping papers and tangles of ribbon. Everyone smiled expectantly when the mother said, "Dear, what do you say now?"

The child answered, "Where are the rest of my presents?"

That may be typical behavior for a four-year-old, but how many of us still ask similar questions? "Is this all I get?" There seems to be an expectation of more—of something better, newer, faster, hotter, bigger, grander. We can be grateful for the things we have, or we can focus on things we don't have and make ourselves and others miserable. Our mind has the power to determine if we'll be satisfied or left wanting more. What is it we want so badly? What is this emptiness we may be trying to fill?

Winston Churchill loved to tell the story of a little boy who fell off a pier into deep ocean water. An old sailor, heedless of the great danger to himself, dived into the stormy water, struggled with the boy, and, finally, exhausted, brought the lad to safety. Two days later, the boy's mother came with him to the same pier, seeking the sailor who had rescued her son. Finding him, she asked, "Are you the one who dived into the water and rescued my son?"

"I am," the sailor replied.

The mother then quickly demanded, "Well, where's his hat?"

One might wonder how a hat could have such importance when a child's life had been at stake, but the story illustrates how many people focus on what's wrong rather than what's right. One of the great truth principles is that the feeling of gratitude is a mighty energy that attracts all manner of good things to us. When we make an effort to practice gratitude as a regular activity, it becomes obvious that life can be good, very good, and then expansively good! The universe responds regularly to gratitude by providing more opportunities, friends, activities, and means for your life to grow and expand. Keep centered in the feeling of thanksgiving. Your thanksgiving is a celebration of the continuity of blessings, leading toward happiness for you.

With great courage, give thanks also for the challenges in your life, for through them you can grow stronger and more aware. The limitations of the realm of appearances often stand in the way of those who do not know this great law of increase through praise and thanksgiving.

One man who had reached the state of consciousness of being

grateful for everything in his life was talking with some friends one day and commented that, if given a nucleus, even though it appeared useless, he could produce something without the use of capital. His friends challenged him to prove his assertion. They found a pile of scrap tin which was about to be disposed of, chided him to begin with that worthless pile, and then left the shop laughing.

The man looked at the pile, concentrated his mind on the tin, and said, "I am grateful for this opportunity to open my mind to spirit. This tin can tell me what it can do, what it can shape and form, and what can come out of it." Then he sat quietly for a few minutes, holding a piece of tin in his hand. There came to his mind a picture of a little matchbox. So he began to cut and bend and pretty soon he had shaped a matchbox. The man called to a boy who was passing by and asked the lad to take the matchbox and sell it for 40 percent commission. The boy sold the matchbox for twenty-five cents. The man, from his share of the profit, bought a bit of paint with which to decorate other matchboxes he had made. Several neighborhood boys were then recruited to sell the colorful tin boxes. Over the course of several weeks, the man's friends were shown the considerable capital that had been realized from the small and seemingly worthless pile of tin scraps. The man demonstrated the capital of creative ideas coupled with an attitude of gratitude.

The psalmist in the Bible proclaims, "Enter his gates with thanksgiving, and his courts with praise!" (Ps. 100:4). The writer is inspiring us to give joyous and full expression to our feelings of thankfulness for the blessings God has given us. And we surely have received many blessings! Here is a heart filled with gratitude and a mind filled with the understanding that God is the source. To "enter into his gates" simply means to have a consciousness that we may be a little part of God's infinity. When we have this quickened consciousness within us, we can become aware of our unity with God's presence, God's life, God's love, and God's divine purpose in the universe and also within every person and every situation.

Thanksgiving leads to giving and forgiving, and to spiritual growth
—SIR JOHN TEMPLETON

Thanksgiving may often be called the "law of gratitude," with fear as its opposite. Gratitude enhances the open-hearted, genuine appreciation for what is wonderful in our lives. Fear can be a contracting force that can take us out of our own power and make us the victim of lack. In the book *Lazy Man's Guide to Enlightenment*, Thaddeus Golas writes, "We think fear is a signal to withdraw when it is really a sign that we are already withdrawing too much."

A Course in Miracles, published by the Foundation for Inner Peace, states that there are two basic forces in the universe—love and fear. Another way of saying that may be thanksgiving and lack. If we recognize these forces when something is happening, we can ride out the negative current much more easily and find our way back to the positive one through the practice of gratitude. *A Course* also describes two ways of learning—the path of joy and the path of pain.

When was the last time you felt grateful for the simple conveniences of your life? Think about it. There is so much in our lives to be grateful for that we often fail to recognize. One hundred years ago, most homes in the United States had outhouses instead of indoor plumbing. Today almost every home in America has a working bathroom. Seventy years ago, it was not uncommon to have the central rooms of a house heated by a pot-bellied stove or a single fireplace, and to close off the other rooms until you went to bed. There was also a time when feather mattresses, so soft you would sink in the middle, were used against the cold.

We often take so many things for granted. It is important to learn the art of looking for and appreciating the real blessings of life, great and small. There is an old saying that "a donkey may carry a heavy load of sandalwood on its back without ever knowing its value; all the donkey knows is the weight of the load." Often we, too, may go through life, feeling only the weight of circumstances, failing to recognize the precious nature of life, simply because we may have a chronically negative attitude. Cultivating the attitude of gratitude can lead to self-appreciation and a more positive mental perception of life.

The Japanese have a remarkable sense of appreciation. The story is told of a grower of chrysanthemums who awaited a visit from the emperor to enjoy his blossoms, of which there were hundreds in bloom. The grower selected one magnificent specimen, then cut down all the others, leaving this one perfect flower. The emperor arrived and sat for several hours quietly gazing at this beautiful flower, letting its beauty have its way with him. Can you imagine being so caught up in appreciation of one flower that everything else fades into the background?

The law of gratitude and thanksgiving is considered an aspect of the universe that deals with the flow of energy. That is, as you give out energy, it returns to you. This works in almost every aspect of life. As you give love, love is drawn to you. It may come back in a different form, but it can return when it is given without manipulation. This law of life is about combining the expectations of the mind with the power of the heart. You create a "mold" for something good in your life, and with the power of gratitude, good things are drawn to you as to a magnet.

"Ask, and it will be given you," says Matthew 7:7. Have you ever noticed that when we hoard our resources, such as friendship, help, or affection, the flow of the energy often stops? But as we give love and appreciation, abundance flows to us.

Have you ever wondered what it might be like if we couldn't appreciate the good things in life, such as spirituality, music, art, drama, literature, friends, dance, sports, nature, and all that makes life worth living? Have you ever considered the possibility that gratitude, thanksgiving, and the power of forgiving could be as creative as other works achieved in the world? Every person may not be great according to the terms of the world, but we can be grateful! True appreciation is a fantastic kind of creativity that can lead to spiritual growth. Let us imbue our lives with love and gratitude. Let us use the laws of thanksgiving and forgiving to bless ourselves and others and make our lives more complete.

Thanksgiving opens the door to spiritual growth
—SIR JOHN TEMPLETON

In the magazine *The Clergy Journal,* C. Thomas Hilton tells the story of Ben Weir. Ben Weir was a Presbyterian minister who had recently been released from five hundred days in captivity in Lebanon. He was held hostage by terrorists in solitary confinement for fourteen months. At first he had nothing to read, no conversation with his captors, and he was thrown back upon his own inner resources. Ben described how he began to remember certain passages of Scripture that were significant to him. He recalled favorite hymns. He described how he used the chain that bound him to the room's radiator as a Protestant rosary, whose links he would use at the day's end, or anytime, to count off and remember all the things for which he was thankful. Yes, he really did say thankful! He described his day by saying, "When I awakened in the morning, I usually could hear the birds twittering, or dogs barking, or other sounds of life going on, and I would respond in a spirit of thanksgiving that God had given me another day with health and strength." There can be no doubt that in Ben's situation, thanksgiving truly did open the door to greater spiritual growth.

Is thankfulness a passive attitude? No, it is active. Give thanks! As we've mentioned earlier, the law of giving and receiving is "give and it shall be given unto you." The law is give and then receive, not receive and then give! The giving is the first activity—the giving of our thanks for the good that is already in our world. Can you imagine what would happen if we prefaced our prayers with "Thank you, God, for . . ."? It is possible our entire approach to prayer would be changed, as well as our outlook on life. Gone would be the beseeching prayers, the supplications, and perhaps many tears. Our focus would be transferred from perceptions of lack to appreciation of the abundance in our lives.

If your spirit of thanksgiving seems to be sagging because of anxieties or a variety of worries, try releasing these limiting and restricting attitudes and begin to affirm the right and perfect outcome for whatever the situation may be.

Carl Holmes wrote:

> A habit for all of us to develop would be to look for something to appreciate in everyone we meet. We can all be generous with appreciation. Everyone is grateful for it. It improves every human relationship, it brings new courage to people facing difficulties, and it brings out the best in everyone. So, give appreciation generously whenever you can. You will never regret it.

And is not appreciation an aspect of thanksgiving?

There is something quite powerful and life-giving in the act of giving thanks. It is a lot like recharging a battery. As you open your mind and let your heart sing for joy, you can receive a recharging of spiritual energy in your mind, body, spirit, and activities of your daily life. There is no greater tonic and perhaps no more potent tonic for our spirit than gratitude. When we are grateful for the blessings we already have, our very attitude of gratitude attracts extra good to us. Thanksgiving is like a powerful magnet that can draw to us friends, love, peace, joy, health, and material good.

Yes, it can be easy to give thanks when we are richly showered with good health, a comfortable living, and many wonderful gifts and experiences. But what about being grateful when the days may seem dark and it might be difficult to see our way? Those are the times when it becomes especially important to give thanks! During the "dark and difficult" times, one woman would pause during her day, sit down, and write three things for which she was thankful. They were

(1) being alive, (2) having a good mind, and (3) having the wisdom to say "Thank you, God!"

Count your blessings every day and they will grow and multiply like well-tended plants
—WILLIAM JUNEAU

In his book *The Positive Principle Today*, Dr. Norman Vincent Peale talks about the power of words, or of word combinations, to affect persons and situations. He describes a seven-word combination that has affected many people he has known. This statement demonstrates the power to erase failure, increase strength, eliminate fear, and overcome self-doubt. He says these seven words can help any individual become a more successful human being in the best meaning of that term. That seven-word formula is this: "I can do all things through God." These words indicate an awareness that the creative power of God can be the motivating energy behind our endeavors.

"Thank You, God, for all my good" is another seven-word statement that can propel us forward in wonderful ways. One secret of a grateful heart may be that thanksgiving lifts us into a higher consciousness where we know that life is good. Ask yourself: "Do I take sufficient time to be grateful, to pour out my thanks for all the blessings in my life?" And where do you begin to count your blessings?

The gifts of life and health—what precious gifts!

Family and friends—how bare and perhaps dreary life would be without these!

Food, shelter, clothing, and daily needs—things we so often take for granted, but what would our lives be like without them?

Daily work—whatever that work may be, it can provide an avenue of creative expression for you at this time.

Depressed moments—possibly, but moments only! They pass, and faith can break through like the sun breaking through the clouds.

Wisdom and understanding—the joy of learning and growing in

awareness. Life, in order to move us forward, often confronts us with situations that we can answer or resolve by growing a little wiser.

Peace of mind—and the opportunity to radiate joy, encouragement, good cheer.

Healing—of mind, body, and spirit. Nearly everyone needs some kind of healing at some point in life. When we believe healing is possible and we become open and receptive to the stream of healing life, healing may occur.

If the circumstances of your life reflect joy and happiness, then praise and thanksgiving can open the door to even greater joy and happiness. If the circumstances in your life seem to reflect the other side of the coin, praise and thanksgiving can help you become aware of a new and exciting current of energy flowing within you that can become a living flame that can consume old negative ways of thinking and believing. The product of continual praise and thanksgiving can be a happy, peaceful, joyous, successful new you! Times of seeming struggle, uncertainty, or problems can simply be the growing pains of that new you emerging and, what is incredible, you can praise and give thanks for the growing pains!

Many people who speak of "living life more abundantly" refer to having a greater abundance of things, which include health and strength, work and play, love and friendship, wisdom for today and security for tomorrow. Have you ever considered that abundant living can include another dimension—a dimension that cannot be engendered by the acquisition of things nor eliminated by their absence? This is the dimension of faith, appreciation, and giving thanks.

When we plant a garden, we often mulch and fertilize the soil. We carefully place the tender plants in the ground and continue to care for them regularly until the mature plant provides the harvest—whether of fruits, vegetables, or flowers. When we count our blessings—expressing our appreciation for life, its lessons, and its gifts—they can also grow and multiply like those well-tended plants.

CHAPTER 16

Praying

More is wrought by prayer than this world dreams of
—ALFRED LORD TENNYSON

RAYER IS COMMUNION between God and a person. Prayer can be a way of life rather than a series of isolated acts. It is an attitude of the soul that, at times, expresses itself in words. But prayer can often be most effective when offered silently from within. Prayer is the recognition by your soul of God in everything it does and says. It is the home life of the soul; it is the work of the soul, the deepest reality and creator of everything. It is the source, the center, and the goal. Prayer's eloquence can be expressed in deeds, and its breath rises in aspiration.

Nothing in your life should be foreign to prayer. Everything, both great and small, may be swept within its sacred circle. The circumference of the circle includes the most remote province of your individual life. The heart and mind that recognize and touch God through prayer can tap a limitless reservoir of universal substance that spirit brings forth into powerful demonstrations or manifestations in your life. In truth, you cannot afford not to pray! When you pray, you move away from outer human personality into the great individuality within, which is the real you.

Your times of prayer are food for the soul and can work wonders in

209

your life. Through the action of meditation and prayer, you can learn to practice the presence of God, or begin to see God as everything in the universe. Closer to home, you become aware that your daily life is contained within God. The sincere desire that goes forth from your heart does not return to you void. One important thing to remember is that prayer may not change God, but it certainly can change *your attitude* about God.

Just as the sunlight floods into a darkened room when the curtains and doors are opened, so does the light of Truth pour into your heart when you become open and receptive to the circumstances of life through prayer. Prayer is like dialing a number on your telephone. It can be the conscious connection you make with God. You call; God answers!

When you have established authority over your thoughts, prayer can work for you—not because you command it but because the very nature of the universe has placed you in the driver's seat! Through positive thoughts and feelings, you have aligned yourself in harmony with life. Prayer is a constructive direction, and it adds to your creative and redemptive power of light and love. When prayer is released with understanding and sincerity, it may invoke healing streams of the life force of God.

Some real blocks to success are feelings of insecurity, inferiority, and unworthiness. Prayer can help remove these blocks. There is no place separate from God! Prayer may be your process of affirming this truth. Dreams and visions may manifest and become realities in your life.

Whatever pathway your life may take, you never can leave the presence of God. What a comforting thought! What a boost this awareness can bring to every need and desire! Approach your time of prayer with the intention of experiencing this presence of God for yourself. Know what it feels like. Truth is individually sought, individually prepared for, and individually received. No effort you put forth is lost or wasted. The supreme laws of life measure your efforts, expose your human self, point out errors, show you the simple truth, uplift your spirit, and enfold your mind, body, and soul with the universal embrace of love.

It is a grand truth that "more is wrought by prayer than this world dreams of." The call to prayer is heard in all languages. Every culture in the world, every civilization—regardless of how primitive—has some kind of spiritual activity that may be referred to as a "prayer process."

We can compare ourselves to a wave in the ocean. A wave is simply a part of the ocean expressing itself as a wave. It has no identity outside the ocean. If you look at this idea objectively, you realize that it would be ridiculous for a wave to go looking for the ocean. The one thing the wave cannot find is the ocean, for the two are part of the whole. The human being, like the wave, may be a movement in God, an activity of the infinite universal flow. So when we look, search, and reach for God, or worry about "finding" God, maybe we have, through our thinking, moved out of the flow. We may be looking outside ourselves for that which can be found within. When, through prayer, we become still, release our thought of the outer world, and look within, we may renew our conscious connection with life, creation, and abundance. And the accomplishments may be wondrous to behold!

By prayer you receive spiritual energy
—SIR JOHN TEMPLETON

Most men and women are convinced that there is a divine power of some sort; but many are not sure what it is, nor do they know how to bring this divine presence and power into their daily lives. Throughout the world, and throughout the ages, there have been spiritually enlightened men and women who have described conscious union with God. Everybody in the world knows *God,* but not everyone *knows* God. For many, God has remained a word, a term, a power outside the self. However, more and more people are becoming aware of the Creator in an intimate and personal manner through prayer.

Prayer has been described as a concerted effort by the physical consciousness to become attuned to the consciousness of the Creator, either collectively or individually. Since the beginning of time, prayer, in some form, has been observed in almost every culture recorded and studied. The desire to attune one self toward a higher point of view is an innate part of the human soul. As we grow from childhood to adulthood and our lives become more complex and our concerns more encompassing, prayer often becomes the last resort for many people. We forget the scriptural imperative to "pray without ceasing."

I attribute a large part of my own formula for success to the power of prayer in my daily life. In fact, I begin all my shareholders' and directors' meetings with prayer. Whatever you do in life—whether you get married, bring a case to a court of law, perform surgery on a child, or buy a stock—it is wise to begin with prayer. That prayer should be that God may use you as a clear channel for his wisdom and love.

The four words *Thy will be done* are the most difficult and yet the most important part of any prayer. Sometimes we have a tendency to ask God to do things for us, hoping he will agree that our requests make sense and will grant them. This relationship with God playing the part of a divine fairy godfather may not always work out to our liking, but it doesn't mean God isn't listening. It may mean that God is wiser than we, or we're not fully understanding the meaning of the words *Thy will be done.*

In C. S. Lewis's book *Letter to Malcolm: Chiefly on Prayer*, he notes that *Thy will be done* doesn't necessarily mean we must submit to disagreeable things that God has in store for us, but rather that there is a great deal of God's will to be done by his creatures. The petition, then, is not merely that we may patiently suffer God's will, but also that we may vigorously *do it*. Lewis also notes the tendency to overlook the good that God offers us because, at that moment, we may have expected something else. But that doesn't necessarily mean some prayers aren't answered, only that God is wiser than we.

By communicating with God on a regular basis, we may receive guidance and the power to understand as well as receiving an increase of energy to do his will. The more we talk with God, the more he reveals himself to us.

In his book *My Favorite Quotations*, Dr. Norman Vincent Peale wrote the following about prayer:

> If you want to utilize the matchless power of prayer, begin praying immediately and continue at every opportunity. I have observed from a number of enquiries that the average person probably spends about five minutes a day in prayer. That is one-half of 1 percent of one's waking hours. Back in the days of Prohibition in the United States, half of 1 percent alcohol was declared by act of Congress to be nonintoxicating. That percentage is also nonintoxicating in religion! If you want to experience the heady energy of prayer, practice it more often. The physician, Alexis Carrel, a spiritual pioneer, advised praying everywhere: in the street, the office, the shop, the school. You can transform spare moments by praying for your need, for everyone and everything you can think of. Then believe that your prayers will be answered. They will be. And prayer is always answered in one of three ways: no, yes, or wait a while.

The family that prays together, stays together
—COMMON SAYING

What images come to your mind as you think of a family praying together? It might be a family of pilgrims giving thanks that their table is full, or a modern family in the face of a crisis. How can the average family apply this principle to their lives and why would they want to?

Let's take a look at this old adage and begin by examining prayer. Charles Fillmore, cofounder of Unity School of Christianity in the United States, speaks of prayer as "entering the silence." He says, "There is a quiet place within us all and by silently saying over and over, 'peace be still,' we shall enter that quiet place and a great stillness will pervade our whole being." So to pray could mean to go into the silent place within ourselves and commune with something wise within us, the result of which can bring peace.

The silent communion may look different to each of us. It isn't so important how we enter the silence as it is that we do. In his booklet *The Golden Key*, Emmet Fox described prayer as "the golden key to harmony and happiness":

> Scientific prayer will enable you to get yourself, or anyone else, out of any difficulty. . . . The ability to draw on this power is not the special prerogative of the mystic or the saint, as is so often supposed, or even of the highly trained practitioner. Everyone has this ability. . . . This is because in scientific prayer it is God who works, and not you, and so your particular limitations or weaknesses are of no account in the process. . . . As for the actual method of working, like all fundamental things, it is simplicity itself. All you have to do is this: Stop thinking about the difficulty, whatever it is, and think about God instead.

When we pray with our families, whether they consist of our relatives or a family of our closest friends, we go together to a silent place of wisdom and peace. It is an experience that can mend hurt feelings, calm anger, encourage love and forgiveness, and help us to remember how important we are to one another.

For a family, prayer can happen when there are no longer words to speak. If you've ever come home feeling hurt or afraid and someone has quietly held your hand, you have entered into the silent place together. Maybe, when you were a child, you sat with your brothers and sisters on a special holiday, feeling warm and safe together or, when you were older, took a quiet walk through the woods with a favorite friend. These are some ways of communing together in prayer. As a family begins consciously to make the choice to pray together in their own way, conflict begins to resolve itself and love increases.

You have the most powerful weapons on earth—love and prayer
—SIR JOHN TEMPLETON

You may be familiar with the inspirational writing called *The Desiderata*. Although the entire writing is exquisitely presented, one statement in particular can be quite beneficial. It states, "Go placidly amid the noise and the haste." This could be particularly relevant to life in a big city with all its hustle, rush, and sometimes confusion, and equally meaningful for smaller towns and areas when we seem to get caught up in the "busyness" of daily life. An important thing to remember is that whatever kind of confusion may be around you, what is within your own consciousness is what counts. And you have available two of the most powerful tools to use—love and prayer.

In the New Testament, Jesus admonishes his followers to "become as little children" and to "love your enemies." No two commands may be more difficult to follow in today's world, confronted as we are with our own negative thoughts, whether in business, within our family, or among our friends. And yet, throughout history, it seems almost impossible not to notice the success of those who have acted on the courage of their convictions to "love thy neighbor as thyself."

Most people now understand the term "the laws of nature," the multitude of principles discovered by scientists, primarily in the last four centuries, explaining or describing the physical universe. However, as mentioned in my book *The Humble Approach*, not everyone yet understands the phrase "the laws of the spirit." There is a difference between laws of the spirit and religious laws, such as those formulated by Moses, Hammurabi, Muhammad, and other ancient lawgivers. More benefits may result in the domains of the spirit if each individual drew up his own personal list of the laws governing spiritual matters. It may be that when we understand and claim as our own some actual laws of the spirit—such as love and prayer—that we begin to build our own heaven.

Once we understand how to express this love to others through our own lives, we may then be better able to direct our prayers to make God's priorities our own. As we learn to share and give and care, love increases. A person who knows how to love does not seem to feel lonely or alone. In this sense, the power of love can become a true weapon against harm. As a friend of mine is fond of saying, "Love given is love received," and happiness is a by-product of that kind of love. This law of life, when put to use through loving expressions and prayer, can guide us in fulfilling our every aspiration, as well as enriching the lives of those around us.

Your prayers can be answered by "yes," but also by "no," and by "alternatives"
—RUTH STAFFORD PEALE

Let's look at this possibility from three perspectives. First, when we become very still and ask for guidance, we may be directed, clearly and unmistakably, with a "yes" or a "no," and often in a way that may not require us to make a decision. Perhaps on an inner level, our decision may have already been made. Even though the immediate result appears to be a failure, or a "no" answer to our prayer, the successful outcome can eventually be revealed by life itself.

Second, when we have done our work, when we have prayed and then followed our inner guidance, we can continue about our daily routines with the assurance that the manifestation of the desires of our heart may progress according to God's perfect plan. This awareness often brings a wonderful feeling of peace and serenity as we trust the flow of divine order in our lives.

Third, a most significant lesson for us may be to realize that no matter how impossible a situation seems, no matter how desperate the circumstances may appear, there can be a blessing for us and for others concerned. And that blessing may come in a manner we have not thought about! These can be alternative possibilities in answer to our prayers.

Sometimes, when our prayers seem to go unanswered, we may feel that we are not in tune with the timeless, unlimited universal Creator called God. But nothing can be separate from God. Everything that touches you, everything that touches each individual in the universe, is a part of God. Scripture tells us that every hair on our head is numbered. We become more aware of God's infinite love as we tune into the silent place within, the realm of God's creation. The divine ideas we receive from God in the silence are like manna from heaven. They pour forth through us ever new, ever alive, ever beautiful, ever more wonderful every day.

We can realize God's presence in our lives as love, wisdom, health, and happiness. We can observe God's presence in the events of our lives as we move safely and easily through many trials. Trials can help us grow, and may come into our lives to offer a greater realization of God's presence and power. As we maintain our trust and peace, our problems are more likely to be solved—sometimes in a mysterious manner, sometimes even at the eleventh hour!

When we allow ourselves to be Spirit-filled, we move into an area of trust and confidence that helps our prayers to be answered. It matters not whether the answer is "yes," "no," or an "alternative," because we can go forward in confidence, if our actions are in tune with the Infinite.

CHAPTER 17

Awakening Spiritual Growth

It is by forgetting self that one finds self
—ST. FRANCIS

UCH IN LIFE depends on the view we take of it. Is it a gently flowing river with trees growing along the bank, or is it people strolling on a sandy beach, or perhaps walking in the midst of a bustling city? The look of things changes as you take a close-up, or a distant, view. When our thoughts are directed toward giving in some manner to others, we expand the horizons of our perspective.

Because we are part of life, we have experiences that are part of life. Some of these may be easy; some of them may seem more difficult. The easy experiences we can meet with rejoicing and the tough experiences we can meet triumphantly. For it is in our nature—as dreamers and builders—not necessarily to accept things as they may appear, but to change them into something better. When we forget self and let sincere caring and love flow from our hearts to others, we have an opportunity to turn a wilderness into a garden, to make the desert bloom, to build dikes against the sea, to change poverty into abundance, sickness into health, war into peace, and to remake ourselves and our world closer to our hearts' desire. We can live in the heart of love, whose infinite compassion encompasses all people, places, and things.

A unique example of putting others first is given by Charles E. Harvey Jr. in a story in *Reader's Digest*. He told about driving for an important job interview and running about fifteen minutes late when he saw a middle-aged woman stranded by the side of the road with a flat tire. His conscience prompted him to stop. He changed the tire and headed for the interview, thinking that he could probably forget about getting the job. Nevertheless, he filled out the job application and went into the personnel director's office. Imagine his surprise when the personnel director hired him on the spot. She was the woman whose tire he had changed on the way to the interview!

Edward was fifty-two years old when he finally admitted that he was an alcoholic. Like many before him, he knew that Alcoholics Anonymous was his only remaining option. It was a move he felt reluctant to make, however. Edward did not want to admit defeat, although he seemed thoroughly beaten, not only physically but also emotionally. He felt embarrassed that others might know he was an alcoholic, although, in fact, everyone who knew him well was aware of his condition.

After a few weeks of attending AA meetings, the fog began to clear from his mind. He kept hearing the strange phrase "You've got to give it away to keep it." The *it* was sobriety, and AA told him that once he attained it, he would have to share it with others. Unfortunately, Edward was a self-centered and selfish individual at that time. He thought to himself, "No way. Whatever it is, as soon as I get it, I'm going to hold on to it and keep it for myself!"

When we hoard things instead of passing them on, they often become of less value. When we choose to get beyond our personal self and act with a loving, generous spirit, then we receive what we're giving away. And more.

But how can we help someone become something he doesn't want to be, or give him something he may not want to receive, even if he may ultimately benefit from it? Perhaps the best way is to lead by example. If we are willing to perform a service for another, others may be more likely to replicate our actions. And now a paradox comes into play. For example, someone who finds it difficult to receive love may not be able to give love. The first step in giving is to receive God's love in order to give it away, for we cannot give what we do not have. In order to be a true giver, our motives for giving must be pure. Give because you genuinely want to give. Give because you believe in life. Give willingly and joyfully, and peace and joy will be your reward.

Let us return to Edward, who truly changed through the gifts that others shared with him. He became an avid sharer of experience, strength, hope, time, and love. He learned to give to others that which was given to him with an open heart and hand. Sometimes what he gives may not be accepted, but the good he is trying to give away returns to him in some manner.

So the ripples of love and giving from the stone thrown in the pond move out, and those of us privileged to watch and experience this movement play a vital role in passing on the good we receive so others may benefit. And when others benefit, so do we.

Laugh and the world laughs with you; weep, and you weep alone
—ELLA WHEELER WILCOX

While there are times when it may not be appropriate to giggle or laugh aloud, your genuine smile is never out of place. Can you think of a time or place when the world could use a little more light and love? Every person has the capacity to bring these vital qualities to life with a smile. While not all of us smile in the same situations or in the same way, we can bring a little more warmth into a sometimes cold world with a smile that brings forth the best part of us. The smile we bring to a difficult challenge in life may infuse it with the light of understanding and with love, which can attract harmonious solutions. It may also inspire those around us to respond in a similar manner. Our smile can make a difference wherever we are!

Studies have shown that it takes far fewer facial muscles to smile than it does to frown. The choice to smile in a trying time may be a decision to take life in a way that is lighter on you and loving to everyone around you. A smile is often the expression of a grateful person. A smile can show your willingness to relax, enjoy the moment, and share in a good feeling no matter what stressful circumstances may be testing you. And when you take life more easily, life may be easier on you, for the energy you might have spent on a frown is freed for more useful purposes.

The spirit to whistle when we may not feel like whistling, the heart to sing when we may not feel like a song, the faith to affirm the goodness of God when we may see few visible facts to justify our affirmation—from these often has greatness sprung, and with these attributes have many victories of life been won. A happy heart may not assure you that you have no difficulties to meet in life's journey or that the world will laugh with you. It does assure you of a happy heart with which to meet each experience that blesses your life. And a happy heart can bear life's strains without falling apart.

Taking it easy could be good advice when you are faced with a difficult situation. Others may not express a great deal of interest in what is happening in your world, and you may feel that you are totally on your own. Your eyes may fill with tears, and laughter and happy times may seem far away at the moment. Being on your own does not mean being deserted. It does not mean that you are without help. It does not mean that you are truly alone. Being on your own may be perceived as important to growth, important to maturity, and important to the expression of your God-given powers and possibilities. Even when we are alone we have God's *power* within us; we have God's *Spirit* always with us. To know this can make the difference between feeling devastated by circumstances or being filled with an awareness of strength and confidence in our ability to carry on and rise above self-doubts. A smile of quiet confidence can return to our faces.

Birds of a feather flock together
—ROBERT BURTON

Often the way we talk, eat, and work arises from observing other people. Thus, if we want good role models, it makes sense to associate with people who display the characteristics we desire. Albert Einstein interpreted this law of life in a similar way. Although many regard Einstein as a peculiar and solitary eccentric, he wasn't. While Einstein was working on his first theory of relativity, he often invited friends to his home, where they discussed physics, philosophy, and literature. Einstein wanted to know all about these things, so he surrounded himself with a group of people who understood these subjects. Thus, Einstein never wasted his time deciding whether it was good to be in one group or another. Instead, he formed his own group of people whom he admired and could use as role models.

It is natural to enjoy the companionship of others of like mind. Like attracts like is a master law of life dealing with the attraction between ourselves and other individuals, places, things, and conditions. We accomplish this linking or connection through our thoughts and beliefs. Most of us are familiar with magnets that attract or cling to a piece of steel or other magnets. Physics teaches us that two magnets can be attracted to each other by their magnetic fields. It has been scientifically established that these invisible fields exist within and outside the body of the magnets. Two such magnets, properly oriented and even some distance apart, will draw together because of the attracting force of the fields between them.

A second law of life applies in cases in which a search for balance exists: as you seek, you attract and are attracted to what will enable you to find what you're looking for. In view of this, it is logical that people who are thinking along similar lines are drawn together. It is also a universal principle that you may attract the ability to become that which you innately desire to be. God knows your potential and provided that innate desire for fulfillment through the use of your talents and abilities. As you recognize and accept that desire, the energy of your mind begins to work in various areas to attract and build the abilities that you need in order to fulfill your desire.

Can you imagine life as an artist, constructing a picture of each of us? We are life's canvas, its colors, its brushes. Artists love their colors and enjoy combining them in skillfully contrasted and integrated ways to increase and vary the forms of beauty. Life loves to paint the picture of God's idea of you on the canvas of your selfhood. Authorities estimate that there are seven billion human beings on this planet, and life needs every one of us to express itself, for life is infinite. Is it any wonder, then, that some of us will be drawn together by the magnetic pull of similarity and the brushstrokes of blending the colors of people, events, and situations into magnificent expressions of God's creativity on life's canvas?

We carry within us the wonders that we seek without us
—ERIC BUTTERWORTH

When you were a baby, you may have been aware of your own needs and desires and nothing beyond them. If you needed food or a dry diaper, you didn't care whether your parents were asleep or needed time to finish their own meal; you simply demanded what you wanted. As you grew, confident that your survival needs would be met, you moved on to other aspects of the world around you. Have you ever watched a baby playing with her toes and fingers? Therein lies a fascinating exploration of a whole new world. You did that as a child, too, and as you gained mastery over each little bit of your physical world, you continued your explorations.

During your childhood, you were perhaps mostly concerned with your parents' expectations. When you started school, you also became concerned with your teachers' expectations. During adolescence, you may have became preoccupied with what your peers thought about you. As an adult, you may have had many opportunities to experiment with creating a satisfying life. Each of these stages prepared you for the time when you could discover the deeper truth: what really makes the difference in the way you experience life is what you believe *about* yourself and what you believe *is possible* for yourself.

The love and approval we first seek from our parents and family, then from other authorities, such as teachers, then finally from our friends, can be felt and experienced more easily if we love and approve of ourselves.

Can you remember an incident from your childhood when you worked very hard to accomplish something? You felt proud, good about yourself; and if your parents or someone else told you how well you did, you knew they were right. You felt affirmed.

Can you now see that what happened was that others merely affirmed what was true about you? Your feeling of value did not come *from* them but was merely confirmed *by* them.

If you are fortunate, you had a teacher or a mentor whom you admired and from whom you wanted to learn. Sometimes you may feel you could never be like that admired person, but you can. The fact that you are attracted to that person can be proof you have the capacity to express some qualities you so admire in another. It works the other way as well. Sometimes we may feel repelled by or hateful toward another. Those feelings can be inner warnings that we, too, may be capable of behaving in that same unattractive manner. At such times, it becomes important to recognize that you can choose to express the loving, kind, caring qualities you possess.

One of the greatest gifts we have to give to humanity and the world can be our own growing consciousness of life. As we rejoice in the refreshing currents of life that flow through us mentally, emotionally, physically, and spiritually, we can bless our world and everyone in it. But we are not likely to rise any higher than we believe we can. And we have such a wide variety of beliefs to choose from that we may sometimes get confused. However, if we believe we are made in the image and likeness of God, a life-giving spirit and therefore master of life, we can seek to develop those wonders within!

Because, as children, our needs are basic and are met by others, it may be easy to believe others always have the answers for us. As we grow and our needs change, we can come to recognize that we have within us everything we need to create lives of joy, usefulness, wonder, and value.

You can build your own heaven or hell on earth
—SIR JOHN TEMPLETON

As a child, do you remember asking the question, "Where do people go when they die?" It may have been an unsettling question, and perhaps you hoped to receive a reassuring answer. The response from adults may have been that "people go to heaven or hell." This statement could have been puzzling enough for you to ask the inevitable next question, "What is that and where is it?"

Many people believed that heaven was a place up in the sky filled with harp-playing angels, where a white-bearded God sat on his throne and made judgments about who had been good and bad, and doled out rewards and punishments accordingly. Hell may have been defined as a fiery pit, where the devil, a horrifying apparition with red skin, horns, a tail, and a pitchfork, made life miserable for the bad people who got sent there. Heaven was where the good people would go to live in eternal bliss, while the bad people would burn in hell forever.

Because, to a child, hell may have seemed like such a frightening alternative, it was important to be as good as possible so we could be assured of a place in heaven, where we would be happy and our needs would be met. However, as we grew and were challenged by the complexities of adult life, we may have begun to doubt whether a reward for our behavior, such as heaven, or a punishment like hell, even existed.

The definitive descriptions of the afterlife we received as children could possibly call for some refinement in light of scientific discoveries of the modern age and our increased sophistication of thought. With maturity, our concepts of heaven and hell may have evolved.

A number of philosophers offer a variety of definitions and descriptions of heaven and hell. Charles Fillmore, cofounder of the Unity Movement, describes heaven as "a state of consciousness in harmony with the thoughts of God. It is the orderly, lawful adjustment of God's kingdom in man's mind, body, and affairs." To him:

> [Hell] symbolizes that purifying fire which consumes the dross of man's character; a corrective state of mind. When error has reached its limit, the retroactive law asserts itself, and judgment, being part of that law, brings the penalty, called hell, upon the transgressor. This penalty is not punishment, but discipline.

The Bhagavad Gita states the following: "Hell has three gates: lust, anger, and greed." Mencius, a Chinese philosopher, wrote: "Heaven sees as the people see. Heaven hears as the people hear."

At times, despite our best and most positive intentions, the experience of heaven may seem to elude us, and the experience of hell may seem to pursue us. This often happens if we compare what we have with what others have and feel either superior or inferior to them. In subtle ways, we may become like yo-yos, with our emotions yanked up or down by the state of someone else's fortune. We may become obsessed by the *form* rather than the *content* of life.

If we judge only the outer appearances of anything, we can create a private hell that permeates the various areas of our lives. To the extent that we look outside ourselves for heaven, we may possibly create a hell of discontent and dissatisfaction for ourselves. What we really want is not "out there," and we may exhaust ourselves in searching hither and yon. We may rail against the world or other people in frustration, but the very real place where we can experience heaven is within our own hearts.

There is an ancient legend about three men, each of whom carried two sacks that were tied around their necks, one in front and one in back. When the first man was asked what was in his sacks, he said:

All my friends' kind deeds are in the sack on my back where they're hidden from sight and soon forgotten. The sack in front carries all the unkind things that have happened to me; and as I walk along, I often stop, take those things out, and look at them from various angles. I concentrate on them and study them. I direct all my thoughts and feelings toward them.

Consequently, because the first man was frequently stopping to mull over unfortunate things that had happened to him in the past, he made little progress.

When the second man was asked what he was carrying in his two sacks, he replied:

In the front sack are all my good deeds. I keep those before me and continually take them out and flash them around for everyone to see. The sack in the rear holds all my mistakes. I carry them with me wherever I go. They're heavy and slow me down, but for some reason I just can't put them aside.

The third man, when asked about his two sacks, replied:

The front sack is full of wonderful thoughts about people, the kind deeds they've done, and all the good I've had in my life. It's a big sack and very full, but it isn't heavy. The weight is like the sails on a ship—far from being a burden, it helps move me onward. The sack on my back is empty because I have cut a big hole in the bottom of it. In that sack, I put all the evil I hear about others and all the bad thoughts I sometimes have about myself. Those things fall through the hole in the sack and are lost forever, so I have no weight to make my journey more difficult.

From time to time, as each of us journeys along the path of life, it is important to examine what we are carrying with us. Are we weighted down by negative thoughts about ourselves? Are we weighted down by lumps of fear that tell us we may not measure up to some artificial standard? Are we weighted down by protective shields and psychological armor that may prevent us from relating to others in a free and wholehearted manner? Do we carry with us those misdeeds of friends and family that may have caused us distress in the past? Do we carry with us false lessons that teach us to look for undesirable characteristics in others and then run the other way when we think we detect one of those characteristics? Are we making our lives a heaven or a hell?

Each of us is born with the freedom to choose the thoughts that direct our lives. We may choose the path we want to walk and what we wish to carry along the way. With this awareness in mind, would it not be preferable to choose thoughts that can form positive attitudes and emphasize our unlimited potential? Negative thoughts and attitudes weigh us down and make our journey through life more difficult.

Our innate goodness is an essential fact of our existence and cannot be taken from us. Neither can it be given to us by someone else. When we perceive this truth, we experience heaven on earth. When we experience heaven within, we naturally are inclined to share that heaven with others through a pure, generous outlook and a loving, positive attitude.

The pen is mightier than the sword
—E. G. BULWER-LYTTON

Some of the old sayings we often hear may not be true. For example, "Sticks and stones may break my bones, but words will never hurt me!" could be 180 degrees off the mark. Sticks and stones *do* hurt; but so do unkind words, and the healing process from damage done by harsh words can take much longer. Wounds to the body can be visible where they may be more easily treated. Wounds caused by harsh words are often hidden inside us, and we may think or pretend they don't hurt. Words can be powerful because we believe them or fear that others believe them.

An emaciated beggar stopped Count Leo Tolstoy, who was out for an evening stroll. The great author, so the story goes, perceiving that the man was hungry, groped through his pockets for some money to give him but found not a single cent. Tolstoy was distraught at his inability to help the man. He took the beggar's worn and dirty hands in his, lamenting, "Forgive me, brother. I have nothing with me to give you." The pale, tired face of the beggar lit up. "Oh, but you have just given me a great gift." He smiled. "You called me brother!"

Perhaps it would be helpful to consider the creative essence of speech, which, scripture tells us, has its derivation in the creative power of sound. In Genesis, God "speaks" the universe into existence: "Let there be light. . . . Let there be a firmament." With a similar potency the Gospel of John begins: "In the beginning was the Word."

Some theologians describe the "word" as God's creative essence ensouling, permeating, informing, and conveying creative energy through all living things, here and now. Could there be a correspondence between the "word of God" and our spoken words? Perhaps we may recall instances when someone spoke sharply to us and we felt the "sting" of harsh words. Fortunately, we can do something to change the hurt. Because the hurt is an inner response, we can turn within to find help.

Remember, your spirit is powerful. It takes words and ideas, sorts them, and provides guidance on how to act and feel. If you remain poised and balanced, putting forth your best effort every day, speaking your most loving and caring words, and, under all circumstances, remaining compassionate, kind, and generous with those you meet on life's journey and if you continue doing your best work and thinking your best thoughts every day, you can meet life with an awareness that can help you take appropriate and successful action.

Keep your mind open to receiving lots of positive messages and loving thoughts because they can be powerful fuel. Be aware of the words that go into your mind, both conscious and unconscious, because words and ideas can be great tools for your mind to use in making appropriate decisions. Remember that a statement spoken in spiritual consciousness can contain great spiritual power. Speaking powerful words of love changes things and outer circumstances as well as consciousness itself.

If we desire to become instruments of a higher consciousness, the laws of life can offer some guidelines to help us attune our words to God's Word. How? Let's look at some things we can do.

1. Speak words of prayer to identify yourself with God.
2. Aim for honest relations with yourself and others.
3. Refrain from gossip and speak only words of truth.
4. Become observant of yourself, of how you write and speak.
5. Speak of others as you would want others to speak of you.
6. Decide for yourself how you choose to respond to whatever judgments or criticisms may come your way. Your spirit and mind belong to you.

We must tap into our spirituality. A soap manufacturer and a minister were talking one day as they strolled along a street. The soap manufacturer raised the question of what various religions have accomplished for the world. He said, "People continue to hate, fight, cheat, and steal, and the world seems no better than if there were no religions."

The minister reflected on his companion's words and pointed to a small boy who was playing in the mud along the gutter, "Look at that little fellow," he commented. "He is covered with dirt. I don't see that soap has done him a bit of good. Look at all the dirty people in the world. Would the world be better off without soap?"

The soap manufacturer replied indignantly, "Well, of course not. Everybody knows that soap is good. You have to use it!"

The minister smiled. "And so it is with spiritual truth. You have to use it to receive the greatest benefits!"

Nothing can bring you peace but yourself
—RALPH WALDO EMERSON

The Bible scripture John 14:27 (KJV) states: "Peace I leave with you, my peace I give unto you. Not as the world giveth, give I unto you. Let not your heart be troubled, neither let it be afraid." These comforting words, attributed to Jesus, seem to indicate that the world can give us a certain kind of peace. It can offer us a lovely country place, away from the hustle and bustle of the city; a quiet and beautiful park tucked amid the city's activities; a peaceful, scenic beach upon which to stroll; or a distant mountaintop where all is serene and still. Although we may travel to faraway places, the journey is made in the company of our own consciousness, and we return home with ourselves. We cannot get away from our own inner being. If we have a problem, we take it with us wherever we may go. On the other hand, if our consciousness is imbued with gentle serenity, then it can also be imbued with power—quiet, inner power.

One way to be successful in the world is to go forth to do what is ours to do with peace in our consciousness. This peacefulness is a state of receptivity that can allow us to be more open to other people. How can we get in touch with this inner peace? A simple exercise can help. Reserve some time each day—even a few minutes can be beneficial—in which you can be alone and undisturbed. Sit in a comfortable chair, close your eyes, breathe deeply and slowly, and let your mind and body relax. Repeat slowly to yourself, "I am now letting go. I am now letting go." Mentally release the events of the day, one by one, until you feel yourself moving into a realm of stillness and peace.

This place of inner stillness and quiet is termed the "Silence." A minister friend described it in this manner:

> In the Silence, we enter an elevated state of awareness, of heightened receptivity, a time of being fully alive to the moment. It may sound strange, but when we are in the Silence, we do absolutely nothing. We are content just to *be*,

and we luxuriate in the ecstasy of being consciously with God. The Silence is a time of stillness when we think neither of the past nor of the future. It is a state when we are detached from the ordinary world. If we are thinking about business, troubled relationships, or any other problem, we are not in the Silence. And yet, although we are not thinking about ideas, concepts, or perceptions, we remain alert. Our receptivity and sensitivity are increased. It is truly an ineffable experience; words are inadequate to describe it.

Anwar Sadat, Egyptian military and political leader, understood the power of peace when he said, "Peace is much more precious than a piece of land." He spoke of the peace that cannot be bought, but that is available to us all, if we so choose. As new buildings and structures may be created from new plans and materials, so, too, can new thought structures be built. Through our peaceful thoughts, prayers, and activities, we can build a consciousness of peace.

There may be times in the life of every person when he feels the presence of the Creator and becomes aware, in one way or another, of an actual transcendental Presence, Power, and Peace. With this awareness often come a liberation and a freedom from negative thoughts and things of this world: its fears, doubts, cares, and problems. The degree of transformation may be immediately apparent in the visible realm, but, bit by bit, it becomes evident in the outer world as well.

Jesus acknowledged this truth and taught about the existence of an inner peace that "passes all understanding," a peace that is not dependent on outer circumstances. As you discover this inner realm for yourself, you eventually realize that it is the only real peace you can ever have. You don't have to travel far to find it; you need only look deeply within yourself. External events can change at a moment's notice and what you thought was peace may suddenly evaporate. But once it's yours, true peace will remain with you—even in the midst of a rapidly changing world. The depth of increasing inner peace can continue to bring forth greater spiritual light, wisdom, and guidance, so that every day is a day of deeper discernment.

You are more defined by what comes out of your mouth than by what goes in
—ANONYMOUS

A middle-aged man attended a male therapy support group one evening when he felt he was at his lowest ebb. His wife was leaving him. His business was teetering near bankruptcy. He had gained weight over the last few years, and his self-esteem wasn't very high. Even his hair was thinning!

The moderator explained the group's purpose for that evening. They would go around in a circle and each man would take a few minutes to explain what wasn't working in his life. On the second round, the participants would discuss what they were going to do to change these situations.

The middle-aged man listened patiently as each of the other group members spoke. When it was his turn to unburden himself, he believed that his was one of the saddest stories in the room. A secret part of him felt almost proud to be so pathetic. As the sharing continued around the circle, the man found himself trying to second-guess why the other group members had come. As he looked around the circle, he noticed that the last person was a handsome young man about twenty years old.

Why, he thought, would such a young man be here? The youngster's face looked sympathetic as he nodded at each person's story. When the time came for him to speak, he was smiling.

"My friends," he said almost wistfully, "I have been diagnosed with terminal cancer." The gasp was audible in the room. "My doctors have given me three to six months to live. I have struggled with this awareness for a month now and have finally made a decision." His voice gained self-confidence as it grew. "I am going to take flying lessons!"

The words hung in the air. *Flying lessons?*

"I have chosen to live!"

The middle-aged man drew in his breath. His mind flew over all the imaginary reasons he had created for this young man to have spoken, realizing that each of them had been trite and pretentious next to the reality of his plight. Then his thoughts rested, for the first time without self-pity, on his own small problems. He felt almost ashamed.

This young man was dying. He would not have a chance to live a long life. "I've lived more than twice the boy's number of years," the man thought to himself, "and what have I really done with my life?" Yet here was a young man, facing a critical situation, with almost a look of triumph, a look of—could he say it?—joy. And what had the young man said? He chose to live!

When the man left the meeting that night, he and the other members of the circle had once again taken up their torch of believing in their own lives. They had seen light in another and had heard words of truth spoken. They were reminded that they had a choice about how they might carry their burdens.

Each of us carries who and what we are within and with us. Sometimes this can be quite visible on the faces of those we pass on the street. At other times, it may be more subdued and hidden from even the most discerning eyes. We cannot know what has happened to another person unless we have truly walked in that person's shoes. But how we perceive a person may often be determined by what that person says. How many times have you seen people who may be lovely in appearance yet speak with language that would curl a sailor's toes?

The Bible says, "Hear and understand: not what goes into the mouth defiles a man, but what comes out of the mouth, this defiles a man" (Matt. 15:10, 11). The sacred Hindu Kaushitaki Upanishads express the wisdom of looking beyond the spoken words in this statements: "Speech is not what one should desire to understand. One should know the speaker." Again, in Psalms, we are made aware of the importance of our words: "Let the words of my mouth, and the meditation of my heart, be acceptable in thy sight, O LORD, my strength, and my redeemer" (Ps. 19:14, KJV).

We are living in a marvelous time when humanity appears to be awakening to a greater awareness of our spirituality. Paralleling this inner awakening often come discoveries in various areas of human endeavor—psychology, physics, science, religion. We are learning that our words can be instruments with which we build and shape our world. In this context, doesn't it seem possible that a statement spoken in spiritual consciousness can have great spiritual power? When we speak affirmations in a time of prayer, we identify ourselves more closely with God.

The spoken word can be like an arrow shot from a bow. It cannot be recalled. We may have said things we regretted, either at the time we made the comment or later. "My words declare the uprightness of my heart, and what my lips know they speak sincerely," proclaims the writer of Job 33:3. Right now can be a good time to begin to exercise the utmost care in the selection and formation of our thoughts and, particularly, our words and speech. We can avoid using words that are negative, ugly, and harmful. We can make it a point to express ourselves in a harmonious, cheerful, tactful, and caring manner. We can avoid gossip, falsehood, and careless and unnecessary talk. We can refrain from trying to force our viewpoint on others through too much talking. Being aware of our words is one way we can add to life only that which may bless and uplift. Remember what an impact the young man's words, "I have chosen to live," made on the therapy group? Who knows how many lives may have been affected, directly or indirectly, by that one simple statement? Who knows the effect your words may have on another? Choose them well!

The greatness is not in me; I am in the greatness
—ANONYMOUS

Sunlight travels ninety-three million miles in a little over eight minutes to reach Earth. It is tasteless, odorless, and, unless a rainbow occurs, invisible. Prismatic droplets of mist can make what was there all along suddenly visible. The rainbow can be a powerful symbol, reminding us that the unseen world holds many treasures for those whose eyes are open.

Many material goods may be designed to distract us from feeling sad when it could be important to our well-being to grieve a loss. Outer appearances may disguise our errors when greater good could come from admitting a mistake. The moment our welfare seems threatened, many of us may rush to the nearest commodity center for a "fix," expecting money to buy for us what it cannot buy—spiritual happiness.

Eventually, though, stabilizing forces bring us back into balance—just as gravity acts on a pendulum's swing. These forces may come in the form of an economic recession, a job transfer, a change in our home life, or a health crisis. These setbacks may be important opportunities to grow spiritually.

Not that a person cannot be materially wealthy and spiritually enriched at the same time. It is not gold or silver in themselves that may be dangerous but rather our attachments to them. We need to ask ourselves, "With what consciousness and purpose do I utilize the things in my world? Am I a slave of materialism, or a good trustee, acting selflessly and ethically in the handling of my worldly assets?"

Apart from its ability to serve the legitimate trading needs of humanity, money can be meaningless. And spiritual belief, divorced from the tangible world, can be naïve. True happiness often comes from bringing a wonderfully creative idea from the world of spirit into the world of matter, enjoying the benefit it can bring others, and then reclaiming it through gratitude. Furthermore, spiritual affluence can operate under some of the same universal principles as material wealth. The physical objects in our everyday world may be merely the manifestations of their spiritual essence. The flow between the spiritual and the material world needs to be honored if we are to live fully and with purpose.

Ultimately, money can be a convenience for organizing and

harmonizing human enterprise. Material wealth can be directed for this higher purpose. We are not the *source* of generosity and fruitful acts. We can be the *vessels* through which these virtues may be poured upon humanity. We are the overseers, rather than the owners of earthly resources.

When we begin to act out of this knowledge of the heart, the masks that conceal truth fall away. Desiring a new car can often be an awareness that the old car no longer functions satisfactorily. When this is recognized, the "newness" of the car becomes secondary. Moving from a larger home to a smaller place may reflect a need to simplify life. Far more than a setback, it can be a reordering of priorities.

If we happen to be spellbound by materialism, all may not be lost. Is not the breaking of a spell often the turning point of many great tales? We can think of the days that may have seemed enchanted as the world initiating us in lessons of abundance and the secrets of the rainbow.

The wise person looks within his heart and finds eternal peace
—HINDU PROVERB

Withdrawing from the world either physically or emotionally does not seem to be the wise person's path to eternal peace. We are placed in this world to deal with it, not escape it; to integrate ourselves with it, not separate into a fragment apart from it; and to find a way to be of benefit and service to the world, not to shun it or harden ourselves to it. However, if you are willing to be present in the world and involved with it, your emotions may not always feel peaceful. We have both positive and negative feelings in our hearts, and our life experiences tend to stir up both. How, then, is it possible to find peace within your heart?

We tend to feel at peace when things are under control. And we do the best we can to control or manage our lives according to our ideas of order. But if inner peace depends on that control, your peace of mind could frequently be at risk. Can you control the economy or energy supplies? Another person's behavior or actions? The choices and destinies of loved ones or others on whom you depend? When you take a long, honest, and sincere look, there may be very little outside yourself that you can control. Therefore, real peace must be an inside job!

A person is truly wise who knows that the heart is the place where lasting peace may be found. The changeability from one day to the next of your personal world, or the world at large, may make the larger world an unreliable source of peace. Try going away to that mountaintop, or to any place that seems serene and carefree to you, and you can still find yourself disturbed over something—a memory, a concern about a current situation, a fear about the future, or a mere gnat flying around—if you fail to realize that peace dwells at the center of your being.

When your world goes topsy-turvy and turmoil threatens, try this exercise. Think about tranquility. Let the screen of your mind reflect whatever the word *tranquility* may bring. A gentle meadow in warm summer sunlight. A placid blue lake at dusk. A fragile butterfly lightly touching a flower. Cool green woods with sunlight filtering through the trees. A majestic snow-covered mountain peak. A fisherman leaning against a tree, nonchalantly watching his float on a gently flowing river. It's your thought. Simply take a moment and become still. Speaking softly to yourself, affirm that deep within you is a place of complete tranquility. It is the secret place of the Most High, where peace and tranquility reign supreme. Nothing—no discord—can enter here without your consent. And you choose peace. You may turn often to this place within where you abide in the presence of God, saying to yourself, "I am poised, serene, and peaceful."

The dance of life continually shifts its tempo, rhythm, and form. As you move with it, you may find yourself facing unimagined situations. This is the flow the dance often uses to carry you beyond limited ideas of who you are and what you are capable of handling.

Practice looking within your heart, not for emotion but to identify yourself with the still point of your essence and, regardless of "accidental elements" existing around you, peace can be found.

If you would find gold, you must search where gold is
—WILLIAM JUNEAU

We often see people searching in the wrong places for the things they desire. Too many of our fellow humans try to find peace and happiness in drugs, alcohol, and sensual excitement. And it doesn't work. If we seek peace, the first place to look is within ourselves. Peace isn't an external condition so much as an internal context. We can progress in consciousness by going on to the next larger context of thought and realization. Becoming aware of the next larger context of life, we may be, by the nature of our being, impelled onward. A higher plateau of consciousness beckons. The desire for a deeper reality to experience the golden truth of reality—not the "fool's gold" of illusion—whispers in our soul that "there is more."

Often true growth requires us to "unlearn" some things in order to reach the higher point of view. It may take a dose of humility and cleansing disillusionment to prompt us to release the old habits and ways of life that bring pain and suffering. Facts can have a fleeting reality of dimension, condition, and circumstances. Transitional growth experiences sometimes pose contradictions to the past. The psyche can learn to reorganize and adapt itself in preparation for entering the next larger context. This could be a new stage in life, a new state of consciousness, or even a radical shift in our personal affairs and environment.

To find the pure gold of truth often means adopting a more universal perspective on life, on yourself, and on everything that comprises your world. The greatness and power of many souls of the past enabled them to see a higher context than perhaps the average person. They knew where to look to find the golden nuggets of truth. Time does not prevent us from knowing these higher truths; our stage of consciousness makes all the difference.

Each day, as we look a little further in our quest for truth, explore a little deeper in the great wisdoms that abound, and search for the golden threads of light and love, we can be led in the path of righteousness. Those in search of an easier, softer way to obtain the important things of life often find cheap imitations or nothing at all. The miner who searches for gold on the beach because the digging is easy may certainly find lots of sand, but it's unlikely that he will find gold. Sometimes we must dig among stones and hard clay to find the treasure we seek. And when we do, we may learn that our efforts have not been wasted.

All sunshine makes a desert
—ASIAN PROVERB

A story is told about a group of children who were playing in the sand, writing their names and spreading shells in simple patterns. The gentle breeze coming in off the water tousled their damp hair, and the swish of the waves was pleasant background for the babble of young voices. Suddenly, one of the boys had an idea.

"Let's make a swimming pool right here," he exclaimed. The other children agreed, and they promptly set to work with shells and shovels and soon had a hole about a foot deep and several feet across. They ran down to the water's edge with their buckets and brought water to fill the hole. But as fast as the children poured the water into the hole, it drained off into the sand.

They surveyed the hole dolefully. Then, the boy who had the first idea had another. "I know—we'll line the hole with shells. That will keep the water in."

The children were busy for a time gathering and placing more shells. Then the bucket brigade started again. But no matter how fast the children worked, they still could not fill the hole with water.

One of the nearby parents had become fascinated with the children's activities and walked over to watch. A little girl saw her father standing nearby and ran over to him. "Daddy, what can we do?" she asked. "We're trying to make a swimming pool, and the water won't stay in the hole."

The father smiled. "Why, of all things, do you want to make a swimming pool?" he asked. "Look at the beautiful one already made for you. You haven't even been in it yet." And he waved his hand toward the expanse of water stretching out as far as the eye could see.

The little girl ran back to her friends, excitedly calling, "Come on. Here's a much better swimming pool than we can build," and she dashed down to the water with her friends.

How much like those children we may sometimes be! The great ocean of life may be before us, but we scurry about on the shore, writing our names in the sand, perhaps gathering shells, and trying to build our own private swimming pools. We forget to look around us and see the many-faceted blessings that are right before our eyes.

For example, what would life be like on earth if we had no clouds, no rain, nothing but sunshine? Sometimes we think we would like to have only sunshine, but without the rain we would be left with a dry, barren planet, incapable of supporting life as we know it.

Our lives seem filled with such variety—sunny days and stormy days, good times and frightening times, pleasure and pain, joy and sadness. Often we try to create only experiences of pleasure and happiness. However, by attempting to exert too much control over our experiences, we set ourselves up for a fearful existence.

We all need balance in our lives. Very few of us would survive an existence that is totally filled with fear, doubts, and negativity. Just as rain nurtures beautiful green grass and sunlight can kindle a sense of warmth and inner peace, so challenges can compel us to seek a greater understanding—engendering new beliefs and ideas about life. Happy times can provide for pleasant memories to relive during the difficult experiences, and, like old friends, good memories can fill the void when we mistakenly feel as if everything joyous has abandoned us.

As a youth, Sidney was raised in poverty on Cat Island in the Bahamas. At sixteen, with less than two years of education and $3 in his pocket, he moved to New York City in search of a better life. When he arrived, the only place he could find to sleep was a rooftop, and his first job was as a dishwasher.

Although he knew nothing about acting, Sidney responded to a want ad listed by the American Negro Theater. Because of his limited education, he could not read all the words in the script. The director interrupted his audition, shouting, "Stop wasting my time."

While that rejection would have stopped and maybe even destroyed the ambitions of most people, the young man walked away more determined than ever. Saving money from his meager dishwasher's salary, Sidney bought a radio. He used it as an educational tool, listening to people's voices for hours, trying to enunciate as clearly as they did. At the restaurant, he found a waiter who was willing to tutor him in reading.

Later Sidney returned to the American Negro Theater, persuading officials to let him take acting lessons. Privately, he resolved to become not only the best black actor but the *best actor*. Sidney Poitier is one of the finest actors of his generation. The rain that fell in his life only served to water the seeds of desire and determination to bring forth a better life and to elicit greater balance in his world.

Reverse the word evil *and you have the word* live
—PHINIUS P. QUIMBY

Why do bad or evil things seem to happen to good people? That question has perplexed artists, philosophers, and religious thinkers throughout the ages. When accident, disease, financial misfortune, or other personal tragedy happens to the morally responsible, it piques our sense of justice, especially when those whose behavior is less than honorable often seem to live problem-free lives, at least on the surface. Wouldn't it only be fair that those who lead upstanding lives should each be rewarded with a life unmarred by tragedy? Instead, we hear repeatedly how some innocents are victimized while some oppressors go free. What flaw in the order of the universe, some people ask with no small amount of bitterness, allows misfortune to plague the existence of good people?

In the fullness of time, the pain of personal catastrophe often gives way to new understanding and inner growth. That which is called "evil" may be typically experienced by the victim as a destructive reversal of fortune that causes unnecessary suffering. For example, an honest, hardworking political candidate is undermined by her opponent's slanderous remarks to the media. A star football quarterback becomes a paraplegic in an accident caused by a drunk driver. These two examples of gratuitously evil acts may invite the beginning of transformation for the victims. From these tragedies can emerge the possibility of a deeper, more meaningful life. "Evil," transformed and reversed, often can indeed spell "live." A good person who passes through a painful experience can mobilize inner resources and open doorways into a new and more expansive and useful life.

In an Old Testament story, Joseph was cast into a pit by his jealous brothers and abandoned to die. He was saved by traders who sold him into Egyptian slavery, where, again, he incurred the wrath and jealousy of some people he met. He was jailed, once more an innocent victim; but instead of destroying Joseph, the prison experience served as a new beginning. He learned to channel his dreams toward constructive ends, and eventually he was able to serve the Egyptian people. To his brothers who sought his forgiveness, Joseph granted it, telling them, "You meant evil against me; but God meant it for good" (Gen. 50:20).

Seeming evil can multiply and triumph when good people become resentful and bitter over their misfortunes, but, just as surely, evil may be overcome when people find it within themselves to transcend despair, forgive ignorance, heal betrayals, love everyone, and go on with a life of spiritual growth. In fact, as was true with Joseph, such transcendence may be the hard road good people travel to become great people.

Great people refuse to be victimized by circumstance. Instead, they often use even the most traumatic event as a springboard for a creative and helpful response to life. From his wheelchair, the paralyzed quarterback mobilized his leadership skills to help handicapped children. The victimized politician spoke her simple truth, and thus exemplified humility to millions. Those who grow in stature through adversity have learned to reverse the word *evil* to the word *live*.

Zeal is the inward fire of the soul that urges you
onward toward your goal
—CHARLES FILLMORE

Each time an opportunity comes your way that allows you to express your talent, welcome that opportunity with open arms! Feel the stirrings of zeal and enthusiasm move within you, providing the impetus to transform that opportunity into a full realization of good. Zeal can often be described as that part of us that generates spiritual motivation, resulting in forward or progressive unfoldment. When Charles Fillmore was ninety-four, he remarked, "I fairly sizzle with zeal and enthusiasm and spring forth to do that which should be done by me." What a tremendous attitude! Zeal can be the inner fire that stirs us into action. It offers the ability to gain distinction through concentrated effort directed toward our goals. Zeal has been called the "impulse to go forward" and "the urge behind all things."

There can be a tremendous energy in doing well what you have to accomplish. Then you can move forward to the next opportunity that may be beckoning. Just as a tuning fork vibrates to the note that is struck on the piano, so each of us vibrates to the notes that sound around us and within us. This has been referred to as the "mirror principle" or the "law of reflection."

There is no need to drag yourself through life bored, tired, or dull.

It is unnecessary to allow yourself to be the victim of erroneous belief, limited thinking, superstitions, ignorance, or fear. You can grow new wings of awareness. Let me share a story with you. The Rockefeller Institute conducted an enlightening series of tests involving parasites (organisms living in or on another living organism). The tests demonstrated to the institute that even the so-called lowly creatures have the power to call upon nature's intelligence for the resources to meet any need. The institute brought potted rosebushes into a room and placed them in front of a closed window. They found that if the plants were allowed to dry out, the parasites, which had previously been wingless, grew wings! After this metamorphosis, the parasites left the dead plants that could no longer provide them with food and drink. The only way the insects could survive was to grow wings and fly, which they did. When their source of food died out, they had to find a means of migrating or they, too, would perish. There is a great line in *A Sleep of Prisoners*, a play by Christopher Fry. It says, "O, God, the fabulous wings unused, folded in the heart." Those fabulous wings are within each of us as mental and spiritual forces, powers, and potentials. Could not the uplifting power of zeal be the invisible wings of spirit that can move us wondrously toward the achievement of our sincere hearts' desires?

Exploring beyond the boundaries of the personal mind, keep asking yourself, "What if?" What would happen if I injected zeal and enthusiasm to a greater degree in my work? In communication with others? In family and personal relationships?

Look at everyday situations with a new perspective of that propelling forward force of zeal. Think of possibilities in various situations, and let your imagination soar. Then engineer these ideas into workable possibilities. A lot of human progress has come from those who keep asking, "What if?" and then add the life-giving ingredient of zeal.

No one knows what he can do until he tries

—PUBLILIUS SYRUS

Each of us possesses patience, tolerance, and perseverance. Life may seem to wall us in, but we have the wings of spirit. We are transcendent creatures and have power to rise above obstacles. When faced with difficult or challenging situations, we can utilize our strength to become calm, wait patiently for confusing and conflicting thoughts to cease, and then move forward with a well-planned strategy for overcoming obstacles. And where we are right now is the best possible starting point. We can overcome almost any limiting situation by being willing to direct our attention in an appropriate manner.

W. Somerset Maugham spent twelve long years as an unknown writer before he got his break. During this period, he endured much frustration and disappointment and a career that seemingly was doomed to failure. But rather than concentrate on the obstacles, Maugham focused on the lessons he learned about human nature and worked these insights into his plays. He kept growing and writing, even though no one showed an interest in his work.

One day a London producer was looking to replace a play that had failed. Searching through his files, the producer came up with a script that had sat unnoticed for some time. It was Maugham's *Lady Frederick*. The play went into production and opened. The producer was amazed that this "fill-in" play was so enthusiastically accepted by audiences and became an overnight smash hit. Soon, everyone wanted Maugham's plays. And he was ready. Within a year, three of his works were simultaneously playing to packed houses, and critics were acclaiming this newfound genius.

When times seem troubled, pause for a moment. Remember the patience and persistence of W. Somerset Maugham.

CHAPTER 18

Finding Joy

*A measure of mental health is the disposition
to find good everywhere*
—SIR JOHN TEMPLETON

AVE YOU EVER noticed how some people seem to be joyful no matter what is going on in their lives? There is a buoyancy to their spirit and a sparkle to their personalities. A kind of glowing field of energy seems to radiate from their faces, their words, even the way they walk. There are others who seem to be predisposed to gloomy, negative thoughts. They seem to live in a perpetual state of unhappiness. What is the difference between a healthy, joyful person and a miserable, gloomy person? Choices! One person is an optimist and the other is a pessimist. The optimist sees the good in all things, builds upon the most hopeful and cheerful view of matters, and expects the best possible outcome in a situation. The pessimist sees only the darker side of life. Both of these are subjective realities. They are attitudes, not events.

Every great endeavor usually has an optimist at its helm. Without optimism, Magellan would never have circumnavigated the globe. Without optimism, Charles Lindbergh would not have made his way across the Atlantic Ocean on the first solo flight, thus opening the way for intercontinental travel.

249

People throughout the world are doing great damage to themselves by holding sickness-producing attitudes, compounded with defeat, fear, guilt, and hatred. A most important technique of good health, especially mental health, is to rid the mind of unhealthy thoughts. Bernard Baruch said, "Two things are bad for the heart: running up stairs and running down people." This is true not only of the heart but of the entire physical being.

One definite step that some people have found helpful in applying positive attitudes to physical well-being is that of *affirmation*, or the use of definite positive statements. Words are dynamite! The words we habitually use are reflections of strongly held thoughts, and thoughts can affect us in every aspect of our being. Forces favorable to our well-being may be stimulated by the constant use of positive words or affirmations. And positive thinking is usually stronger than negative thinking, just as faith is stronger than fear.

Properly employed, affirmations may improve your health, lengthen your life, rejuvenate your body, increase your happiness, bring you success, and give you the most important gift of all—peace of mind. Here are some examples of affirmations that have been used successfully by others:

1. My entire being is filled with radiant health. I think health. I practice health. I feel health.

2. I am a child of God. In him I live and move and have my being. I am strong, vital, and joyous. The kingdom of God is within me and I am grateful.

3. I feel wonderful today. This is going to be a happy day of my life!

As within, so without
—HERMETIC PRINCIPLE

All of us live in two worlds. We inhabit both an inner and an outer world. Most of us develop a preference for one world or the other.

Some people turn almost exclusively to the inner world, while others direct their thoughts and interests toward the world of externals. But in order to be happy and well-integrated people, it becomes important to function in *both* worlds with ease and satisfaction—to achieve balance in how we live.

In his work *Happiness: Essays on the Meaning of Life*, Carl Hilty writes about happiness and balanced living: "The paths by which people journey toward happiness lie in part through the world about them and in part through the experience of their own soul." This is another way of saying that our happiness lies in the development of our two worlds—the inner one and the outer one.

We may feel that we have built up a busy and successful outer life, so free from problems that we seldom feel the need to fall back on our inner resources. However, regardless of how good life may seem, how filled with multiple interests, events, and congenial people, the outer world is not enough. Those inevitable times arrive when we are thrown back upon ourselves and our inner resources. Most people want to know how to rise above hurt feelings and injured pride. They want to experience self-realization and the full development of their innate powers and abilities. Nothing the outer world offers can compensate for the satisfaction of the hungers and desires of our souls.

On the other hand, some people have built an inner world that provides more happiness than the outer one. It may be easier to create a thought world of pleasure, harmony, and accomplishment than to build a meaningful life in the larger world. For some, it is easier to love people if they can avoid intimate contact with them. It may also be easier to be great doers in the world of thought than to put forth the effort and experience the disappointments that go with outward accomplishment. It is often easier to feel that we are children of God than to prove it. But there is work to be done and a multitude of things that call us forth from our inner seclusion.

To live successfully in the outer world we need to live successfully in the inner world. Almost everyone desires friendships and the comforts of life. And what we want within we can have in our outer lives if we are willing to follow through with action. It isn't enough to wish for people to love us. It is important to be kind, helpful, compassionate, and thoughtful to others. We must do more than long for worldly success. We must develop the skill, the interest, and the perseverance that contribute to achieving the elements of such success. God has given us transcendent powers and it is our choice whether to express them or not.

Truth teaches us to relate the inner to the outer, to integrate the spiritual with the physical, to unify our thoughts, feelings, and actions into a harmonious whole. What appears in our outer world—friends, jobs, opportunities, schools, career—reflects what is happening inside ourselves. Almost every successful person will tell you that he first thought out his moves in the inner consciousness. The door to success opens from within. Combinations of circumstances can arise as the result of conscious union with the inner forces of being.

Appearances are often deceiving
—AESOP

It is important to train yourself to look beyond appearances and perceive what is before you with clarity and openness. Begin now to use the attributes you already have—whether they are special talents or abilities, material possessions, or special opportunities for service to yourself and to others. Do the most you know how to do with your present awareness and abilities. Let the guidance come from *within* rather than from outer appearances. Take one step at a time and begin with the step immediately ahead of you. Use what you already have to good advantage. Clear the way in your mental and emotional consciousness and in the activities in your life for the abundant good you earnestly desire. Give things the "light" touch with a gentle sense of humor and air of positive expectancy.

Clarence Darrow, a lawyer renowned for his conduct of labor litigation and murder cases, would often look at the lighter side of life. This attitude often provided a balance with the intensity of his work efforts. On occasion, reporters would tease Darrow about his disheveled appearance. Darrow, in good humor retorted, "I go to a better tailor than any of you and pay more for my clothes. The only difference is that you probably don't sleep in yours!"

We often admire a person who seems calm and collected, poised and self-controlled, a person who is not given to fits of temper and outbursts of anger when something disturbing occurs. A very competent teacher once said that habits and inclinations are as teachable as Latin and Greek and much more essential to happiness. Some people think they have no control over their emotions, no power over the way they react to certain situations or conditions in their lives. But we do have this power. The calm person we so admire may be working just as diligently as we are to overcome a situation. Appearances do not always speak the truth of a situation. Once, when someone commented on his amazing achievements, Sir Isaac Newton remarked:

> I do not know what I may appear to the world; but to myself
> I seem to have been only like a boy, playing on the seashore
> and diverting myself in now and then finding a smoother
> pebble or a prettier seashell than ordinary, while the great
> ocean of truth lay all undiscovered before me.

Rather than placing your focus on outer appearances or illusions, step forward with inner assurance to make the most of every day. You can make the commitment to be honest, steadfast, and true to the laws of life with your own development and growth, knowing that positive results must then manifest themselves in other areas of your life. With a peaceful mind and a song of joy in your heart, you can step forth each morning with a smile on your lips and wings on your feet to greet the world and all with whom you come in contact.

In this manner we go forth to meet our good. With a strong faith, we place our family, friends, loved ones, and acquaintances in God's care, knowing they, too, are enfolded in abundant love. Should unexpected situations occur, we can remember that at any time in our lives, at any place in our experiences, or wherever we may be, we can begin anew with an increased awareness as we allow the wisdom of spirit to flow through our minds. Loving thoughts, peaceful thoughts, optimistic thoughts are like a strong shield from which destructive forces glance off like wisps of straw.

A smile breeds a smile
—TED ENGSTROM

Most of us tend to be drawn to those who have a positive outlook on life. An optimist has a reason to smile, and his smile reveals his faith in life. The pessimist, on the other hand, thinks he has no reason to smile and lives his life without smiles, without faith, and often alone. The ability to smile in the face of life's adversities has escaped the pessimist. He has unconsciously chosen to ignore the many blessings life has given him.

When we learn to smile in the face of life's adversities, we can overcome our problems more effortlessly. Ella Wheeler Wilcox wrote:

'Tis easy enough to be pleasant,
When life flows along like a song;
But the man worthwhile is the one who will smile
When everything goes dead wrong.

There are three simple words that almost seem to have magical properties for developing a positive attitude in our lives. *Feel supremely happy!* When you let yourself feel supremely happy—regardless of outer appearances—your whole body changes. Your thoughts, your facial expressions, your health, your attitudes—everything about you changes for the better. It is possible to achieve a similar state of mind as does the mystic when he taps into universal power. If you persist with this feeling and attitude until it becomes a vital part of your life, you can be in harmonious communion with the universe—and all because you are thinking and believing the power of thought energy behind these three little words: *Feel supremely happy!* Living life with a smile enables us to see the joy of life, no matter what is going on around us. We can spread that joy with a simple smile.

When the bullet that began the American Revolution was fired at Concord, it was called "the shot heard 'round the world." Your smile, aimed in the direction of any hostile emotions, could be the smile felt around the world. "Brighten the corner where you are." The world needs your smile.

Happiness is always a by-product
—SIR JOHN TEMPLETON

The Constitution of the United States says that every person is entitled to life, liberty, and the pursuit of happiness. Innately, we know that our purpose in life is to be happy, because we seek happiness with all our hearts. Yet, sadly, we are often seeking it outside ourselves. Happiness never seems to yield to direct frontal attack. The happiest people give happiness to others. Happiness is not found by seeking it; it is a by-product of trying to help others. We can only attain happiness by trying to give it away.

Hugh Black, who for thirty years was a professor of practical theology at the Union Theological Seminary in New York, said:

> It is the paradox of life that the way to miss pleasure is to seek it first. The very first condition of lasting happiness is that a life should be full of purpose, aiming at something outside self. As a matter of experience, we find that true happiness comes in seeking other things, in the manifold activities of life, in the healthful outgoing of all human powers.

One example of this statement is to develop your talents and become excellent in a particular line of work, and happiness and success will follow from the blessings you bring to others.

Happiness comes from the work, the endeavor, the pursuit of a goal—the *giving*. Production, not consumption, is at the core of happiness and success.

Perhaps Mother Teresa of Calcutta epitomized better than anyone the concept that happiness can be achieved by what you do. She believed in showing love to those near you and to those who cross your path every day. Spiritual awareness shines through in her comment, "How can we love God if not through others?" A powerful reward of loving service is the deep inner knowing that you have given the greatest gift—yourself—and that is a happiness money cannot buy.

Laughter is the best medicine
—NORMAN COUSINS

When the United States entered World War II in 1941, patriotism was at a high point, and young men by the thousands rushed to recruiting offices, eager to serve their country. Movie stars were no exception, although some who applied were not accepted. Comedian Bob Hope was turned down as a recruit. The country's leaders felt he could serve a better purpose with the USO, entertaining the troops. He protested vigorously that he didn't want to receive any preferential treatment, but the government stood firm. Government officials could not possibly have known at the time what a wise decision they made.

Hope and his group of entertainers logged millions of miles and gave thousands of performances for the troops in Europe and Asia. These men and women risked their lives many times by performing in combat zones. They visited the hospitals where the wounded were treated and brought joy to many people. Always the positive entertainer, Hope didn't dole out sympathy or pity. He would ask a wounded serviceman questions such as, "Did you see our show, or were you already sick?" The therapeutic value of laughter was never questioned by those who received his visits. Laughter can be a doorway from misery to joy.

When a person laughs, many good things happen. Muscles relax, breathing becomes deeper, the bloodstream is more fully oxygenated. Pain and gloom are forgotten, or at least put into proper perspective. It's difficult for a person who is shaking with laughter to think negative thoughts. Often the most serious of matters can best be solved by giving the situation "the light touch."

We are all travelers on the pathways of life. How tremendously valuable is the power of joy and laughter to enliven our soul as we go forward to meet our goals. Laughter can lift us over the high ridges and lighten up the dark valleys in a way that makes life much easier. A happy heart generates a force field of love and joy in which doubt, fear, disaster, and dismay have no power to interrupt the universal flow of good. And in some instances, laughter has been considered to be a high form of prayer. Truly, when you are in the consciousness of the joy of the spirit, you are praying from the very heart of your being.

Laughter can be immensely uplifting in a tense situation. In September 1862, President Abraham Lincoln called a special session of his closest advisors. When they arrived, he was reading a book. At first he paid little attention to their entrance, then started to read aloud to them a piece by the humorist Artemus Ward, titled "A High-Handed Outrage at Utica," which Lincoln found very funny, and he laughed heartily at the end. But no one joined in. The cabinet members sat in stony disapproval of the president's seeming frivolity. Lincoln rebuked them, "Why don't you laugh? With the fearful strain that is upon me night and day, if I did not laugh I should die, and you need this medicine as much as I do." Then, turning to business, he told them that he had privately prepared "a little paper of much significance." It was the draft of the Emancipation Proclamation!

Those who bring laughter also seem to be its beneficiaries. Although we can't all be professional comedians, opportunities may be available to share our laughter and good humor with everyone we meet. We can visit hospitals, convalescent centers, and homes for the aged and give of the joy of our spirit. The people who live in these homes are often terribly lonely. They may feel forgotten by the ones they love, and visitors are welcome, especially those who bring moments of healing laughter.

For those who may feel unsure of themselves as natural wits or stand-up comedians, books, DVDs, and audiotapes can be shared. The sharing is the important part. It can brighten a lonely person's life; it can improve your relations with those close to you. Bringing laughter is better than any "spring tonic" for yourself. Laughter is the best medicine!

Happy relationships depend not on finding the right person,
but on being the right person
—ERIC BUTTERWORTH

In the fairy tale *The Sleeping Beauty*, the heroine is saved from her seemingly endless sleep by a kiss from the handsome prince, who whisks her away to his palace where they live happily ever after. This same idea is portrayed in *Snow White* and in countless other stories. Many films and novels continue to follow a similar plotline. Many people grow up believing the false information given to us by television, radio, film, and the printed word that something or someone can rescue us from our mundane lives and turn us into all that we want to be. Even our parents may inadvertently give us the impression that the right person can make everything just fine. Young women dress up like fairy princesses in white lacy dresses on their wedding day, propagating this myth even further.

Why, then, do so many people seem discontented in their marriages and relationships? Why do people divorce and then often remarry someone who may resemble their previous spouse? Could it be because they remain the same within? So they continue attracting the same painful and unsatisfactory relationships for as long as they maintain the same old attitudes.

When a person begins to work on changing himself from within, he begins to attract different types of people and experiences into his life. The junkie who is using drugs associates with other drug users. When he reforms himself and starts to change his attitudes, he starts associating with a different sort of person. This is because he is changing from within.

Most people think of love as some sort of power outside themselves that will "take them away from all of this." Sadly, that is not the case. Love exists only within our own hearts, and to have happy relationships we must first become truly loving people. And as we fill our hearts with love by expressing love toward others in thought, word, and deed ("acting as if" until we make it happen, if necessary), that love can heal our own lives, help to solve our problems, and enable us to feel good about ourselves.

In Alan Cohen's book *The Healing of the Planet Earth*, the following passage sheds a beautiful light on how love is the real key to success in all our endeavors, whether it be work, relationships, family, achievements, or harmony among the nations and peoples of the world:

> The real secret of success is love. We must love ourselves enough to know that we are worthy to succeed. We must believe that those around us want us to win at life, and that our winning can only support their winning. We must know that God wants us to be happy in all the arenas of our lives. We must understand that there is no need to struggle, strain, or live in pain or a state of lack. These hellish conditions are but signals that we must try another way. We must never settle for less than whole and holy abundance in our health, relationships, and livelihood. We are not born to scratch the dirt with chickens—we were born to soar with the eagles!

Outward beauty is transient, but inner beauty lasting
—SEYYED HOSSEIN NASR

Almost every day, in a magazine or on television, we can see a handsome man and a lovely woman, often hugging, always smiling, and, without exception, selling something. The message: you can be just like us if you buy this product! But, of course, in real life it may not be true that you can be beautiful, happy, loved, and popular just by using the right product, driving the right car, or wearing a designer label.

Do you know someone who may buy all the "right" things and still not be liked? The beautiful, happy, lovable part of you comes from within. It remains unaffected by clothes, cars, or other outer accoutrements. Beauty is more than skin deep. It begins at the center of your spiritual being and is reflected in our faces, postures, mannerisms, speech, and tone of voice—all the qualities that are recognizable as uniquely you.

Beauty often lies in your attitude toward other people, perhaps toward those who may not be popular or cannot afford the "right" clothes, expensive cars, or other possessions. Can you see beyond the clothes or cars to the deeper identity of the person? Do you make an effort to get to know the being within?

Many of the most influential people in history rose from humble beginnings, without the material goods and advantages others may enjoy. They called upon the richness of their minds, the depths of their creativity, their high respect for the worth of others, and expressed their willingness to stand apart from the crowd. St. Francis of Assisi, Mahatma Gandhi, and many others, who on the inside were truly beautiful and rich in spirit, chose to live in poverty.

Back in the 300s BCE, Kungfutse asked the Chinese philosopher Mencius, "We are all human beings. Why is it that some are great men and some are small men?"

Mencius replied, "Those who attend to their greater selves become great men, and those who attend to their smaller selves become small men."

"But we are all human beings," Kungfutse continued to inquire. "Why is it that some people attend to their greater selves and some attend to their smaller selves?"

Mencius replied:

> When our sense of sight and hearing are distracted by the things outside, without the participation of thought, then the material things act upon the material senses and lead them astray. That is the explanation. The function of the mind is thinking: when you think, you keep your mind, and when you don't think, you lose your mind. This is what heaven has given to us. One who cultivates his higher self will find that his lower self follows in accord. That is how to become a great man.

The contributions of truly great people to our lives can be measured not by the size of their bank accounts but by the depth of their spirits. They may not have been leaders in the popularity polls or included in the *Forbes* 500 list of the wealthiest people, but their contributions often changed lives and can continue to do so as long as truth is valued.

It is important to figure out how you want to live your life, and one way to start is by answering these questions in preparation for the years ahead. Is what you are doing now going to be appropriate and beneficial in thirty years—in fifty years? While being grateful for your present life, what are you doing now to prepare for that future time? What are you doing to leave the world a better place than you found it?

Love yourself by being the very best you can possibly be. Treat yourself as a close friend, one for whom you want only the best of everything—respect, honor, solid relationships, and the joy of a life well-lived. These things will be yours by living honorably, at the highest level of which you are capable.

Happiness comes from spiritual wealth, not material wealth
—SIR JOHN TEMPLETON

When people who have become instant millionaires by winning a large lottery or receiving an unexpected inheritance are asked how their lives changed since receiving the money, some respond that life has become more complicated. A lot of money is at their disposal, but instead of finding happiness, new problems arise.

If we have not developed a reservoir of spiritual wealth, no amount of money is likely to make us happy. Spiritual wealth provides faith. It gives us love. It brings and expands wisdom. Spiritual wealth leads to happiness because it guides us into useful or loving relationships.

It is easy to determine our material wealth, but to determine how wealthy we are spiritually, it is important to look at our lives. What are our relationships like? Have we learned how to love and accept others for who and what they are without reservation? Have we learned how to forgive and forget perceived wrongs done to us? Do we value all of life and the many forms through which it expresses itself? Have we used our talents to the utmost? The answers to these questions can offer us a fair estimate of the extent and quality of our spiritual wealth.

We may think that happiness is a result of happy circumstances. A more mature view of happiness is that it is a by-product of sharing our good and serving others. It is a sense of doing a job well, honest communication with another, visiting someone who may be ill, or sharing a sense of humor. Happiness is a spiritual principle that we can grasp and use, regardless of our outer circumstances.

It isn't necessary to wait for circumstances to bring happiness. When we try to give it to others, it returns to us multiplied. We can make our own joy, and let it act upon circumstances! One of the great paradoxes of life is that a happy heart draws to itself what it needs for happiness.

Spiritual wealth can be a pathway to true and lasting happiness because with it, we have a resource to provide for what we need. If we take inventory and find ourselves lacking in spiritual wealth, we can replenish the supply. Within us can be found the necessary tools for building productive and happy lives. We can access the ability to be useful and, thereby, enjoy life, regardless of what may be taking place around us.

Material comfort may be a positive force in our lives, eliminating any concern about being hungry, paying bills, or educating our children. When the economy is strong, material wealth can be a dependable source of security. What happens if the economic situation weakens, however? As we develop our spiritual wealth, we can fall back on our inner security as a source of strength. It is like a "blank check" that can be honored anytime. Should we lose our savings and financial resources, then our spiritual wealth can help us recover and recoup our losses. With spiritual wealth as the foundation of our lives, we gain a deep and abiding peace that can't be obtained with material wealth alone.

If you truly desire happiness in your life, consider these three important guidelines.

1. Happiness can be the *cause* as well as the *effect* of bringing more good into your life.
2. Happiness increases through use, because when you think, speak, and act with joy, there is little room for anything less in your life.
3. You can cultivate happiness through service to others.

Healthy minds tend to cause healthy bodies, and vice versa
—SIR JOHN TEMPLETON

Take a look at any of today's newsstand magazines, and chances are one of the leading articles focuses on managing stress. Stress is one of the leading causes of illness in today's world, and more and more doctors and scientists are discovering vital links between body, mind, and spirit.

Emotional stress can weaken the immune system, making the body more susceptible to disease. Dr. Ronald Grossarth-Maticek, a Yugoslavian oncologist, published the results of three studies, begun in the 1960s, that stirred international excitement. On the basis of interviews and questionnaires given to a large group of men and women, he assigned people to one of four personality types. By following their medical histories for ten to thirteen years, he found evidence that certain aspects of mental and emotional behavior may be linked to cancer or heart disease.

Disease-prone people often exhibit emotional dependence, passivity, and dissatisfaction with their key relationships. They tend to be unduly influenced by the way others respond to them and may find it difficult to improve unsatisfying relationships. They also often seem unable to take the initiative in forming or maintaining close emotional ties with others.

Louise Hay, author of *Heal Your Body*, says, "I find that resentment, criticism, guilt, and fear cause the most problems in ourselves and our lives. Whatever is happening 'out there' is only a mirror of our own inner thinking."

Tests have shown that people who develop heart disease often have problems handling anger, either by failing to control it or by over-controlling it so that their feelings may not be adequately expressed. Frustration, fear, and helplessness are also emotions that may create disease in the body.

So where do we look for an answer? Unfortunately, there are no easy answers. It could be important, however, to have some strong stress relievers at the top of our list. First, spend some time out of doors. The beauty of the earth can stimulate joy, thanksgiving, and healthy thoughts.

There have been many stories in recent years of terminally ill patients who may have literally laughed themselves back to health. Those men and women had nothing to lose when they began a systematic program of watching funny television shows and reading humorous books. Without realizing it, they may have stimulated their immune system and helped to conquer, or at least stabilize, their disease.

Meditation can be a proven method of achieving a more relaxed state of consciousness. Findings reported by Stanford University researcher Kenneth Eppley review the effects of transcendental meditation. He reports that "TM has consistently beneficial effects on anxiety."

Another proven method for reducing stress can be owning a pet. Long-range studies with the elderly and the ill confirm that having a dog or a cat to stroke and love increases happiness and extends longevity. Mother Teresa of Calcutta often provided animals as therapy for mentally ill children.

In order to be happy, healthy, and stress-free, you must believe in yourself and your right to happiness and health. Louise Hay writes:

> Our subconscious mind accepts whatever we choose to believe. Life is very simple. What we give out, we get back. I believe that all of us are responsible for every experience in our lives, the best and the worst. Every thought we think is creating our future. Each one of us creates our experiences by the thoughts we think and the words we speak.

Habit is the best of servants, the worst of masters
—J. JELINEK

Everyone has habits. Getting up in the morning, doing the things that create order in your environment, eating nutritious meals, exercising your body, practicing good hygiene, getting enough sleep—all these are habits. These habits enable you to function at full strength both at work and play. Habits of courtesy create natural good manners that make others comfortable in your presence. Consistent practice enables you to develop a skill or talent like music, sports, painting, crafts, or writing.

A habit is a pattern of behavior we have acquired that has become so automatic it may be difficult to modify or eliminate. Many habits are unconscious, and we no longer have to think about where, when, how, or whether to do things. It almost seems as though they're done outside of our conscious will.

Habitual behaviors can certainly be helpful. We rarely need to think about the way we use our bodies to walk, run, and climb stairs. We automatically know how to hold a pencil, a fork, or a cup. Drivers may get into the habit of operating the accelerator, brake, and turning signal of a car efficiently, never giving the process a second thought.

Habits of politeness—such as saying "Hello," "Please," "Thank you," "You're welcome," and "Excuse me"—promote harmony as we communicate with each other in our daily routines. Hygiene habits also aid us in our journey through life. Bathing our bodies, brushing our teeth, and eating nutritious foods in the proper amounts contribute to healthy bodies. Keeping our clothing and living quarters clean and neat are habits that can promote self-esteem and success. Once learned, these good habits often become beneficial, although perhaps unconscious, ways of life.

The habits of doing routine things in a certain order can sometimes ensure completion of a project. For instance, putting everything you need for work in the same place near the door before you go to bed at night can help you get a smooth start the next morning. If, before you leave the house each day, you form the habit of taking a few seconds to visually scan the room and think about what you need to take with you, time and possible embarrassment could be eliminated. Thinking about what needs to be turned off (like stoves) or unplugged (like curling irons) can help keep your home safe.

Still, not all habits are helpful, and bad habits can become cruel masters that are detrimental to our well-being. Smoking, drinking, and taking drugs can rapidly develop into habits that sabotage our health and our relationships with others. While the dangers of addictive drugs are obvious, sometimes habits that are much more subtle can be just as detrimental to our development into successful individuals.

The habit of thinking negatively about ourselves and our opportunities is self-destructive, as can be the habit of daydreaming instead of concentrating on our work. Procrastination is an insidious and self-defeating habit that has ruined many lives. Blaming other people or circumstances for our failures can become a habit that may prevent us from moving forward toward the completion of our goals.

By the time a behavior pattern becomes a habit, it can feel so familiar that it seems to be a natural part of us, but, in fact, habits are learned and practiced. Just as we have learned them over time, we can "unlearn" these practiced behaviors. By observing yourself, you can become aware of the habitual ways you think and act that could be harmful. When you're conscious of a habit you want to change, you can unlearn it by replacing the automatic behavior with a different, more thoughtful response. You may make mistakes or slip back into old ways, but it's important not to give up. Simply correct your behavior as soon as you're aware that you've slipped back into the old habit. Determine how to be the master of your habits, so that your habits can be useful servants to you.

Joy provides assurance, envy brings loneliness
—SIR JOHN TEMPLETON

When things go awry—perhaps your car was acting up and didn't want to start, an anticipated lunch date fell through, or you forgot an appointment you really wanted to keep—you have the key to turn it around. Your attitude! Just like so many other things in our day-to-day living, the "bad-day" syndrome or "good-day" experience can be outgrowths of our general attitude toward life. We can get so involved in examining and dwelling on the unfortunate, minor irritations of living that we may miss or disregard the small delights that occur just as frequently and regularly.

Joy may be difficult to define, but we know it when we experience it; and we know it when we lose it. Some people find great joy when they are involved in doing things that bring others happiness, when they knowingly live in harmony with the laws of life, when their thoughts, feelings, and actions are honest and honorable, and when they have a quiet and peaceful conscience.

When the Rev. Sabine Baring-Gould, author of the hymn "Onward Christian Soldiers," was pastor of the North Devon Church in England, he used to delight in taking visitors around the church and churchyard and pointing out to them the things of special interest.

He never failed to show them the tomb of a predecessor of his, which was set just inside the churchyard wall. The tombstone had been erected by grateful members of the parish, and it listed the ways in which the pastor had faithfully fulfilled his ministry of caring and loving service.

When Baring-Gould asked visitors if they noticed anything unusual about the stone, the more observant visitors would remark, "Why, yes! There is no name on it! Who was this person?"

"That's the point," said Baring-Gould. "Generations of schoolboys have sat on the bank above the stone, and their feet have gradually worn away the inscription of the name on the top line. So we don't know who the person was, only what he did!"

People may not remember who we are, but if there is some piece of service, some word of encouragement, some deed of mercy that we have contributed to their lives, that is our true memorial. To be thought of as a happy, joyous, loving, caring, compassionate person could be one of our greatest compliments and most important accomplishments.

If you have lost the ability to feel joy in living, try your best to regain it. It is vital to your well-being. Real joy is a deep and lasting quality that helps transcend difficulties and restores a zest for life and living no matter what happens. Remember that joy and strength can walk hand in hand to help us meet and overcome whatever challenges come our way.

Joy is not in things, but is in you
—SIR JOHN TEMPLETON

How beautifully the great teacher Jesus trod the path of joy! He said, "These things I have spoken to you, that my joy may be in you, and that your joy may be made full" (John 15:11).

Joy is an experience almost everyone seeks, but the question becomes, Where do we find it? The seed idea of joy is hidden within you! If you desire to walk the paths many master teachers trod, you can walk the path of joy. And this becomes easier to do when you sincerely love people.

To exude joy and to instill happiness in our lives, we must first believe that we were meant (created) to live happy, fulfilling lives. This belief then progresses to become an attitude or a habitual way of looking at life and responding to it. This habitual way of looking at life can then allow us to recognize that persons, places, things, and situations can hold possibilities that may simply be awaiting our discovery. By making a full circle of joy—from an idea that we accept to the expression of that idea in our lives—we not only must communicate this joy to others and bring the blessing of joy expressed, but we also then gain a wonderful feeling of confidence in knowing that others may receive happiness from the expressions we give to life!

When Jesus said, "Let your light so shine before men, that they may see your good works and give glory to your Father who is in heaven" (Matt. 5:16), he may have been talking about letting the joy of the spirit shine forth from us. Charles Fillmore held the idea that "life for every person should be a journey in jubilance." When we think of the pain and suffering, the poverty and hardship, the personal and worldwide conflicts that seem to abound, these words may seem to be the height of pure Pollyannaism. However, Fillmore's statement is a concept that touches the very heart of truth.

Joy comes not from outer things or experiences but from our inner consciousness. Within each of us is an unborn possibility of abounding joy, and ours is the privilege of giving birth to it at any time. It is the little fire of spirit that one may smother but never quite extinguish.

Happiness pursued, eludes; happiness given, returns
—SIR JOHN TEMPLETON

We can initiate the flow of good in our lives by first appreciating our own uniqueness. Then, we need to feel secure enough in recognizing and knowing ourselves that we can look for and appreciate that same uniqueness and diversity in others.

Be aware of the power of your words. Sometimes loving and positive words may be the greatest gift we can give. Look with sincerity for the special talents of others, and tell them the good you see. Give encouragement when it is needed. Be a pleasant reminder of past accomplishments, joys, and triumphs. Be appreciative and accepting. Be willing to say, "I love you."

Forgive generously. Learn to say, "I'm sorry," when it needs to be said. No matter who may be right or wrong, these words, spoken sincerely, can be a gift that projects happiness to everyone involved.

Be kind. Happiness can be a phone call to a friend who may be lonely or ill or facing a difficult time. It may be listening, without giving advice, to someone who needs to talk, helping with a chore, running an errand, or anticipating a need.

Can money and possessions be gifts from our own well of happiness? Yes, when they are given with a joyful heart. Sharing what we have with those who are in need can multiply our happiness if our motivation is appropriate. We should give with the idea of sharing or easing another's pain or hardship, and not to glorify a false sense of benevolence, or to get our name in the paper, or provide a good tax write-off.

Like the man who hungered after happiness, it may be easy to mistake "getting" with "being." Adding anything to our lives in a material sense only gives a very fleeting, and often false, sense of contentment. The paradox of achieving personal peace and happiness may be that what we are looking for is already within us, and by giving it away, we experience it most powerfully for ourselves.

CHAPTER 19

Pursuing Your Dreams

Hitch your wagon to a star!
—RALPH WALDO EMERSON

YOUNG WOMAN who had recently graduated with honors from a good college aspired to write novels, but her ideas kept ending up as short stories. The thought of such an ambitious project as a novel seemed overwhelming. One day she confessed to a friend how discouraged she was, and he suggested that she needed a larger vision for her work. He advised outlining a series of novels that would include and develop the powerful stories and characters that were already living in her imagination. He recommended that the outline incorporate a plan that would unfold over several years, or possibly over her lifetime.

Following his advice, the writer built scenarios around the characters and projected how the various stories would mesh together, and expanded that idea to include how the novels would emerge, one after another. Her outline became a design for an exciting and successful career. When the plan was completed, she could easily see her work expressed in a larger context and realized where she needed to begin. Her first book was mentally clear. The young woman began to write and, by the time the first novel was published, she was well into the second.

273

A wise friend helped her realize that the problem was not with her writing ability but stemmed from a limited vision of who she was and what she could accomplish. Her expanded vision helped her fulfill her heart's desire, which resulted in a productive and joyful career.

In her book *The Longevity Factor*, Lydia Bronte, PhD, describes how Millicent Fenwick held the high vision. Millicent Fenwick's most important career peak began shortly before her sixty-fifth birthday, when she was elected to the U.S. House of Representatives. Born and raised in the state of New Jersey, Fenwick married in 1929 at the age of nineteen and began a family. She undoubtedly thought her life would be spent comfortably as a housewife, much as her mother's had been. But the marriage did not work out. Divorced in her early thirties, she found herself with no professional or career training (she hadn't even finished high school), two young children, and a huge burden of debt run up by her former husband.

Spurred on by desperation and her sense of responsibility, she spoke with another friend, who put her in touch with someone at *Vogue* magazine, and she landed a position on their staff. There she wrote the *Vogue Book of Etiquette*, which became quite popular and widely used. Meanwhile, she was gradually repaying the financial obligations left over from her marriage and putting her children through school.

During the years when she was at *Vogue*, Fenwick gradually became active in public life. When she moved back to New Jersey after her children left home, she was asked to join a local recreation commission, which became highly successful under her chairmanship. It was then suggested that she run for local council. At first she was doubtful. But, to her surprise, she won! This initial success encouraged her to run for higher office, and it led eventually to a seat in the House of Representatives in 1974. Fenwick served four terms in the House, with distinction, before launching a bid for a Senate seat in 1982. Although this campaign proved unsuccessful, she was appointed the following year as U.S. ambassador to the UN Food and Agriculture Commission in Rome.

Like Fenwick, we, too, need to think big and aim high when planning our goals. Ambition can sustain us—with our thoughts and hopes up in the stars—while traveling along the path toward success. And the journey may take some time to accomplish. Many famous and successful entertainment stars, whose names and faces we see everywhere, spent years in clerical or restaurant jobs while waiting for an opportunity to express the talent they were convinced lay within. People who became successful in business may have tried many ideas and faltered before they discovered the idea that worked. Many of the innovations that change our lives were once the dreams of inventors who, at first, came up against seeming dead ends and sometimes the skepticism of family and friends.

These successful entertainers, businesspeople, and inventors had one quality in common. To realize their dreams, ambitions, and individual growth, they managed to see the bigger picture of their lives. They believed in themselves and aimed for the best.

The price of greatness is responsibility
—WINSTON CHURCHILL

If you hope to accomplish great things, begin by accepting responsibility for the smaller things facing you today. The student who fails to do homework assignments or to take on extra research in school subjects may not develop the ability and the knowledge needed to be successful as an adult. The young person who fails to act caringly and responsibly at home and with friends may often fail in crucial relationships—professional and personal—later in life because compassion and understanding were too long left to others. A business may fail because the record keeping and other areas of exacting work have been neglected.

How capable do you feel at this moment in your life? There are certain steps that are important to take in order to accomplish your goal. First, it is important to know what may be keeping you from making the progress you desire. Ask yourself the following questions;

respond honestly from the depth of your being; and write your response in your journal for further consideration:

- ► Do you habitually feel sorry for yourself?
- ► Do you hesitate overly long when making changes in your life?
- ► Do you lack the faith in yourself (in any way) to accomplish great things?
- ► Do you fear what people may say if you move out of the rut you may have made for yourself?

Answering "yes" to any of these statements represents some success-crippling habits that can cause roadblocks to the inflow of your abundance. A great antidote for any of the above success-cripplers can be to take responsibility for your life and begin to count your blessings daily. Counting your blessings is important because you cannot be aware and grateful for the abundance you have already received and feel deprived at the same time. Free yourself from any self-imposed bondage by taking full responsibility for your life.

Taking responsibility nurtures self-confidence, and self-confidence can help you be a more interesting and attractive person. Best of all, the more you believe in yourself, the more power you possess to attract good things to yourself. Dr. Viktor Frankl said that on the West Coast of the United States we should erect a "statue of responsibility" to balance the Statue of Liberty on the East Coast. It might be even better to erect statues of both standing hand in hand, on both coasts. Those who speak constantly of their right to freedom must understand that an irresponsible act does not bring greater freedom but only greater bondage to the action. One law of life says, "If we are to enjoy freedom, we must accept responsibility."

Self-control wins the race
—ANONYMOUS

Can you imagine what it was like to live in the world when it took a month or more to cross the Atlantic Ocean? When you might have had to wait months in San Francisco for a letter to arrive by Pony Express from New York? When you had to travel long distances over bumpy dirt roads to the nearest town to buy a new pair of shoes? The slow pace of life in the nineteenth century may be difficult to comprehend today when e-mail and texting transmit messages in seconds, and the local mall is only minutes away by car. Cutting-edge technology allows us to do almost anything instantly.

The ability to do something quickly can be useful, but speed isn't everything. In the long run, using what you have to the fullest degree is the way to attain lasting success.

Do you sometimes envy people who seem to have it made without even trying? They have the money, looks, talent, connections, and they're on the fast track to success; but you may seem to plod along, making progress one small step at a time. It's important to remember that it's not *what* you have, but what you *do* with what you have that counts. You may be tempted by instant success, but history has proven that "slow and steady" translates into lasting progress over the long term. Cheng Yi, a Chinese scholar, said, "If one concentrates on one thing and does not get away from it . . . he will possess strong, moving power." If you want to back a winner in today's fast-paced world, remember the law that perseverance and self-control win the race.

Minds are like parachutes—they only function when they are open
—DICK SUTPHEN

A closed mind can have an important effect on your future. Two high school seniors, Bill and John, were invited to an open house at a college they both were interested in attending. They joined a group of students who were discussing physics. Bill broke in, talking confidently as though he had a good grasp of the subject, although he had never studied physics and his knowledge was superficial. John was as ignorant of physics as Bill, but he listened carefully to the discussion, which had to do with atomic structure and the origin of the universe.

Before long he realized the ideas he held concerning the subject were different from those being discussed by the college students—different and not very well informed.

Bill, who had acted as if he knew it all and whose ignorance was exposed, went home and told his parents he didn't want to attend "that stupid college." John, on the other hand, read as much as he could on the subject of physics. Even though physics was not his prime subject of interest, he realized that he didn't fully understand the principles involved, so he made the effort to learn. He followed this up by reading a book recommended by his high school librarian. He ended up attending the college and graduating in the top quarter of his class.

While you should not turn away from values and ideas you have good reason to believe are true, it is important to continue learning and growing mentally. A narrow mind can be the straightest avenue to a narrow life. Listen to others better informed than you are, and don't be afraid to ask questions. Reading can increase your knowledge and open doors of learning and understanding.

Let's look at the parachute analogy in the title of this essay. A parachute used when jumping out of an airplane is constructed with a small pilot chute that is released first to activate the larger chute, which is tightly packed within its protective cover. A handle is attached to a rip cord that must be forcefully pulled to release the pilot chute, which then fills with air and provides the initial power to pull the tightly packed main chute from its container.

Your mind is like a parachute—unless you open it, it remains tightly packed and inactive. It does take courage to open the parachute of your mind to the mysterious unknown, but once accomplished, life unfolds wondrously before you.

A closed mind is a sad waste of possibilities when a person chooses inaction over progress. One of the important purposes of this book is to encourage you, the reader, to open yourself to the joys and wonders of your existence. It is with sincere hope that you will accept the challenge to continue a lifelong pursuit of progress toward awareness of the spirit within you.

If we look at some of the great minds that have given humanity wonderful discoveries and inventions, in many instances we become aware of an open and questing mind.

Ross Bagdasarian, creator of the singing group Alvin and the Chipmunks, first conceived of the chipmunks after nearly running over one on a country road. He named them Alvin, Simon, and Theodore, after a trio of record executives.

In 1950 Frank McNamara ate a fancy meal in a classy New York restaurant and realized as dessert was served that he had no available cash. Embarrassed, he phoned his wife to come pay the check. Shortly thereafter, he borrowed $10,000 and founded Diner's Club—the first credit card accepted by restaurants.

J. M. Haggar, founder of the Haggar Company, was inspired by Henry Ford's idea of the production line and mass production. Using the ends of suit fabrics instead of denim, Haggar made a new kind of dress pants he called "slacks," and in the process, J. M. Haggar revolutionized the clothing industry.

Our minds are our creative center, and when we are open and receptive to thoughts and ideas, our accomplishments can be tremendous.

Fortune knocks at the door of those who are prepared
—ANONYMOUS

By the time Dean began his second year of college, he was considering a career in education, so he scheduled a session with his counselor and professors in the education department of his college to plan his course of study for the next three years. His advisors convinced him to work toward a master's degree and perhaps even a doctorate. Realizing, however, that many valuable lessons were not learned in the classroom, Dean considered the kinds of extracurricular activities and part-time work that would best prepare him for his chosen career.

He became active in the Student Education Association and other campus activities geared for education majors, but he wondered how his part-time job as a salesman in a department store would fit with his goal of pursuing education as a career.

Dean liked his job, and his employer was very supportive of his commitment to get an education. He worked out a schedule that allowed Dean to earn the money he needed and yet have the time he required for study. Another benefit of the job was his ability to buy shoes and clothing at a discount. Dean's salary was on a par with other jobs available on a part-time basis, and he decided that the support of his employer was worth a great deal, even though his actual work seemed to have little to do with his life's goals.

Dean pondered what he could do at work to advance his career. He noticed that the new people hired had no idea how to utilize their time advantageously when they were not busy with customers. He knew from his own experience that even though the owner attempted to train them well, he had many other priorities. New clerks were quickly left on their own. Dean created a checklist of items that would have been helpful when he was new to the job. He made notes of questions new employees asked and listened closely as they dealt with customers.

In a few short weeks, Dean accumulated pages of notes and recognized he had the bare bones of an employee training manual. He presented his boss with a rough draft of the manual, asking him to read it through and make suggestions and comments. Dean proposed to write the book, which would then be printed and circulated to all new employees. His boss enthusiastically endorsed the plan and gave him a raise. Three years later, when Dean was applying for graduate school, his employer's sincere and strong recommendation became the deciding factor in Dean being granted a substantial scholarship to a university that was preeminent in the field of business education. Dean's good fortune was not a matter of luck or fate, as many of his classmates thought. It was a clear result of his applying his interest, skill, and energy in every facet of his life. Dean had used all the resources available to him; consequently, he was given the chance to be successful.

Even in the little things, in the seemingly insignificant events of life, it is important to be prepared. Opportunities to learn new things can be readily available if we open our eyes to truly see. Almost every moment offers opportunities to grow, to expand in consciousness.

By asserting our will, many a closed door will open before us
—SEYYED HOSSEIN NASR

Paul's large family owned and operated a successful cattle ranch in Montana for three generations. Along with his friends and neighbors, he shared a love of the land and the livestock. Paul respected ranching life and assumed, as did others, that he would continue this vocation as an adult. He studied agribusiness at the nearby college and worked on the ranch during summers and school breaks.

After taking a scuba diving class at the college, Paul began to feel pulled in another direction. His underwater experience was in a swimming pool and a large, silty river, plus a big field trip to the ocean two states away. For Paul, who had never learned to swim, a major challenge was the course requirement to swim one mile. He had to take a swimming class on the side and run daily (not his favorite activity) to develop the necessary physical endurance to pass the test.

Some of Paul's happiest moments as a child were when he watched Jacques Cousteau's television program about the undersea world. The French oceanographer seemed more at home underwater than on land, and his inventions and contributions to undersea exploration intrigued Paul. He began thinking more and more about this fascinating realm. He read everything on it he could find and sent for additional literature to feed his growing interest. He daydreamed about exploring coral reefs and identifying exotic fish. He talked of the sea with wonder, awe, and increasing knowledge. Eager to explore tropical waters, Paul withdrew his savings and flew to the Cayman Islands to dive during a spring break—an adventure that opened up a beautiful new world.

Paul's family thought his attraction to the sea was only a passing interest, like others he'd had over the years. When he began investigating dive schools around the country, however, they were concerned. This area of Paul's interest had no relation to their world, and they doubted its practicality. They loved Paul very much but saw his activity as a flight of fancy and a waste of money. Paul held deep love, respect, and loyalty for his family, and, like most young people, he cared about their approval. He suffered from the conflict between what he felt guided to do and his family's wishes for him. In addition, the schools were far from home, and he knew he would miss his family.

Ultimately, he made a decision: he chose the school he thought would be best for him and sent in his application. The school was expensive, but Paul worked long and hard at unpleasant jobs; he lived simply and saved his money. Because few people understood or supported his goal, he knew he was regarded as "different." Time passed, full of delays and setbacks. At times his dream seemed far away, and he wondered if circumstances were telling him to give it up and settle for something more "realistic." But Paul knew what he wanted and persevered in his efforts.

Three years passed before Paul finally entered school. He applied himself and graduated at the top of his class, earning the school's first recommendation for a job at a dive resort in the Bahamas. After valuable experience there, he was invited back to join the school's teaching staff. He took more schooling and became qualified to instruct instructors. From the additional education, Paul discovered his love of the scientific aspects of his work, which opened up further avenues of potential.

His success fed on itself and created more success. Paul is now respected as one of the top people in his field. Not only is he in demand as a teacher, but he also writes articles for publication; co-owns a dive shop; travels around to trade shows; and has become an accomplished underwater photographer. He meets people from all over the world. He knows he can go anywhere he likes and enjoy work and friends. Paul's family is very proud of his accomplishments, and he enjoys his trips home to see them. He may be different, but he's the most interesting person they know—and one of the happiest!

Paul's story is a wonderful example of listening to our inner guidance, making a decision about what you want to do, and moving toward your goal in the best way you know how. He exemplified the idea of focusing his mind on a point of power, which is similar to allowing the rays of sunlight to flow through a magnifying glass until the concentration of the rays actually causes combustion—lighting a fire with a piece of glass. When strong desire is concentrated, it becomes a powerful means of manifesting that which you desire or precisely envision. And even difficulties can provide the strength of overcoming. Ask yourself: am I willing to commit to an activity strongly, or is my will fragile or weak? Remember, where there is a will, there is a way!

Every ending is a new beginning
—SUSAN HAYWARD

Nature demonstrates that almost everything occurs in cycles. The earth rotates on a daily cycle. The moon revolves around the earth on a monthly cycle, and the earth revolves around the sun in an annual cycle. During the year, the four seasons take us from cold to warm and again to cold as plants and animals cycle from a dormant to an active stage and then, as another winter approaches, again become dormant. Tides flow daily toward, and away from, the shore. Each day closes with a sunset, which is followed by a sunrise. Winter ends; spring begins. And so it goes. Every beginning has an ending, and all endings herald a new beginning: life out of death.

Kofi Awoonor, the Ghanaian writer, stated, "In our beginnings lies our journey's end." Our lives also have seasons and cycles. Each of us experiences an endless flow of beginnings and endings. Every season of our lives has a beginning and an ending that leads to a new beginning. Childhood ends and adolescence begins; adolescence ends and adulthood begins; young adulthood ends and middle age begins; middle age ends and old age begins.

We generally like beginnings—we celebrate the new. On the other hand, many people resist endings and attempt to delay them. Much of our resistance to endings stems from our unawareness, or inability to realize, that we are one with nature. Often we don't feel the joy of an ending, perhaps because we forget that in each ending are the seeds of beginning. Although endings can be painful, they are less so if, instead of resisting them, we look at time as a natural process of nature: as leaves budding in the spring, coming to full leaf in the summer, turning red and gold in autumn, and dropping from the trees in winter. It can be comforting to realize that we are an integral part of the great scheme of nature. And nature's great scheme involves change.

In his book *Mastering Change*, Leon Martel described how we now have the capacity to communicate simultaneously with every person on earth. Someone has noted that it took five months to get word back to Queen Isabella about the voyage of Columbus, two weeks for Europe to hear about Lincoln's assassination, and only 1.3 seconds to get the word from Neil Armstrong that a person can walk on the moon! Old eras of communications end and new ones begin.

The more we allow ourselves to trust that every ending is a new beginning, the less likely we are to resist letting go of old ideas and attitudes. The less resistance we have, the less pain we experience in making the journey through the many cycles of our lives. Many people have a fear of change. Yet our divine self is calling us to grow, to become more, to expand our horizons, and to experience the kingdom of heaven. Life demands change. We can choose to flow gracefully or to resist and become immobilized in fear. We can coast downhill, but mountain climbing is the journey of the soul.

For a moment, imagine that you are a caterpillar. You have this strange urge to spin a cocoon around your body—certain death! How difficult it must be to let go of the only life you have ever known, a life of crawling on the earth in search of food. Yet, if you are willing to trust, as caterpillars seem to do, the end of your life as an earthbound worm may be the beginning of your life as a beautiful winged creature of the sky.

The powerful potential behind change lies in the possibility that each new beginning will bring us greater joy and freedom than we have ever known. Whether or not that actually happens—whether or not we continue to grow through the cycles of our lives—is largely up to us. We play a part in what happens by choosing how we see our changes, our beginnings, our endings. We can see each ending as a tragedy and lament and resist it, or we can see each ending as a new beginning and a new birth into greater opportunities. What the caterpillar sees as the tragedy of death, the butterfly sees as the miracle of birth.

Material progress needs entrepreneurs
—SIR JOHN TEMPLETON

We are blessed to live in a time when anyone who desires to organize a business and is willing to take the steps necessary for the project to unfold can experience the freedom and opportunity to be an entrepreneur. And world progress needs entrepreneurs. If there is a blueprint or guideline to follow, getting started may not be difficult. The value of a definitive plan is easy to understand, for it can help us to avoid wasting precious moments. Dedication to the goal and earnest hard work are important values that can help manifest the dream. The advice of Harlow Herbert Curtice, an automobile manufacturer, was:

> Do your job better each time. Do it better than anyone else can do it. Do it better than it needs to be done. Let no one or anything stand between you and the difficult task.

I know this sounds old-fashioned. It is, but it has built the world.

Psychiatrist W. Beran Wolfe put it this way:

> If you observe a really happy man, you will find him build-
> ing a boat, writing a symphony, educating his son, growing
> double dahlias, or looking for dinosaur eggs in the Gobi
> Desert. He will not be searching for happiness as if it were
> a collar button that had rolled under the radiator, striving
> for it as the goal itself. He will have become aware that he
> is happy in the course of living life twenty-four crowded
> hours of each day.

And isn't "living life" an important foundation for building our dreams? Within you, within the creative genius of your mind, lies the real land of opportunity. Within you lies the insight, the foresight, the strength, courage, faith, freedom, and ability to accept and express your opportunities. From the circumstances around you, from the situations in which you may find yourself, from the relationships in which you may be involved, you can be creative!

Choose carefully and devote much thought and prayer to whatever you desire. Be sure your desire is worthy of your energy, your time, your creativity, and can bring a blessing of service to others. Know what you desire to accomplish, and plan—step-by-step, day by day—how to achieve your goal. We start at the beginning and work our way to the finish line. If we are open and receptive, the resources needed are provided.

What is necessary to become an innovator? First, recognize that you have within you the power to be creative. Next, be willing to try new experiences, to discover new fields that may enlarge the scope of your activities. Being open and receptive can teach us much about the world and help sincere and creative individuals become innovative entrepreneurs. Success-bound people find it important to believe in themselves, because the frontier exists inside them. Jesus's teaching concerning this is found in Luke 17:20–21, where we are reminded that "the kingdom of God is not coming with signs to be observed . . . for behold, the kingdom of God is in the midst of you." This is the true frontier that we must explore: our own inner being, our own divinity.

Progress depends on diligence and perseverance
—SIR JOHN TEMPLETON

The ability to endure is an important ingredient in realizing success, in business as well as in other areas of our lives. Often, we resolve to exercise regularly, lose weight, spend more time with our family, or eat more nutritiously. The commitment, however, is often forgotten because, over the long haul, we may fail to demonstrate the endurance needed to reach our goals. We may be tempted to spend valuable time pursuing interests that give pleasure while neglecting our long-range priorities.

The ancient Chinese sage Lao Tzu set down laws of effective living that he discovered after years of meditation and careful observation of life. He called his invaluable teaching the *Tao Te Ching*, or *How Things Work*. Many of his teachings reflected the effects of diligence and perseverance. One meaningful example is described in "The Ripple Effect" from the *Tao*:

Do you want to be a positive influence in the world? First, get your own life in order. Ground yourself in the single principle so that your behavior is wholesome and effective. If you do that, you will earn respect and be a powerful influence.

Your behavior influences others through a ripple effect. A ripple effect works because everyone influences everyone else. Powerful people are powerful influences.

If your life works, you influence your family.

If your family works, your family influences the community.

If your community works, your community influences the nation.

If your nation works, your nation influences the world.

If your world works, the ripple effect spreads throughout the cosmos.

Remember that your influence begins with you and ripples outward. So be sure that your influence is both potent and wholesome. How do I know that this works? All growth spreads outward from a fertile and potent nucleus. You are a nucleus.

Doesn't this "bigger picture" offer inspiration for diligence and perseverance? In order to realize the wonderful feeling of accomplishment that comes with meeting our goals, the ability to endure hardship is essential. So don't give up easily! You have the ability to make striking progress in pursuit of your goals. If we truly want to be all we are capable of being, we must be committed, and we must prepare ourselves to endure—to be a strong finisher in the race of life.

Perseverance makes the difference between success and defeat
—ANONYMOUS

Imagine a goal you strongly desire as resting at the summit of a steep and slippery mountain. Next imagine a heavy stone placed on your back just before you begin to climb. How do you feel the higher you climb? Excited? Tired? Frustrated? If you fail to reach your goal the first time or even the second, what keeps you going?

The answer may include many qualities, but at least one of them is perseverance. To persevere is the ability to persist in, or remain constant to, a purpose, an idea, or a task in the face of obstacles or discouragement. Removing obstacles in the path leading to your goals can be difficult and frustrating, leaving you with a desire to abandon the goal and the energy and belief required to achieve it. Perseverance is the voice within, constantly urging you that "if at first you don't succeed, try, try, again."

Reaching a goal may require repeated attempts, each one bringing you closer to achieving the objective, while in the process of reaching other goals as well. Among these may be personal redirection or the achievement of a greater good not initially planned.

George Washington Carver, born about 1864, had a dream of enriching the depleted soil of the southern United States. He persevered in getting an education when to do so was extremely difficult, especially for a black man. Rather than give up, he continued with his efforts, and in 1896 earned an MS degree from Iowa State University. Afterwards, he persuaded Southern farmers to plant soil-enriching peanuts and sweet potatoes instead of cotton. After achieving initial success, he went on to discover more than three hundred uses for the peanut, thus encouraging a steady market for the crop.

At the age of twelve, Thomas A. Edison became a railroad newsboy, and at age fifteen he earned a living as a telegraph operator. He studied and performed experiments in his spare time. Although he fathered many useful inventions, it cost him more than $40,000 in unsuccessful experimentation to produce the first incandescent lamp in 1879. Over a period of fifty years, he filed for 1,033 patents. He continued to try and try again.

With the kind of effort exemplified by George Washington Carver and Thomas Edison, not only do we come closer to our goals but, in the process, we also learn about ourselves. Through perseverance we discover virtues we may not be aware of in ourselves. At the same time, we may discover areas in our personalities that need further development before our goal can be reached. We gain satisfaction as we master tasks that lead to success. In the process of persevering, we boost our inner strength. We develop our spiritual muscles when we continue working faithfully toward what we consider success.

Only in the dictionary does *success* come before *work*. Though failure seemed to be his constant companion, Abraham Lincoln never stopped reaching for his dreams. Many of his detractors found little in Lincoln's background to suggest that as president he could bring the Civil War to a successful conclusion. Here was a man who had faced a series of failures: the death of his mother and sister when he was a child; the death of his sweetheart; a nervous breakdown; the death of three of his young sons; defeat as a candidate for the Illinois state legislature in 1832; a failed business partnership in a general store; a large debt to be paid off after a partner died; defeat as a candidate for Congress in 1843 and, again, in 1844; rejection of his nomination as commissioner of the general land office; defeat as a candidate for the Senate in 1855; defeat as a vice-presidential candidate in 1856; and defeat by Stephen Douglas for a Senate seat in 1858.

When asked how he overcame so many personal defeats and failures in his life, Lincoln attributed his success to his undying faith. He said, "Without the Divine Being, I cannot succeed. With that assistance, I cannot fail." Lincoln found solace and comfort from his belief in God and from reading the Bible.

Thomas Edison was not a religious man but believed in a "supreme intelligence." Lincoln had very little schooling and was described as a "wandering, laboring boy," who grew up without an education. Edison had only three months of formal education. One of Edison's teachers called him "addled," so his mother pulled him out of school and taught him at home. Later he said that formal school bored him.

Dedication is another attribute of success. Edison said, "Genius is 1 percent inspiration and 99 percent perspiration." He was never discouraged when he didn't get results even after countless experiments. When a friend consoled Edison after his repeated failures to make a storage battery work, he said, "I have not failed. I've just found 10,000 ways that don't work." In his later years, when asked how his developing deafness was affecting him, he said, "I find it easier to concentrate now."

When we pursue a goal, we may sometimes encounter setbacks. There are many men and women throughout history who achieved incredible success only after trying, then trying again and again. We can do the same.

Leave no stone unturned
—EURIPIDES

While turning over the stones along your search for direction and movement toward your goals, do not allow the process itself to make you lose sight of what you are striving for. Frantically wasting energy in trying to move enormous obstacles blocking your way can sometimes be an exercise in futility. Calmly allowing your inner guidance to suggest an alternate course of action often shows greater wisdom.

Leaving no stone unturned, Noah Webster spent twenty-five years compiling the first dictionary of the English language. Robert E. Peary tried for twenty-three years to reach the North Pole before succeeding in the early 1900s. Songwriter Irving Berlin received only thirty-three cents for his first song, yet remained undaunted until he ultimately received international recognition for his music.

Diligence can often produce startling success that, at first, may seem to stretch the imagination. Before he was able to set sail, Christopher Columbus left no stone unturned in acquiring financial backing for his expedition. He convinced Spanish monarchs Ferdinand and Isabella of the viability of his plan to sail westward to reach India and, after the initial voyage, made several further exploratory expeditions. His diligent pursuit of a new trade route to the Indies resulted in the discovery of entirely new lands—the Americas.

Madame Curie spent her entire adult life conducting scientific research. Her diligence in the laboratory resulted in the discovery of the elements radium and polonium and laid the groundwork for nuclear physics and theories of radioactivity. In her case, one stone overturned became a stepping-stone to the next discovery. Madame Curie was the first person to be awarded the Nobel Prize twice.

Expand your awareness and perspective. Expand yourself by doing more, giving more, being bigger in your thinking and feeling. Words found in the New Testament may strengthen us in our efforts. "God did not give us a spirit of timidity, but a spirit of power and love and self-control" (2 Tim. 1:7). Renewed and refreshed, keeping in mind the power within, you may have greater strength to follow the counsel of Euripides and continue to "leave no stone unturned."

Your dreams can come true when you activate them
—SIR JOHN TEMPLETON

There are dreams . . . and there are dreams!

Elias Howe, American inventor of the sewing machine, was experiencing a major problem in determining the appropriate location for the eye of the needle in his new invention. He was rapidly running out of money and ideas when, one night, he had a peculiar dream. He was being led to his execution for failing to design a sewing machine for the king of a strange country. He was surrounded by guards, all of whom carried spears that were pierced near the head. Realizing instantly that this was a solution to his problem, Howe awakened and rushed straight to his workshop. By nine o'clock that morning, the design of the first sewing machine was well on the way to completion!

Dreams, or magnificent ideas, have often played a major part in discovery, and discoveries have fulfilled many dreams. Jonas E. Salk, the American virologist who developed the first effective antipolio vaccine, worked hard to publicize his discovery, but he received no money from the sale of it. Someone once asked him who owned the patent. He replied, "The people. Could you patent the sun?"

The structural formula for benzene eluded Kekule von Stradonitz, the German chemist, for a long time. He claimed that the initial insight came to him in 1858 while he was dozing on a London bus traveling to Clapham Road. He saw atoms dancing before his eyes and then things like snakes, which contorted and took their tails in their mouths, thus creating rings. The ancient alchemical symbol of the snake biting its tail suggested that the two ends of the benzene chain were joined in a circle, prompting Kekule to accurately express the chemical makeup of benzene.

These examples of dreams, visions, ideas—whatever you may wish to call them—exemplify an important truth. In each instance, the person took some kind of action to bring the dream to fruition.

From Rebecca Clark's book *Breakthrough* comes a stirring description of a dreamer. Does it call to the vision within you?

Who are the dreamers? They are the souls who are the architects of the world's greatness. Their futuristic vision lies seeded within the rich soil of their adventurous souls. The dreamers never see the limiting mirages of so-called fact. Their vision can peer beyond the veils and mists of doubt and uncertainty and pierce the walls of time.

Makers of empires have fought for bigger things than crowns and higher seats than thrones. They are the Argonauts, the seekers of the priceless fleece—the Truth. Through the ages, they have heard the voice of destiny call to them from the vast unknown. Their brains have wrought all human miracles. In place of stone, their spires stab the old world's skies and with their golden crosses they kiss the sun.

They are the blazers of the way—who refuse to wear doubt's bandage on their eyes, who may starve and chill and hurt, but who hold to courage and hope because they know there is always proof of Truth for those who try. They know that only cowardice and lack of faith can keep the seeker from his chosen goal; but if his heart be strong and if he dreams enough in sincerity, he can attain the goal, no matter that men may have failed before.

CHAPTER 20

Discovering Your Life's Purpose

He who has a "why" for which to live, can bear with almost any "how"
—FRIEDRICH NIETZSCHE

IN HIS BOOK *Man's Search for Meaning*, Austrian psychiatrist Viktor Frankl documents the profound power that a life purpose exerts over an individual under even the worst of circumstances. Frankl, who survived the Nazi concentration camps, described how prisoners who felt they had nothing to live for succumbed, while those who perceived themselves as having a mission to complete struggled to survive. Deprived of all external supports that might give life meaning, these survivors came to realize that, in Frankl's words, "it did not really matter what we expected of life, but rather what life expected of us." Their sense of an inner purpose pulled them through the most horrible physical and emotional experiences so that they might make their unique contribution to the world.

Every one of us has a purpose in life beyond our immediate interests and gratifications, though that purpose frequently goes undiscovered. Since God has given us everything potentially, we need to learn how to discover His gifts by making them spiritually active in our lives. Many people devote their entire lives to the pursuit of greater ease and pleasure. Those who have not found the "why" that gives meaning to existence may achieve material success, yet the real

295

goodness of life eludes them. One true meaning of life lies in sharing our particular qualities of greatness with others.

There is a simple way you can discover your special purpose in life. Draw up a list of all the qualities you value in yourself and that other people admire in you. If you're a humorous person, you have the ability to uplift and entertain. If clear thinking is your strong suit and you're skilled at developing ideas, accept this as a gift that can benefit those around you in many ways. Since we sometime think of ourselves as lacking in good qualities, it is important to dig a little to unearth those skills and talents that may lie hidden.

Next, examine the ways in which you interact with other people and make a list of those ways that work the best. Does it excite you to teach someone a skill that will help him? Do you enjoy simply listening while someone shares a problem with you? Are you happiest when organizing a group for a project, or perhaps when encouraging someone who feels hopeless about herself and her life?

Finally, imagine what your world would be like under the best of all possible circumstances. Would it be clean, peaceful, and productive? Form a mental picture of the world that you'd like you and your loved ones to live in, and write down that vision in as much specific detail as possible.

Your mission in life is to have a "why" to live for, to use your best qualities in the service of the kind of world in which you would like to live. That is your purpose. This is what life expects of you. And when you live according to your purpose, setting goals that support that purpose, you may find the pieces of your life drawn together into a strong internal whole. Then, no matter how difficult life's experiences may prove to be, you will be able to endure and even prevail.

Where there is no vision, the people perish
—PROVERBS 29:18 (KJV)

The ancient proverb, cited above, reflects the truth that everyone needs dreams and goals in order to live life fully and satisfactorily.

If we don't have a specific goal in mind or we don't know where we want to go, we may end up in places not of our choosing. Establishing goals, along with guidelines on how to achieve them, helps to keep us focused and energized and often makes our lives more interesting, useful, and successful.

The story of long-distance swimmer Florence Chadwick illustrates the importance of keeping our goals in sight. Chadwick swam the English Channel in both directions and set international records. She then attempted to become the first woman to swim across the Catalina Channel. On the day slated for the Channel swim, Chadwick faced heavy seas. However, because she had trained in the Persian Gulf, she was in peak condition and prepared to do battle with the surging waves. Along with the rough weather, Chadwick encountered chilling cold. That was a problem, but, again, her training made a big difference. She was accustomed to cold water and her trainers had greased her body to help insulate her from the elements. In addition, Chadwick's trainers, rowing alongside her, were able to sustain her with hot soup from a thermos and comforting words of encouragement as she fought the cold, rough sea.

Yet, with all her planning and superior training, the one thing Chadwick and her trainers had not anticipated was fog. As a fog bank descended, visibility closed to only a few feet, obscuring the horizon and the distant shore. Chadwick started to flounder. With the loss of visibility, the ice-cold, heavy waves seemed to grow to towering proportions. Chadwick began to suffer cramps in her arms, legs, feet, and hands from the severe cold. Her muscles screamed in pain as she battled the huge waves. Finally, she asked her trainers to bring her onboard and take her ashore.

Later, when she was warm and dry, newspaper reporters asked her if she knew that she'd been only a short distance from the shore when she gave up her valiant effort to break the record. She responded that even though her trainers told her the same thing, it simply hadn't made a difference to her. "You see," she said, "I lost sight of my goal. I'm not sure I ever had it firmly in mind."

When we have no goal, or when our vision of the goal is obscured, we may lose our sense of purpose. Even when we've prepared ourselves well and have an aptitude for a given activity, poorly directed efforts can rob us of vital energy. We end up running around in circles. Unless we formulate specific goals that dovetail with our purpose in life, and unless we keep a clear vision of these goals in mind, we may eventually falter and fail.

Once you have your purpose clearly in mind, explore the various ways you can make it happen and visualize the process you believe can work best. Set goals, do what it takes to accomplish them, and enjoy the process.

'Tis the part of the wise man to keep himself today for tomorrow, and not venture all his eggs in one basket
—MIGUEL DE CERVANTES

Helen Keller once said, "I do not simply want to spend my life, I wish to invest it." For many people throughout the ages, human life was simply spent in doing what was necessary for survival. The hand-to-mouth existence of our prehistoric ancestors precluded their deep consideration of the future. At that time, to live through a single event may often have been an accomplishment.

As human civilization mastered survival, life became more refined, and the pursuit of a life to be spent in comfort, ease, and physical pleasure preoccupied many people. In the developed state of our world today, many people have the prospect of an extended life span and the assurance of luxuries undreamed of a hundred years ago. We can spend our lives doing a moderate amount of work to obtain a maximum amount of comfort, if that is our desire. Yet those people who are on the leading edge of human evolution realize, as did Helen Keller, that the greatest happiness in life comes not from the comforts and pleasures that money can buy but from the investment of the days of our lives in a purpose that transcends purely personal interests.

Each of us has a purpose for living beyond our own survival and pleasure. Every individual is like a thread in a beautiful tapestry with a vital contribution to make, not only to the sustenance of life as we know it, but in the creation and development of more beneficial expressions of life. Investing, rather than spending, our lives involves the commitment of our resources—ideas, love, talents, time, energy, money—to those activities that support our larger purpose. We think about how we can contribute to the overall good, focus on our talents, and then invest our energies in our chosen work. The return on a wisely made investment is happiness and usefulness.

Investment of time, energy, and resources can be exciting. Whether you oversee a worldwide organization or a simple project in which you have invested yourself successfully, you can share in the success with the knowledge that, in some way, it might not have happened without your contribution. When you see your investment joining with others' to make a positive difference in a community, in a state, in a country, or in the world, you gain a sense of the power that like-minded individuals have to effect change. The return on a successful investment can be a tremendous motivation to invest again and again.

Although you may be delighted with the success of an initial investment, the experienced investor advises you to concentrate in more than one area and share your resources with many deserving organizations or people. Depending on a single investment or any kind of human relationship breeds a watchful concern, based on a fear of loss. If you have one friend to whom you devote most of your energies and affections, then you come to expect a lot from that person. And what if your friend, for some reason unrelated to you, cannot fulfill your expectations when you need it? For some people in this situation, disappointment and resentment, which puts a strain on the friendship, may result. In this scenario, your investment may not provide a positive return. If, however, you invest yourself in several friendships, when one friend cannot fulfill an expectation, there may be others available to provide nurturing and support. Because you do not depend solely on one person, you can have the blessings and rewards of many friendships. The author of Ecclesiastes writes: "Cast your bread upon the waters, for you will find it after many days. In the morning sow your seed, and at evening withhold not your hand; for you do not know which will prosper, this or that, or whether both alike will be good" (Eccles. 11:1, 6).

You have the ability to formulate an idea, plan ahead carefully, and then invest yourself totally in the work at hand. Investment in those endeavors that fulfill a higher purpose are vital to achieving happiness in life. You have much to give, so give it to as many as you can.

A soul without a high aim is like a ship without a rudder
—EILEEN CADDY

A ship with properly trimmed sails can travel in any direction in relation to the wind, except directly into it. While the set of the sails determines the most efficient use of the available wind, the rudder enables the ship to travel in a specific heading. Without a rudder, the ship can do little more than blow aimlessly downwind.

What is true of the wind-powered boat is also true of people. There are many things you can do to contribute to your success. You can cultivate a charming personality, develop a dynamic appearance, and receive a fine education. Making these preparations are like setting your sails. However, without a rudder, a proper steering device, you still may fail to get anywhere in life. You need a goal, a purpose, an ideal that can steer you in the direction of your choice.

Many people seem to work hard throughout their lives, earning a minimum of personal and professional satisfaction. But often the problem is that they engage in aimless thought and useless activity, rather than steering themselves in a charted direction. Like a rudderless ship, they blow helplessly on the winds of circumstance, wasting their precious mental energy, failing to build vast knowledge and expertise. Feeling ineffective, they often live in a chronic state of unhappiness. High aims and clear purposes, however, act as a rudder for the unlimited potential of your mind and help you move in directions that can build your reputation and bolster your usefulness. As effectiveness and productivity increase, feelings of uselessness, of drifting, diminish.

Consider how Samuel Colt, inventor of the revolver that bears his name, got the idea for its revolving cylinder as a sixteen-year-old seaman, as he watched the helmsman turn the ship's wheel—each spoke aligning with a clutch that held it fast. It pays to be observant while reaching for high vision!

If you choose carefully and navigate your course with care, you can move in positive directions. Chances are you might set your sights on many things before you find the direction you really want to pursue. That is perfectly natural. We often gradually evolve into the field that best suits our deepest interests and abilities. Each time you set and attain a specific goal, you learn that much more about the dynamics involved in taking command of your life. Then, when you find the things you most want to do, you are prepared to reach out and attain your goals. No longer is success a mystery that only comes to others. You can be well acquainted with it and ready to seize the moments of opportunity that come your way.

Make yourself necessary to the world and mankind will give you bread
—RALPH WALDO EMERSON

Ralph Waldo Emerson, in many of his masterful essays, pondered this formula. He was expected to follow in the steps of his father and grandfather as a Unitarian minister. Although he did become an ordained minister, Emerson was not content to minister in the ways of his forefathers. He recognized that his gift was different. Fired with enthusiasm to reveal his ideas on morality, self-reliance, and the soul, Emerson began to write. His ideas were new to many people, and his audience began to grow. Before long, he met with success, and today, his influence in American literature and culture is profound. Emerson bravely stepped forth and created a need for what he had to give the world by making his talent available.

Like Emerson, if you find the special talent you have to offer and use that talent to produce something the world can use, the world will supply your needs. What activities bring you great joy? What activities do you perform well? What flows easily for you? If you could do whatever work you desired and had some assurance that you wouldn't fail, what would you do? What are your goals? You may wish to revisit them and think of a way people could benefit from what you have to offer . . . and then offer it! You might find, as did Emerson, that what it takes is a taste of something good—something you have to offer the world—and people will find themselves hungering for more.

With the sheer driving force of advancing technology, it becomes increasingly clear that opportunities are available in many areas for those who feel an inner pull to be of service. For example, the environment, the physical sciences, the economy, health and medicine, education, communications media, religion, charity, philanthropy, and volunteerism are but some of the areas changing with advancing technologies. The evolution of humanity and the universe seems to be vast in its conception, yet curiously experimental and tentative, a truly creative work in progress. If you choose, you can be a conscious part of that creative process. We have come a long way from the cave shelters of the Ice Age, but it may well be, in God's great plan, that we have vastly further to travel. Science is beginning to reveal a creation of awesome magnitude, intricate beauty, and order, and we sense that what lies beyond our perception is vastly greater still.

There are abundant opportunities for those who elect to make themselves necessary to the world. The rewards are not only the "bread" provided, but an inner awareness of your contribution to God's purpose and to the uplifting of the human race through loving service.

Freedom is a fact of life
—ANONYMOUS

To be fully alive and living—not just existing—in today's world, it is important to allow ourselves to be in a harmonious flow with the people and events around us and still continue moving in the direction of our sincere desires for our lives. Often, we stuff ourselves into habitual ways of doing things. Then, if things don't go in the direction we expect, we get upset. One way to be free is to break the molds of old ways of thinking and rigid ways of doing things.

In *Man's Search for Meaning*, Viktor Frankl tells of his own experience in a Nazi concentration camp. He reflects on the irony that he never felt so free as he did during that dreadful period. How could that be true? Even though all obvious freedoms had been stripped from him and he was living in constant threat of sickness, torture, and death, he discovered a depth of freedom inside himself that he had never before experienced.

If we come to understand that freedom is inescapable, that understanding can serve us well in living a happy and productive life. In the middle of one of the most restrictive environments imaginable, Viktor Frankl discovered this truth about freedom. He learned that no matter where life might take him, no matter how terrible the external conditions might be, he still had the freedom of his own thoughts and attitudes. He could choose to see with the eyes of a free spirit.

If your thoughts sometimes turn negative, do you feel this is the result of some external force? That you have no future because someone is coercing you to follow a particular path? Do you feel you could be happy if only others would change? Or are you choosing to look for the meaning and the good in every situation? As long as we cherish our freedom to think and be, it can never be taken away from us.

You will know them by their fruits
—MATTHEW 7:16

We realize how rich we are when we pause to count our blessings. The wonderful substance of God flows in and through us and extends from us in every direction. Truly, there is no place we can go where we are not bathed in the infinite sea of the substance of the universe. There may be a number of ways to open the channel for our good to flow *to* us, but have we looked recently at the many ways good can flow *from* us?

During his ministry, Jesus told those who were near, "You will know them by their fruits" (Matt. 7:16). Later, the apostle Paul tells us what those good fruits are: "The fruit of the Spirit is love, joy, peace, patience, kindness, goodness, faithfulness, gentleness, self-control; against such there is no law" (Gal. 5:22–23).

The fruits of the Spirit are available for every person, all the time, and in every circumstance or situation. God has packed these good possibilities away in the divine ideal for every person, just as God has hidden within every watermelon seed the possibility of a delicious, full-grown melon. The good fruits of Spirit have been given to every one of us, but it is our job to cultivate them and bring them into abundant harvest in our lives. How can we do this? Let's take a closer look at each of the "fruits."

Love has been called our "human rose." In our soul-soil, too, flowers grow, and none more beautiful than love! Love is more than affection. It is that magnetic, attractive force that binds families, friends, states, and countries together. Love is an inner quality that beholds good everywhere and in everyone.

Joy is the happiness of God expressed through his perfect idea, humanity. We find that joy and gladness are strength-giving, especially when our minds are fixed on being a channel for good.

Peace is more than freedom from strife—it is a positive assurance that only the good is true.

Patience is the attitude of mind characterized by poise, serenity, inner calmness, and quiet endurance—especially in the face of trying or upsetting conditions. The gift of patience has its foundation in faith.

Kindness is one of the gentle expressions of love. We grow in grace when we share our loving-kindness with all of creation.

When we establish an enduring consciousness of *goodness*, we can see many problems disappear as darkness before light.

Faithfulness is being always reliable, honest, and inspiring confidence in your neighbors.

Gentleness brings calmness, quietness, and humility.

Self-control is the starting point of all control. When we begin to grasp our self-control through prayer and thrift and planning ahead in daily living, life begins to take on deeper meaning.

Misfortunes can be blessings
—SIR JOHN TEMPLETON

An old story tells about missionary David Livingstone, who lived among the natives in a small, primitive African tribe. He suffered from a rare blood disease that required him to drink fresh goat's milk daily. During a visit to the village, the tribal king became enchanted with Livingstone's goat. Now, it was the local custom that everything belonging to the villagers was automatically considered to be the king's property if he so desired. Having no choice but to honor the village custom, the missionary offered his goat to the king, knowing that he had just given away the very thing his life depended on.

The king appreciated Dr. Livingstone's gesture and, in return, handed him what appeared to be a long walking stick he had been carrying. As Livingstone turned away to go home, he sadly lamented to his house servant that he was afraid he wouldn't be able to live without his daily supply of goat's milk. The servant quickly turned to Livingstone and said with a gasp of surprise: "Master, don't you realize what the king has given you? That's his scepter, and anything you desire in the entire kingdom is yours!"

How many times have we faced a disappointment or misunderstanding in our relationship with a colleague, family member, or friend? Whatever the difficulty, it is important for us to realize that a positive outlook can make a difference, can turn a "stick" into a "scepter." A poor evaluation at work can actually lead to a promotion if you accept it as a positive challenge to do a better job.

Throughout history there are countless examples of famous scientists and explorers who set out to prove one thing and failed, but who went on to discover something more significant. For example, Christopher Columbus was trying to find a new trade route to China and Japan. Imagine his disappointment when, instead of landing in Asia, he found himself thousands of miles away from his original destination on some strange, unknown landmass, later called America. This failure, however, would eventually earn him a permanent place in history as one of the world's greatest explorers.

Challenges have a way of cropping up when we least expect them, and because they seem constantly to surprise us, we may not be prepared to handle them in an appropriate manner. Regardless of the appearances of the situation, however, the truth is that God is there in the midst of the confusion, ready and willing to respond to our needs. Often when we feel unprepared, we may become alarmed, confused, frustrated, irritated, and perhaps even frightened and angry. These emotions can be overcome when we "stand firm and see the salvation of the Lord."

By turning our thoughts around, we can turn our own lives around. If we let negative ideas and fears invade our minds when our plans fail, our world may be filled with self-doubt and insecurity. Once we become aware of how often we limit ourselves through negative attitudes, we can begin to concentrate on positive thoughts. A consistent, positive attitude—turning a stick into a scepter—can allow us to turn an impossible situation into a positive opportunity to find happiness and success.

Work is love made visible
—KAHLIL GIBRAN

With movement into the adult world often comes work. *Work* can be defined in so many ways: employment, occupation, task, labor, toil, and the like. To some people, the ideal occupation seems to be the one that doesn't keep them too occupied. But what if we take a closer look at this activity that may consume a considerable amount of our time? J. H. Patterson said, "It is only those who do not know how to work that do not love it." Henry Ward Beecher wrote:

> Why do birds sing? Because the song is in them, and if they did not let it forth, they would split; it must come out. It is the spontaneity and the urgency of this feeling in them that impels their utterance. Why should men work? Because their hearts want some outlet to give expression to the feeling of earnest sympathy that is in them. Where a man has a strong and large benevolence, he will always be busy, and pleasantly busy.

Did these writers tap into some great mysterious understanding? Perhaps they simply learned the principle of "swimming with the tide" of possibilities. A minister friend once said that we are here to work out our soul's destiny, and the work we do can simply be an avenue through which this may be accomplished. If we keep poised and balanced, doing our best every day, realizing that under all circumstances it is important to be compassionate, kind, and generous with those we meet on life's journey and, if we continue doing our best work and thinking our best thoughts every day, we can gradually wear away concerns over problems, as the swimmer wears away concerns over the water. We learn how to meet new situations, and this awareness helps us take successful, correct action.

There seems to be a simplicity in what we seek to do when we dedicate ourselves to the doing. When we choose to accept into our consciousness only what uplifts, but do not reject that which we may not understand, we do those things that are to be done by us in a more loving state of mind. And that which we do in a loving state of mind can become love made visible through our work.

An artist can become so enmeshed in the design of a painting and the flow of the palette of colors that hours may go by without her noticing the passage of time. A surgeon can become so focused on his work that the healing energy of the universe flows through his intelligence, his love for the great calling, and his hands. An assembly-line operator in an automobile manufacturing plant can feel satisfaction in knowing that his work contributes to a safe vehicle for those who will drive the cars he helps build. A worker in a furniture manufacturing company can feel an inner joy in knowing that the end product of his craftsmanship may grace a home for many years.

Thomas Edison often ate and slept in his laboratory and worked there for eighteen hours a day. But it wasn't toil to him. "I never did a day's work in my life," he exclaimed. "It was all fun!" A humorous story is told about former U.S. President Lyndon Baines Johnson and his love for his work. The Senate worked hard and late when Johnson was majority leader. One weary senator complained to a colleague, "What's the hurry? Rome wasn't built in a day." "No," the colleague replied, "but Johnson wasn't foreman on that job!"

On one level, a career can be described as a job that sustains your interest while you make enough money to support yourself in a comfortable lifestyle. But a career can be much more than that; it can be a vocation. The word *vocation* comes from the Latin root "to call." Your vocation, then, is a calling and, in a very deep sense, finding your vocation is a matter of finding yourself. When you have found your calling, you can give love through your work. In fact, love may be the key to success in mastering your vocation. It directs you to those special talents you can give to the world and shows you how to share them with others.

A vocation is more than putting in hours to earn a paycheck. Rather, it can be your most valuable asset and the greatest gift of yourself and your talent that you can offer the world. Every useful work can be a ministry of service in your chosen field.

For every effect, there is a cause
—HERMETIC PRINCIPLE

Cause and effect has often been called the law of sequence, the balance wheel of the universe. Several sacred scriptures refer to this activity.

In the Bible we read, "Whatsoever a man soweth, that shall he also reap" (Gal. 6:7, KJV). Sound familiar? In the Bhagavad Gita we find, "Find the reward of doing right, in right." Also from the Gita comes the statement, "No man shall escape from acting by shunning action; and none shall come by mere renunciation to perfection."

Confucianism: Confucius was asked, "Is there one word that sums up the basis of all good conduct?" He replied, "Is not *reciprocity* that word? What you yourself do not desire do not put before others."

From the Hebrew Scriptures we read, "Cast your bread upon the waters, for you will find it after many days" (Eccles. 11:1).

The Qur'an tells us, "Wrong not and you will not be wronged."

In the book *The Psyche and Psychism*, Torkom Saraydarian writes:

> The Inner Presence and the presence in nature may be called the Law of Cause and Effect. This law is an energy field extending throughout the Cosmic planes, and any action upon this energy field creates a corresponding reaction relative to the level and intensity of the action. Thus a wish, a desire, an aspiration, a thought can be an act of prayer, a form of action which creates the corresponding reaction from the energy field, from the Law of Cause and Effect.

These expansive and universal understandings of cause and effect indicate a very important truth: we are usually responsible for the things that happen to us. We may not be fully comfortable with this fact because a lot of people do not want to take full responsibility for their lives. It is often easier to blame our parents, our neighbors, our friends, our spouse, the government, or some other organization.

But you and I are responsible for what happens to us. Can this not also mean that we have vast and unlimited opportunity to create, or cause, our lives to be the way we desire? This idea can be exciting! Whatever situation may be present in our lives, we can create a positive experience from the set of circumstances before us. How? Through the power of choice.

Yet what about *chance*? A lot of people grow up with the belief that chance, or luck, or even accidental happenings contribute, for better or worse, to our lives. One woman was in an automobile accident and refused to accept any responsibility for the collision, even though she failed to stop at the traffic sign and received a citation. Another woman was stopped at a traffic signal when she was rammed from behind by a speeding car. Being familiar with the laws of life and how they operate, she proceeded to move calmly through the circumstances by communicating with the other driver, filing the police report, and getting her car repaired. The other driver's insurance paid all related bills, and her life continued on. She did wonder what this little interlude was all about, but had the wisdom to realize that it's not what happens to you that is most important but how you handle the situation.

Can we bring a new scientific perspective to the age-old question of purpose? In the last forty or fifty years, the number of scientists raising philosophical and religious questions as a result of recent scientific discoveries has multiplied. Albert Einstein openly and movingly spoke of the religious attitude as essential to good science, and Sir James Jeans said that "the universe was beginning to look not like a great machine but rather like a great thought."

If there is such order and purpose in the cycling of the planets of our solar system around our Sun (which we don't fully understand), can there not also be a potency and purpose to our individual lives that we may not presently understand?

Every useful life is a ministry
—SIR JOHN TEMPLETON

God's universe operates in rhythm and harmony and beauty. It is like the musical theme of a symphony in which the composer is the life and essence. It may be difficult to imagine the vastness and the orderliness of the stars, planets, and solar systems. It is so much more accurate than any human mechanism and has been maintaining its schedule for thousands of years, bringing the seasons and changing length of days according to a great plan. This perfect order and system can be found in even the smallest things.

Humanity is included in that universal plan. The infinite wisdom and harmony that flow through the universe also flow through the mind and affairs of humankind. As we choose to live our lives in a useful manner and in harmony with the laws of life, what we do can become a meaningful ministry of service to others.

Oftentimes, when people hear the word *ministry*, they think of a church or a government office. In truth, however, everything productive that you can accomplish in life is a ministry. By loving your work—whatever that work may be—and holding the attitude that it may be accomplished from the perspective of doing a good job for others, you are fulfilling a ministry of service. And the world needs many more ministers of service who are willing to dedicate their energies to the job at hand!

Every effort contributed to helping another is a way of saying yes to life. And saying yes is a profound form of successful behavior, which can bring an increase in happiness. To the one who faces the light, the path is bright. It is the person who faces the other way, the way of selfishness, who may ultimately walk in his own shadow as it falls upon the path before him.

It takes courage to rise above the status quo, a bravery that each of us must learn in our own way. Thomas Huxley said, "We live in a world which is full of misery and ignorance, and the plain duty of each and all of us is to try to make the little corner he can influence somewhat less ignorant than it was before he entered it." Life is made up not necessarily of great sacrifices or high-level duties, but of little things. The smiles, the kindnesses, the commitments and obligations and responsibilities that are given habitually and lovingly are the blessings that win and preserve the heart and bring comfort to ourselves as well to others. This is the ministry of service performed by every useful life.

The way you think about the physical mechanism through which you express your being determines the way in which it can work for you. Wouldn't you like to improve yourself? How would it feel to know you were making a real contribution to your world? Would you like to feel that because of you and your work someone's life was blessed?

The secret of a productive life can be sought and found
—SIR JOHN TEMPLETON

We learn not to be surprised at wisdom that comes from unexpected sources. In the process of dealing with today's world and its many complexities, some people seem to have developed increased tension, greater nervousness, deeper fears, and more profound anxieties. The profession of personal counseling has expanded exponentially over recent years in an effort to assist people in these situations. This work is largely performed by psychiatrists, psychologists, clergypeople, social workers, and physicians. We are learning that the condition of our emotional health can indicate whether or not we will have peace, serenity, and strength in our daily lives. And mental, emotional, and spiritual health are essential to successful living.

In determining how to handle some of the stresses in life and learn more about ourselves as individuals, we gain fruitful insights from the Plains Native Americans. Experts say each person had an important part to play in the life of their tribe. At an early age, the young people participated in an activity known as the "vision quest." It emphasized self-denial and spiritual discipline, extending to a lifelong pursuit of wisdom of mind, body, and soul. The Plains Native Americans believed that through the proper preparation for the vision quest—prayer, fasting, meditation, the ceremony of the sweat lodge, and spending time in solitude—individuals could receive a special vision of their purpose in life. The personal revelatory experience received during the vision quest then became the fundamental guiding force for the individual. The dogma of tribal rituals and the religious expressions of others became secondary to the guidance for living a productive life that a Plains Native American received from his personal visions. The vision quest, as a fundamental guiding force, reflects certain universal aspects of the experience and invites comparisons with the *samadhi* of the Yogi, the *satori* of the Zen Buddhist, Dr. Raymond Bucke's *cosmic consciousness*, and the *ecstasy* of the Christian mystic.

Are you struggling with a sense of unfulfillment? Do you have a feeling that you're here on earth for reasons that elude you? A lot of the world's creative work has been done by people under whatever conditions they had to work with. Begin to practice the belief that you *do* have a significant part to play in life and take steps to discover what it is. How? Each time an opportunity comes your way that will allow you to express your talent, welcome that opportunity with open arms. Since good things may be attracted to you when you put what you know and believe into action, it is important to practice what you know. Imagine what it might feel like to live a productive life and then assume that attitude. Go forward to meet life with self-confidence and self-assurance. Do what you are doing so well that people are amazed at how talented you are. Let the joy in your heart give great inspiration and good cheer to others. Let your caring and consideration for others be reflected in your thoughts, words, and actions.

CHAPTER 21

Celebrating Success

If at first you don't succeed, try, try again
—WILLIAM EDWARD HICKSON

HEN THOMAS A. EDISON, working in America, and J. W. Swan, working in England, invented the electric lightbulb, the end seemed to have been reached in that kind of experimentation. A safe means of lighting streets and buildings now existed. What further uses could there be for the electric lightbulb?

After a time, however, researchers developed new types of lightbulbs that made use of ultraviolet rays and infrared heat rays. Still others were developed that killed bacteria in the air, and, before long, these were produced in numerous styles and sizes for use in hospitals, schools, homes, and even in chicken coops! Then came the blessings of halogen, fluorescent, and CFL bulbs.

These are only a few of the uses discovered for what, at first, seemed to be a simple and self-contained invention. To this day, researchers continue to search for new and better ways to make use of the electric lightbulb. There is a lesson here that can be applied to our own lives. Often, when we reach a high level of performance, or achieve a breakthrough in our profession, we're so proud of ourselves that we rest on our laurels. We stop trying to do better.

Success can be defined in many ways, and it is important to realize that your individual definition needs to be clear in your mind.

315

Once you have established your personal vision of success, you can begin the process of achieving your goal. Many successful people can attest to the multitude of difficulties they overcame on the journey to their destination. Sometimes the obstacles seem insurmountable, but when that happens, clearly bring forward your original vision to your conscious mind. Repicture your dream repeatedly until you have the courage and patience to await the next development. Often patience and anticipation are precisely what is required for new breakthroughs.

Success is often based on a high level of striving, day after day, in everything we do. It's important to understand that we never actually "arrive." Success isn't a destination but rather a journey. It's a journey of seeking and learning in each situation, trying to better ourselves as human beings. Like the researchers who continue to find new ways to use electricity, we must struggle to perform at maximum capacity, even though we may sometimes fail and make mistakes.

Self-control leads to success
—SIR JOHN TEMPLETON

In the drama of life, we may not always know or understand the plot. Sometimes the script seems pointless. We may fail to grasp the grand scope of the universal dramas in which we may be participating. At that point, there could be an attempt to blame the director, the producer, perhaps even the playwright, for the situation. However, in the universal drama of life, there are no bit players. And there is no one to blame. Life can seem like less of a muddle if we read the script correctly and become aware that we have unique qualities and can bring gifts to the "show" that no one else can.

One time at a county fair, a farmer exhibited a pumpkin grown in the exact shape of a two-gallon jug. "When it was no bigger than my thumb," he said, "I stuck it in the jug and just let it grow. When it filled the jug, it quit growing." What the glass jug did for the pumpkin, our thoughts do for our lives. We may grow as big and become as creative as the things we think about and believe in. But we stop growing at the limit of our thoughts.

One of the first things we need to do is to banish the thoughts that say the control of our lives is held by another. We have a built-in control tower called the faculty of free will, and nothing can move into our mind unless we are willing to place the "stamp of approval" on the delivery.

The law of responsibility applies in every area of our lives. For example, if we choose to abuse our bodies with drugs or alcohol, we must recognize the cost of this decision. We must ask ourselves if the drugs and alcohol are worth the cost in sickness and wasted time.

You may ask: "How can I take control of my life when I am faced with such inner turmoil and confusion and my problems are so overwhelming?" One thing we can do at once is take the same thought energy we have expressed in "How can I take control?" and turn it around into the thought, "I am one with the wisdom of God; I know what to do, and I do it." One of the best ways to exhibit the self-control that leads to success is to know that faith, not fear; love, not hate; joy, not sorrow; peace, not tension; freedom, not bondage is the role we choose to play.

Enthusiasm facilitates achievement
—SIR JOHN TEMPLETON

George Joe was a high school student in a town in northwest central Texas, an area famous for its love of high school football. In small schools, there often aren't enough players to field separate teams for defense, offense, and special teams, so each person must do double duty or even triple duty. George Joe did quadruple duty. He was the quarterback on offense, running and passing the ball expertly; a cornerback on defense; a kick returner on receiving teams; and a punter on kicking teams. Even more remarkable was the fact that he was usually the *smallest* man on the field, standing barely five feet, six inches tall, and weighing no more than 140 pounds. He didn't possess great speed, although he was quick and agile.

How did a small boy hold so many jobs on a team that had a history of winning year after year? He had a great love for the game and exhibited boundless enthusiasm. He poured every ounce of his energy and ability into each play, and he did it joyfully. George Joe was 50 percent inspiration and 50 percent perspiration, and a thrill to watch!

One of the most respected and famous former American presidents, Theodore Roosevelt, had a vision of American ships being able to go from the Pacific to the Atlantic Ocean and back without having to make the arduous trip around the tip of the South American continent. There were many difficulties to overcome. First was the opposition of his own countrymen who lacked the vision to foresee what a great boon to shipping the proposed canal would be. There was also the opposition of other world leaders who didn't wish to see the United States in control of such a project, and the Latin American leaders who opposed the intrusion of the United States in their domain.

Teddy Roosevelt was not deterred by any of these problems. He was enthusiastic about his vision, and through negotiation with the governments of Colombia and Panama, gained the right to build a canal across the Isthmus of Panama from Colon on the Atlantic Coast to Panama City on the Pacific Coast.

The problems did not end there, and the whole effort was almost brought down by mosquitoes carrying yellow fever. President Roosevelt solved the problem in his typical fashion. Medicine was found to fight the disease and insecticides to fight the insects. He wanted the canal to be a showplace to attract tourists as well as shipping, and he realized that people would not visit places where their health was at risk. When it was completed, the Panama Canal was a model of sanitation, a tribute to the enthusiasm and determination of Theodore Roosevelt.

The boy who loved football and a president of the United States both understood, and profited from, an important law of life: that enthusiasm facilitates achievement.

Real success means not to remain satisfied with any limited goal
—SEYYED HOSSEIN NASR

The dictionary defines *success* both as a favorable or satisfactory outcome and as the gaining of wealth, fame, and rank. Opportunities for success can come in many ways—for example, graduating from college, winning a football game, getting high scores on a test, or going out with someone you like. These are easy and measurable ways of sharing what the outer world terms "success."

There are far more subtle ways of achieving success that can be equally as spectacular, even if they aren't accompanied by social fanfare. You certainly can feel successful when you help a friend who needs your assistance, maintain a confidence you promised to honor, stay on a diet or exercise program, and refuse to give in to peer pressure because someone whose high opinion you desire may be persuasive. In fact, honoring the personal commitments you've made with yourself may be a higher form of success than all the fanfare because it is an inner, personal experience.

The author and speaker Wayne Dyer commented, "Success is a journey, not a destination, and half the fun is getting there!" So how do we "get there" and what makes the difference between a life filled with struggle and one that is full of earned pleasure? Two of the most fundamental laws of the universe—the *law of inertia* and the *law of attraction*—may help place that question in a more clear context.

The law of inertia states: "It is easier for something in motion to stay in motion. Conversely, once an object (or person) is at rest, it is easier to stay at rest." This is like saying that 50 percent of doing a task is beginning it. Once the task is begun, the law of inertia can propel you to finish it. In fact, it may often be more difficult *not* to finish the task—to stop in the middle—than to keep on going. On the other hand, when you are at rest—unmotivated or quiet or withdrawn—it can be easier to stay there than to make the effort to move ahead.

Once you overcome your initial inertia to stay at rest, you can use the energy of the inertia of motion to succeed at the goal you commit to beginning. Thus the law "success breeds success" may be reflected in your continuing to create what you have created in the past, or what you are creating in the present.

The law of attraction, which also breeds success, states that "like attracts like." It is a law that deals with the attraction between ourselves and other individuals, places, conditions, and things. We accomplish the manifestation of this law through our thoughts and beliefs. They bring to us, through the law of attraction, the people who are part of our universe—relatives, friends, enemies, work associates, and others with whom we come in contact. Our thoughts and beliefs also bring to us, through the law of attraction, the situations that become an important part of the creation of our personal world. This law functions like a boomerang, bringing back to us whatever we project onto others, either for good or ill.

You have options, then, of things that may be attracted to you in your universe. They are easy: what you like and what is like yourself. By becoming the person you most admire—a person of honesty, integrity, and compassion—you can attract those of similar values. Your "inner success" can create your "outer success." It is important to keep personal commitments, because the loyalty and honesty reflected in such behavior can return to us.

By focusing on the good in yourself and in others, people will enjoy being in your presence. They will treat you as a successful person because you help them feel good about themselves. As you begin to walk along the pathway of life by seeking inner guidance and developing and using your ideals, choices, and purposes for the highest good, your confidence increases as expressions of truth and faith. These qualities lead to greater understanding that the process of positive thinking works, and you may transform your life into a wonderful journey. Success is indeed a journey and not a destination, for a destination means the journey is over. And life is ongoing!

What appears to us as the impossible may be simply the untried
—SEYYED HOSSEIN NASR

Al kali, the Arab philosopher and philologist, said, "If you cannot accomplish a thing, leave it and pass to another which you can accomplish." But frequently we throw in the towel because it may seem expedient to do so. Is it *really* easier to assume that a stubborn problem cannot be solved than to put time and energy into finding a solution? Is it ultimately more rewarding to give up on a quarrelsome colleague than to seek a common meeting ground with him? *Impossible* may indeed be a convenient word, but can it facilitate the achievement you desire?

In fact, the impossible is merely the untried. What about the person who uses the power of the mind to overcome a stuttering problem; to graduate from college with *two* engineering degrees in spite of being told he was dyslexic; to lift herself out of a dysfunctional family or relationship, and proceed to enjoy a balanced and successful life? These people prove the possibility of the seemingly "impossible."

We must often search for answers to our money needs, our friendship and spiritual needs, and our needs at school and work. It is certainly more important to make efficient use of our time rather than to complain that there aren't enough hours in the day. We can only find a solution to our time crunch if we say to ourselves, "Yes, it's possible. It can be done."

Rebecca was born without a left arm from below the elbow. Fortunately, her parents were supportive as well as loving, and they believed that the impossible is simply the untried. As a result, Rebecca learned to swim, to ride a bike, to shuffle a pack of playing cards, and to tie her shoes. She grew up with a sense of pride, with a belief in her abilities, and with a desire to be useful to others.

What would happen if we choose to look, with fresh vision, at the word *impossible* and change it to *I'm possible!* The alphabetical letters are the same, but the difference is reflected in the punctuation, pronunciation, and emphasis. How can you know something is impossible if you've made little attempt to achieve a desired result? The understanding distills down to personal responsibility and a willingness to exert effort in a particular manner toward a particular goal.

Success feeds on itself and creates more success
—SIR JOHN TEMPLETON

Success takes practice, and successful people start practicing when they are young. Many times the things at which we're naturally gifted are the hardest for us to claim as a success. We may say to ourselves, "If I can do it so easily, why can't everyone else? If I can do it, it can't be that hard." Listen to the acknowledgment you receive from parents, teachers, employers, and friends. Don't brush it off as if they're just being nice. They may be telling you that you are a success right now. Answer with a sincere "Thank you."

We are often our own harshest critics, and we have a tendency to hear only criticism from others and not their praise. Practice hearing both compliments and constructive remarks from those who have good advice to offer. As you begin to recognize and build on the success you're experiencing now, you may discover that this is a feeling you can create again and again in various aspects of your life.

A story is told about a little boy who called at a house, selling picture postcards for a quarter each. The man who answered his knock asked the lad what he was going to do with the money he earned.

"Oh," he said, "I'm raising $100,000 for our new church building."

The startled customer responded, "Do you expect to raise it all by yourself?" The young man answered with a straight and serious face, "Oh, no, sir. There's another little boy helping me!" This young man had the spirit of success at an early age!

Knowing right now—feeling inside right now—that you're successful, whether you're a singer in the church choir, a waitress in a restaurant, the coach of the softball team, or the budding mechanic spending every spare moment in the garage rebuilding the engine of that antique car, will prepare you for greater and greater success. Success is not a onetime event. It is an accumulated series of wins and other experiences that create a successful life.

You are on the road to success if you realize that failure
is only a detour
—CORRIE TEN BOOM

How can we best define success? Does it simply mean that there was a task before us that we accomplished? If that is the case, then we could call walking down the driveway and retrieving the mail a success. Minor matters, regardless of how trivial, could be defined as successes as long as they were completed. Yet success means so much more. Success comes when we face a challenge and struggle against odds to meet that challenge. Historically, success often followed a series of failures.

For example, many of the greatest Americans experienced their share of failures. Abraham Lincoln suffered a staggering defeat in his first election campaign, and he was considered a bumbling speaker. Yet he became one of our greatest presidents, a leader whose speeches are still regarded as masterpieces of political persuasion. William Faulkner experienced a number of rejections as a young writer by publishers who had no understanding of his innovative narrative style, but despite repeated failures, Faulkner went on to become one of the South's foremost novelists and to win the Nobel Prize in Literature.

Because learning is a process that may result in a failure of one kind or another, failure is essential to success. We need to study our failures, to learn from them, and then to make a new attempt. Eventually, this process leads to success. However, if you give up at the first failure, then you've learned nothing, and you've gained no skill that can improve your subsequent efforts. You are seldom defeated by failure when you understand that failure is part of a natural process leading to success. You can then accept failure as a mere detour and not a dead end.

If we want to succeed, we should consider blazing new trails rather than going down the worn-out paths of former triumphs. In *A Treasury*, W. R. Beattie presents the idea that real success can be enjoyed in the process of building—in the drafting of the plans, laying the foundation, selecting the materials, measuring the many parts, and then dovetailing them together. He felt a person's greatest joys often came from the anticipation of each day's accomplishments and the satisfaction gained from a task well done.

For a moment, consider a most important room in your "house of living"—the room of your mind. What you are depends on what is in this room. You are—first and foremost—a spiritual being, so the plan for your inner room should be exquisite, comfortable, and satisfying. This place can represent a sanctuary of loveliness and peace. Its furniture consists of your thoughts. The walls must be sturdy in faith, with the colors showing forth the beauty of strength and courage, joy and peace, love and goodness, praise and thanksgiving, and positive, confident, success. Most important, the light of wisdom must fully illuminate this room, for it is in this inner room that you shape your world, and it is here that you may fashion the self that you give to the world.

*A man can fail many times, but he isn't a failure
until he begins to blame somebody else*
—JOHN BURROUGHS

There is a key distinction between failing and being a failure. Few things are learned in life without failing at least once. Did you learn to roller-skate without falling a few times? Did you learn to ride a bike without losing your balance? Chances are you didn't. You may have wanted to be able to do those things so intensely that you quickly put unsuccessful attempts behind you and kept trying. Soon you acquired the skill to do the thing you wanted. Even though you may have failed many times in the process of learning, you were not a failure. Failing simply became an open door to try again!

In life, it sometimes seems as if there may be someone or something that causes us to fail. It is not unusual to feel that another person or a circumstance may have prevented us from achieving our goals. Would it be more meaningful to analyze our own preparation and effort, and perhaps admit that we could have done better? Ask yourself whether you did the best you possibly could have and be fearless in admitting mistakes and oversights. Simply resolve not to repeat the error, forgive yourself for the mistake, and move on. Remember as you learned to ride the bike, as you kept trying and persisted, you got better and better until bike riding became almost as natural as walking.

There is no one to blame, not even ourselves. The person who gets stuck in self-blame or in blaming others or circumstances often slows his or her own recovery and risks becoming a failure instead of simply having a temporary setback. Rather than feeling sorry for yourself or being angry at others ask, "What now? What else can I do to accomplish my goals?"

If we waste time and energy blaming others, we may not see what we need to learn about ourselves in order to grow and achieve better results from our efforts. We can fail many times, but our failure does not have to be final. Those who fail are not failures, unless they let blame and self-pity prevent them from reaching their goals.

Winston Churchill did not become prime minister of England until he was sixty-two years old, and then only after a lifetime of defeats and setbacks. Many of his greatest contributions came when he was a senior citizen. And in 1962, the Decca Recording Company turned down the opportunity to work with the Beatles. Their rationale? "We don't like their sound. Groups of guitars are on their way out." Of course, the Beatles turned that failure into monumental success.

Remember this important statement: regardless of what may seem to be happening, there are new opportunities. There is a way to inner peace and stability. There is a way to rise above seeming failures and become a success. There is a way to the right attainment of many good desires of your heart. There is a way.

Preparedness is a step to success
—SIR JOHN TEMPLETON

If we are to succeed in life, it becomes necessary to bring our methods of operation into an orderly process. And preparedness can often be considered the first step in the order of success. A familiar adage states that "chance favors the prepared." Opportunity knocks at the door many more times than people may realize. If the moment of opportunity is not seized, it may be because people don't recognize it or are unprepared to seize it.

Eleven-year-old Jeremy was ready and eager to seize the moment. In preparing for a fishing trip to Canada with his father and some of his father's friends, Jeremy insisted on buying a heavy-duty rod and reel so he could catch a big fish. Not wanting to dampen the boy's enthusiasm and knowing he could use the equipment for a deep-sea excursion he was planning, the father purchased the equipment.

When the other men saw Jeremy's new fishing equipment, they joked with him. "You planning on catching a whale, Jeremy?" one of the men asked.

"I'm gonna get me a big pike," he responded confidently.

"Well, you could sure get a big pike with that rig," another said, laughing. Jeremy was undaunted by the men's seeming lack of confidence in him.

Four days on the lake produced little for the men and the boy, and Jeremy's fishing rig became the butt of many a friendly joke. Then, suddenly one of the men shouted, "I have something!" His pole arched and strained. A moment later the pole quickly straightened and the line went limp. The line had broken! The disappointed man muttered that he should have come prepared with heavier equipment.

As the fishing party was about to return to the cabin after another day on the lake, Jeremy's line suddenly tightened. At first he thought he had hooked a log beneath the surface of the water. But then the line began to move with a force that almost frightened him. He had hooked his big fish!

Forty-five minutes later, he hauled his pike into the boat—a thirty-two pounder! The men were flabbergasted, envious, and respectful, because Jeremy taught them that if you want to catch a big fish, then you had better come prepared!

Far too often, people do not prepare themselves for success. While they wish success would favor them, they may put just enough effort into life to get by, thinking that if by chance something big comes along, they'll grab it. But if you're not prepared for success, you may find it difficult to hold on to the opportunities that come your way. Success requires understanding, fortitude, and foresight.

As an exercise, ask yourself from time to time what you are doing to prepare yourself for success. Have you established and become fully committed to your goals? Are you willing not only to cultivate the soil and plant the seed but also to nurture and care for the tender shoot and the young ear as it appears? Are you willing to go the extra mile and devote the energy and attention that the opportunity calls for? Are you willing to stand by your convictions, your principles? Are you prepared to stand alone, if necessary? Have you trained yourself to recognize opportunity when it knocks?

I appreciate the story of the young man who, a number of years ago, was seeking a job as a Morse-code operator. He found an ad in the paper and went to the office address that was listed. When he arrived, it was a large and busy office, and there was a certain amount of hustle, bustle, and noise, including the chatter of a telegraph key in the background. A sign on the wall instructed applicants to take a seat and wait until they were summoned to come into the inner office. More than half a dozen applicants were waiting ahead of the man in our story. This could have been discouraging, but he figured he was prepared for the job and had nothing to lose, so he sat down along with the others to wait. After about two or three minutes, the young man stood up, walked over to the door where the sign was hanging, and walked right on in. Naturally, the other applicants perked up and started looking at each other and muttering. Within about five minutes the young man came back out the door with the employer, who said, "You gentlemen may go now. The position has been filled."

At this, several of the applicants grumbled, and one spoke up and said, "I don't understand. He was the last person to come in, and we never even got a chance to have an interview, and yet he got the job. That's not fair!"

The employer said, "I'm sorry, gentlemen, but all the time you've been sitting here the telegraph key has been ticking out the message in Morse code, "If you understand this message in Morse code, come right in. The job is yours." Apparently none of you heard it or understood the message. He did. The job is his."

In *The Templeton Plan*, I describe how strong spiritual values can help us as we search for financial success, personal success, and a happy and fulfilled life. If your basic values are rooted in spiritual principles, or laws of life, success is more likely to follow. By incorporating these laws of life into your code of behavior, you're on your way to becoming a fulfilled human being. You learn to give freely of yourself and to love without fear. Following the laws of life can give you a greater chance of succeeding at anything you attempt to do.

Continue to read, to learn, and to experience new feelings and ideas. Show initiative at an early stage in a situation. Observe others. Listen carefully to others. Use whatever degree of intelligence you possess to the fullest. Remember that to help yourself is to help others. Ask yourself if you are using your talents and abilities in the wisest way. Do you live consciously, embracing and putting into practice the virtues of honesty, bravery, humility, gentleness, loyalty, and hope? Learn more about the virtues of life and what they mean in *your* life.

Look for the positive in what may seem to be a negative situation. Learn how to live in harmony with others in ways that may lead to productive change. These things are part of "being prepared" and often lead to success.

Bibliography

Adams, Brian. *How to Succeed.* New York: Taplinger, 1969.

Alexander, Denis. *Beyond Science.* Philadelphia: A. J. Hoffman, 1973.

Allen, James. *As a Man Thinketh.* Marina del Rey, CA: DeVorss, 1983.

Asimov, Isaac. *Asimov's Biographical Encyclopedia of Science and Technology.* 2nd rev. ed. Garden City, NY: Doubleday, 1982.

Bachelder, Louise, ed. *The Little Flowers of St. Francis of Assisi.* Mount Vernon, NY: Peter Pauper Press, 1964.

Barnet, Lincoln. *The Universe and Dr. Einstein.* New York: Athenaeum, 1948.

Braden, Charles Samuel, ed. *The Scriptures of Mankind.* New York: Macmillan, 1952.

Bucke, Richard Maurice, MD. *Cosmic Consciousness.* 1st ed. New York: Causeway Books, 1900.

Burtt, E. A., ed. *The Teachings of the Compassionate Buddha.* New York: New American Library, 1955.

Burtt, Edwin A. *The Metaphysical Foundations of Modern Science.* New York: Harcourt Brace, 1925.

Canfield, Jack, and Mark Victor Hansen. *Chicken Soup for the Soul.* Deerfield Beach, FL: Health Communications, 1993.

Capra, Fritjof. *The Tao of Physics: An Exploration of the Parallels between Modern Physics and Eastern Mysticism.* Berkeley, CA: Shambhala, 1975.

Charon, Jean. *Man in Search of Himself.* London: George Allen & Unwin, 1967.

Chatterji, Mohini M. *The Bhagavad Gita.* New York: Julian Press, 1960.

Clark, Rebecca. *Breakthrough*. Unity Village, MO: Unity Books, 1977.

———. *Macro-Mind Power*. West Nyack, NY: Parker, 1978.

———. *The Rainbow Connection*. Unity Village, MO: Unity Books, 1983.

Cohen, Alan. *The Dragon Doesn't Live Here Anymore*. South Kortright, NY: Eden, 1981.

———. *Joy Is My Compass*. Somerset, NJ: Alan Cohen, 1990.

Colton, Ann Ree, and Jonathan Murro. *Owe No Man*. Glendale, CA: Ann Ree Colton Foundation, 1986.

Covell, Ralph R. *Confucius, the Buddha, and Christ*. Maryknoll, NY: Orbis Books, 1986.

Curtis, Dr. Donald. *Helping Heaven Happen*. York Beach, ME: Samuel Weiser, 1992.

Dalai Lama. *Worlds in Harmony: Dialogues on Compassionate Action*. Berkeley, CA: Parallax Press, 1992.

dePurucker, G. *Wind of the Spirit*. Pasadena, CA: Theosophical University Press, 1984.

Dolphin, Lambert. *Lord of Time and Space*. Westchester, IL: Good News, 1974.

Dyer, Dr. Wayne W. *The Sky's the Limit*. New York: Pocket Books, Simon & Schuster, 1980.

———. *You'll See It When You Believe It*. New York: Avon Books, 1989.

Eliade, Mircea. *A History of Religious Ideas*. Vol. 2. Chicago: University of Chicago Press, 1982.

Esterer, Arnulf K. *Towards a Unified Faith*. New York: Philosophical Library, 1963.

Fadiman, Clifton, gen. ed. *Little, Brown Book of Anecdotes*. Boston: Little, Brown, 1985.

Feldman, Christina, and Jack Kornfield, ed. *Stories of the Spirit, Stories of the Heart: Parables of the Spiritual Path from around the World*. San Francisco: Harper, 1991.

Fillmore, Charles. *The Revealing Word*. Unity Village, MO: Unity Books, 1959.

Foster, Michael B. *Mystery and Philosophy*. London: SCM Press, 1957.

Fox, Emmet. Make *Your Life Worthwhile*. New York: Harper & Row, 1942.

Gaer, Joseph. *What the Great Religions Believe*. New York: Dodd, Mead, 1963.

Gibran, Kahlil. *The Prophet*. New York: Alfred A. Knopf, 1923.

———. *A Second Treasury of Kahlil Gibran*. New York: Citadel Press, 1962.

Goldsmith, Joel S. *Practicing the Presence*. New York: Harper & Row, 1958.

Greenberg, Rabbi Sidney, ed. *A Treasury of the Art of Living*. Hartford, CT: Hartmore House, 1963.

Greenlees, Duncan. *The Gospel of Zarathustra*. India: Vasanta Press, 1951.

Hart, Michael H. *The 100: A Ranking of the Most Influential Persons in History*. New York: Hart, 1978.

Heider, John. *The Tao of Leadership*. New York: Bantam Paperbacks, 1983.

Kaplan, Juston, ed. *Bartlett's Familiar Quotations*. 16th ed. New York: Little, Brown, 1992.

Keyes, Ken, Jr. *Handbook to Higher Consciousness*. Berkeley, CA: Living Love Center, 1975.

Lelly, Charles D. *The Beautiful Way of Life*. Unity Village, MO: Unity Books, 1980.

Martin, Nicholas R. M. *Operator's Manual for Successful Living*. Marina del Rey, CA: DeVorss, 1988.

McWilliams, John-Roger, and Peter McWilliams. *Life 101: Everything We Wish We Had Learned about Life in School—But Didn't*. Los Angeles: Prelude Press, 1991.

Mitchell, Stephen, ed. *The Enlightened Heart: An Anthology of Sacred Poetry*. New York: Harper & Row, 1989.

The Oxford Dictionary of Quotations. 3rd ed. New York: Oxford University Press, 1979.

Peale, Dr. Norman Vincent. *The Amazing Results of Positive Thinking*. New York: Prentice-Hall, 1959.

————. *A Guide to Confident Living.* 1948.

————. *My Favorite Quotations.* New York: Harper-Collins, 1990.

————. *The Positive Principle Today.* Carmel, NY: Guideposts, 1976.

Pennington, M. Basil, OCSO. *Centered Living: The Way of Centering Prayer.* Garden City, NY: Doubleday, 1986.

Petras, Kathryn, and Ross Petras, comp. and ed. *The Whole World Book of Quotations: Wisdom from Women and Men around the Globe throughout the Centuries.* New York: Addison-Wesley, 1994.

Price, John Randolph. *The Planetary Commission.* Austin, TX: Quartus Foundation for Spiritual Research, 1984.

Ramacharaka, Yogi. *The Kybalion: A Study of the Hermetic Philosophy of Ancient Egypt and Greece.* Des Plaines, IL: Yoga Publication Society, 1940.

Reader's Digest Association. *Great Lives, Great Deeds.* Pleasantville, NY: Reader's Digest, 1964.

Russell, Lao. *LOVE.* Waynesboro, VA: University of Science & Philosophy, Swannanoa, 1966.

Russell, Peter. *The Global Brain.* Los Angeles: J. P. Tarcher, 1983.

Schweitzer, Albert. *Reverence for Life.* New York: Harper & Row, 1969.

Shah, Idries. *Tales of the Dervishes.* New York: E. P. Dutton, 1969.

————. *The Way of the Sufi.* New York: E. P. Dutton, 1969.

Shanklin, Imelda. *What Are You?* Unity Village, MO: Unity Books, 1929.

Shinn, Florence Scovel. *The Game of Life and How to Play It.* Self published, 1925.

Smith, Huston. *The Religions of Man.* New York: Harper & Row, 1958.

Strong, James. *Strong's Exhaustive Concordance of the Bible.* New York: Abingdon Press, 1890.

Templeton, John Marks. *The Humble Approach.* New York: Seabury Press, 1981.

————, with James Ellison. *The Templeton Plan.* New York: Harper Paperbacks, 1987.